Sunset

ITALIAN

COOK BOOK

BY THE EDITORS OF SUNSET BOOKS AND SUNSET MAGAZINE

LANE PUBLISHING CO. • MENLO PARK, CALIFORNIA

ACKNOWLEDGMENTS

Our special thanks go to Cynthia Scheer for her help with recipe development and photography. We also extend thanks to Dr. Marcello Bottai, of Tenuta Le Velette, Orvieto, Italy; to Conte Dr. Sigmund Fago Golfarelli of Rome; and to the Italian Trade Commissioner in San Francisco, who assisted with food and wine research.

For her help in staging the photographs in this book and on the cover, we thank Evelyn Newell; and we appreciate the assistance of C. Edda Ritson in checking Italian recipe titles. For sharing props for use in photographs, our appreciation goes to Allied Arts Traditional Gift Shop; BFJ's Collectanea; Biordi Italian Imports; Good Cooks & Co.; House of Today; Peet's Coffee, Tea & Spices Co., Inc.; Ramona's Restaurant; Taylor & Ng; William Ober Co.; and Williams-Sonoma Kitchenware.

Cover: Veal & Chicken Cannelloni (Cannelloni alla Bona), streaming with teleme cheese, is a pasta entrée in the great tradition of Italian cooking. A simple green salad and crusty bread complement the rich entrée. The recipe is on page 30. Photographed by Nikolay Zurek.

Photographers: Glenn Christiansen: 18. **Jerry Anne DiVecchio:** 7 left. **Cynthia Scheer:** 7 right top and bottom. **Tom Wyatt:** 2, 23, 31, 42, 47, 55, 58, 91, 99. **Nikolay Zurek:** 10, 15, 26, 50, 63, 66, 71, 75, 78, 83, 86, 94, 102.

Editor, Sunset Books: David E. Clark

First printing September 1981

Edited by
Jerry Anne DiVecchio
Home Economics Editor, Sunset Magazine

Coordinating Editors:
Anne K. Turley
Cornelia Fogle

Special Consultant:
Linda Anusasananan,
Assistant Editor, Sunset Magazine

Design:
Cynthia Hanson

Illustrations:
Carole Etow

Photo Editor:
Lynne B. Morrall

We've tucked all kinds of gifts from Italy's kitchens into this cook book, including such delectable desserts as Lemon Ice (page 105), with its pert flavor that dances delicately on the palate and provides the perfect finalé for many an Italian dinner.

CONTENTS

1

VEAL CUTLETS FROM BOLOGNA, FRESH NOODLES IN CREAM

VIVA ITALIA!

FROM ROME, PERFECT PIZZA FROM NAPLES—WELCOME TO

E BUON GUSTO!

ITALY'S MANY KITCHENS!

From earliest Roman times to the present day, Italians have shown the world what it means to eat well. Ancient Romans recorded, bite by bite, their incredible gustatory extravaganzas. The Medici family of Renaissance Florence is credited with carrying the Italian kitchen to France—setting the discriminating French off in new gastronomic directions.

Of course, the Italians' love of good food isn't confined to elaborate, sophisticated dishes. Indeed, it's their appreciation of the perfect slice of prosciutto, the sweet perfection of fresh, ripe fruit, and the noble wedge of well-aged cheese that gives the Italian way with food its down-to-earth foundation.

Today the influence of Italian foods is felt in kitchens—sophisticated and simple—around the world, but perhaps nowhere as naturally as in the American home. Italians immigrating to the New World brought with them a style of cooking that in many cases has become so totally embraced, its roots would be forgotten if the Italian names did not cling—spaghetti, ravioli, pizza, scaloppine.

Looking back, of course, you realize that relationship has been a reciprocal one. Hundreds of years ago, the

Touring Italy's many kitchens unlocks a treasure trove of recipes. Like a gallery director selecting the best of the collection for display, we've chosen a tantalizing array of Italy's prize culinary works of art. Selection was not easy—Italy has so many wonderful dishes.

Each chapter—from appetizers to desserts—contains a range of recipes. You'll find dishes for relaxed family meals, such as Sausages with Peppers (page 69), as well as elaborate dishes such as the cheese-blanketed Cannelloni alla Bona (page 30) shown on the cover. Whether you're in the mood for a hearty minestrone set forth on a red-checked tablecloth or in the mood for carpaccio (Italian steak tartare) presented in the latest high-tech decor, you'll find the right recipe in our collection of Italy's treasured dishes.

Americas gifted Italy with tomatoes for sauces, beans for minestrone, corn for polenta, and other foods now found all over Italy, such as turkey, potatoes, and peppers.

REGIONAL SPECIALTIES

In the cooking of Italy today, regional differences are still very distinct, and each region treasures unique dishes, foods, and a philosophy of cooking. In this book we've tried to point out such local distinctions when possible, calling attention to them in recipe titles and introductions. You can use the map on page 5 to pinpoint these specific regions and their major cities.

In general, you can expect the cuisine of northern Italy to use butter for cooking, whereas olive oil tends to be used in the South. Northern Italy is more the domain of fresh egg pasta; rice is also more popular in the diet of this area. In southern Italy, on the other hand, tubular pastas of the macaroni family—many in fanciful shapes—reign supreme. Also, the sauces of the North are at once creamier and lighter than the earthy tomato sauces of the South.

Much of Italy—north and south—produces wines in abundance. A dish with strong regional association will usually be complemented by a wine from the same area. You will find a brief guide to Italian wines, as well as some of their New World counterparts, on page 16.

LOVE OF SIMPLY GOOD FOOD

One of the most impressive qualities in the Italian approach to cooking is a regard for the food itself. A ripe melon or peach is savored for its intrinsic perfection. Meat is seasoned with the intent of enhancing, but never disguising, its basic goodness. A dish as simple as a few slices of pink prosciutto with juicy figs may be given as much praise as a complex pasta dish that is assembled in several stages.

The Italian flair for the dramatic is often assisted by a special piece of equipment that enhances the presentation of a dish. Just imagine zabaglione poured, steaming, from a glistening round-bottom copper pan; espresso hissing in its convoluted pot; fettuccine streaming from a pasta machine in golden ribbons.

You also might want to purchase a spaghetti cooker with a lift-out basket that offers an easy way to drain pasta. Or consider a spaghetti rake — a long-handled, wooden utensil with pegs poking out of one end to lift long strands of hot cooked pasta from boiling water. A ravioli rolling pin (page 22) helps you turn out plump little cushion-shaped ravioli.

Fortunately for us, such tools— at one time hard to find—are now available in cookware shops just about everywhere. Though certainly not essential for good Italian cooking, they add enjoyment to the process.

ITALIAN MEALS AND MENUS

In Italy the main meal may be midday or evening. For special occasions it begins with one or more vegetable, meat, and fish dishes—an antipasto assortment that is, in effect, a sit-down appetizer course.

However, you might prefer presenting these foods in another room before inviting guests to be seated. An Italian apéritif, or dry or sweet vermouth, might precede or accompany this stage of the meal.

Next comes soup or a pasta or rice dish served with an appropriate wine. The main course is meat, poultry, or fish, typically accompanied by a vegetable; bread is always on the table. Salad follows, succeeded in leisurely pace by cheese or fruit. The delicious parade usually ends with a tiny cup of rich, dark espresso coffee.

What sort of other meals during the day could balance such a feast? For supper or lunch one might choose something starkly simple—maybe a soup or frittata, with salad, cheese, or fruit.

Whatever Italian meals or dishes you choose to prepare, shopping for ingredients presents few challenges if you live in a metropolitan area. A large supermarket will provide all you need for most recipes, while a good Italian delicatessen can offer the rest. Some ingredients, such as Italian sausage, can be made at home; directions are on page 72. So stock your kitchen with such necessities as olive oil, garlic, Parmesan cheese, basil, oregano, and fennel and anise seeds, and let your cooking tour begin.

ITALY

This guide is intended to help you pronounce some of the more difficult Italian words in this book. We've also included very brief definitions derived from the context in which the Italian words are used.

Word	Pronunciation	Definition
ABBACCHIO	ah BAH kyoh	lamb
AGLIO	AHL yoh	garlic
AGNELLO	ahn YEH low	lamb
AL DENTE	ahl DEN teh	to the tooth
ASIAGO	ah see AH go	a sharp cheese
BACCALÀ	bah kah LAH	salt cod
BAGNA CAUDA	BAHN yah COW dah	a vegetable dip ("hot bath")
BASILICO	Bah SEE lee koh	basil
BEL PAESE	BEL pah AY say	a table cheese
BIETOLE	bee EH toh leh	Swiss chard bundles
BISTECCA	bee STEH kah	beef steak
BOLOGNESE	boh loh NYEH seh	in the style of Bologna
BRACIOLA	brah CHO lah	flank steak
BRICIOLE	BREE cho leh	crumbs
BUCATINI	boo kah TEE nee	a pasta
CACCIATORA	cah cha TOH rah	hunter-style
CALZONE	kahl TSOH neh	filled bread
CANNOLI	kahn NOH lee	a pastry
CARCIOFI	kar CHO fee	artichokes
CARPACCIO	car PAH cho	beef appetizer
CASARECCIO	cah sah REH cho	home-style bread
CASTAGNE	kah STAHN yeh	chestnuts
CHIANTI	kee AHN tee	a red wine
CIALDE	CHAHL deh	anise cookies
CINGHIALE	cheen gee AH leh*	wild boar
CIOPPINO	cho PEE noh	seafood stew
CIPOLLE	chee POL leh	onions
CONIGLIO	koh NEEL yoh	rabbit
COPPA	KOH pah	a sausage
COTEGHINO	koh teh GEE noh*	sausage
FAGIOLI	fah JOH lee	beans
FETTUCCINE	feh too CHEE neh	pasta noodle
FIORENTINA	fyoh ren TEE na	in the style of Florence
FOCACCIA	fo KAH chah	flat bread
FONDUTA	fon DOO tah	cheese sauce or dip
FONTINA	fon TEE nah	a cheese of Piedmont
FORMAGGIO	for MAH joh	cheese
FRAGOLE	FRAH goh leh	strawberries
FREGOLATI	freh goh LAH tee	crumbs
FUNGHI	FOON gee*	mushrooms
GENOVESE	jeh noh VEH seh	in the style of Genoa
GIARDINIERA	jahr dee NYAIR rah	pickled vegetables
GNOCCHI	NYOH kee	dumplings
GRANCHIO	GRAHN kyoh	crab
GRIGNOLINO	green yo LEE noh	a red wine
INGLESE	een GLAY seh	English-style
INSALATA	een sah LAH ta	salad
LENTICCHIE	len TEEK yeh	lentils
LINGUINE	leen GWEE nee	pasta noodle
MAIALE	my AH leh	pork
MARE	MAH reh	sea
MARINARA	mah ree NAH rah	a sauce ("sailor-style")
MASCARPONE	mas kar POH neh	cream cheese
MELANZANE	meh lahn TSAH neh	eggplant
MILANESE	mee lah NEH seh	in the style of Milan
MORDERE	MOHR deh reh	to bite
MOSTACCIOLI	mohs tah CHO lee	a pasta tube
MOZZARELLA	moh tsah REH lah	a cooking cheese
ORECCHIETTE	oh reh KYET teh	pasta ears
ORVIETO	or vee AY toh	an Umbrian wine
OSSO BUCO	oh soh BOO koh	veal shanks
PANCETTA	pahn CHET tah	an Italian bacon
PANDOLCE	pahn DOL cheh	sweet bread
PANE	PAH neh	bread
PANETTONE	pah neh TOH neh	sweet bread
PANFORTE	pahn FOR teh	a confection
PARMIGIANO	pahr mee JAHN oh	in the style of Parma
PASQUA	PAHS kwah	Easter
PATATE	pah TAH teh	potatoes
PAVESE	pah VEH seh	in the style of Pavia
PEPERONCINI	peh peh rohn CHEE nee	small green peppers
PESCE	PES sheh	fish
PIGNOLI	peen YOH lee	pine nuts
PINZIMONIO	peen zee MOH nyoh	type of salad
PIZZELLE	pee TSEL leh	star cookies
POLLO	POHL loh	chicken
POMODORI	poh moh DOH ree	tomatoes
PORCHETTA	por KET tah	roast suckling pig
PROSCIUTTO	proh SHOOT toh	a flavorful ham
PRUGNE	PROON yeh	plums
RICOTTA	ree KOH tah	cheese
RIGATONI	ree gah TOH nee	pasta tubes
RIPIENI	ree PYEH nee	stuffed
RISOTTO	ree SOH toh	rice dish
SALSICCIA	sal SEE chah	sausage
SALTIMBOCCA	sahl teem BOH kah	a veal dish
SCALOPPINE	skah loh PEE neh	small thin pieces
SCHIACCIATA	skee yah CHAH tah	flat bread
SOAVE	soh AH veh	a white wine
SOGLIOLE	sohl YOH leh	sole
STRACCIATELLA	strah cha TEL lah	a soup
STRACOTTO	strah KOH toh	stew
TACCHINO	tah KEE no	turkey
TAGLIARINI	tahl yah REE nee	pasta noodle
TAGLIATELLE	tahl yah TEL leh	pasta noodle
TALEGGIO	tah LEJ oh	cheese
TONNATO	tohn NAH toh	(cooked with) tuna sauce
TORTELLINI	tor teh LEE nee	stuffed pasta
TRIPPA	TREE pah	tripe
UMIDO	OO mee doh	stewed
UOVO	WOH voh	egg
VERDICCHIO	ver DEEK yoh	dry wine
VERMICELLI	vehr mee CHEH lee	thin spaghetti
VITELLO	vee TELL loh	veal
VONGOLE	VOHN go leh	clams
ZABAGLIONE	tzah bahl YOH neh	dessert of beaten eggs
ZUPPA	TSOO pah	soup

*Use hard "g" as in "go."

To market, to market, to buy—anything from artichokes to zucchini. As you can see from these three scenes, the fresh-air market is still very much a cherished part of Italian life.

Laden with greens, a cheery, red-wheeled clean-up cart (top right) testifies to the freshness of produce in Rome's Campo di Fiore market near the Piazza Navona. Above, baskets brimming with beautiful ripe fruit tempt summertime shoppers in Milan. Banners flying over the weekly outdoor market in Alba (lower right) herald the autumn truffle fair held annually in this Piedmontese town.

2

APPETIZERS &

CAPONATA, CROSTINI, ARTICHOKES BAKED WITH CHEESE OR BATHED

FIRST COURSES

IN DRESSING, TENDER PROSCIUTTO WITH MELON. HAVE A LITTLE MORE?

HOT VEGETABLE DIP
BAGNA CAUDA
(Pictured on page 63)

The ancient custom of eating from the same dish to signify the spirit of good fellowship is probably most beautifully represented by bagna cauda, or "hot bath," as translated from the Piedmontese dialect.

It is just plain raw vegetables dipped, **but not cooked,** in a mutually shared bowl of bubbling butter and olive oil made bold by garlic and anchovies.

People often consume an astonishing quantity of bagna cauda—it's so easy to justify taking your fill of the fresh, crisp vegetables because very little of the rich sauce actually sticks to each morsel.

½	cup (¼ lb.) butter
¼	cup olive oil
4	small cloves garlic, minced or pressed
1	can (2 oz.) anchovies, well drained and finely chopped
	Vegetables (directions follow)
	Thinly sliced French bread or sliced crusty rolls

In a 2-cup heatproof container, place butter, oil, garlic, and anchovies.

The style and spirit of Italian eating shows itself in the varied ways a meal may begin—maybe a basket of raw vegetables with the bubbling "hot bath" (dipping sauce) called Bagna Cauda (this page), or perhaps a collection of savory foods, either hot or cold, classed as antipasto.

A delicious variety of Italian cold meats, from prosciutto to the many different sorts of salami, often appears at the opening of a meal, frequently in combination with melon or figs (see page 13).

Other possible openers include artichokes, a seafood salad, and the elegant presentation of thinly sliced beef known as Carpaccio (page 12). Still another possibility is an antipasto assortment—a selection of several appetizers—so popular in many Italian restaurants. Such fare makes very pleasant nibbling with wine or cocktails, and can also provide a tantalizing light lunch or supper with bread and cheese.

Place over low heat until butter is melted; keep hot over a candle or alcohol flame, keeping heat low enough to prevent browning or burning the sauce. Present sauce with an attractively arranged basket of the vegetables and another basket containing the bread.

To eat, hold a vegetable piece in your fingers and swirl through sauce; hold a slice of bread under the vegetable to catch any drips as you prepare to eat the vegetable. Eventually the bread soaks up enough sauce to become a tasty morsel, too. Makes 8 to 10 servings. (You can double the recipe for 16 to 20 servings or triple it for 24 to 30 servings.)

Bagna Cauda Vegetables. You'll need 1 to 2 cups vegetable pieces per person, but you'll have to estimate quantities while vegetables are still whole. Choose a colorful assortment and cut as suggested below to keep a right-from-the-garden look. Cover and chill if prepared ahead. Sprinkle with cold water just before serving.

Artichokes: Use small artichokes, 2 inches or less in diameter. Break off small outer bracts; cut thorny tips from remaining bracts with scissors. Trim stem ends. Keep in acid water (1 tablespoon vinegar to 1 quart water) until ready to serve. To eat, bite off tender base of each bract.

Cabbage: Cut red or green cabbage in half. Cut vertical gashes in each half. Break off chunks to eat.

Carrots: Leave an inch of stem; peel. Cut carrots on diagonal, not quite through, into short sections. Break apart to eat.

Cauliflower: Cut out core, keeping head whole. Break off flowerets to eat.

Cherry tomatoes: Dip with stems.

Green beans: Snap off ends and remove strings. Leave whole to eat.

Green or red bell peppers: Cut out stem end and pull out seeded center, then cut peppers vertically down just to base in 8 to 12 sections. Break to eat.

Mushrooms: Trim stem ends. Leave small mushrooms whole. Cut large ones, through cap only, into 4 to 6 sections; break to eat.

Radishes: Cut off root ends and all but one or two leaves to hold for dipping.

Turnips: Peel and cut, not quite through, into thick slices. Break apart to eat.

Zucchini and yellow crookneck squash: Trim ends; cut, not quite through, into short sections. Break apart to eat.

FRIED ARTICHOKES, ROMAN-STYLE
CARCIOFI ALLA GIUDIA

Resembling withered roses, these artichokes are an intriguing blend of crisp, crusty exterior and tender, sweet interior. Serve as a first course or with simply cooked meats or poultry.

4	medium-sized artichokes (2¾ to 3¾ inches in diameter)
	Acid water (1 tablespoon vinegar to each 1 quart water)
	Salad oil
	Salt and pepper

To prepare each artichoke, cut stem flush with bottom. Holding a sharp knife parallel to side of artichoke,

cut away tough outer leaves, leaving only tender base of leaves attached to artichoke bottom. Cut off and discard top third of each artichoke and remaining leaf tips. Firmly press top side of artichoke against a flat surface to open leaves. With a spoon, scoop out choke; immerse artichoke in acid water until all are prepared.

Into a wide frying pan over medium heat, pour salad oil to a depth of 1 inch. Shake moisture from artichokes and pat dry. Add artichokes to oil (do not crowd) and brown on all sides, then turn artichokes, top side down, in oil and press firmly to open leaves and let hot oil reach interior. Return artichokes to upright position, reduce heat to low, and continue cooking until artichoke base is tender when pierced (about 15 minutes). Drain well and serve hot, seasoned with salt and pepper. Makes 4 servings.

WARM LIVER PÂTÉ
CROSTINI ALLA FIORENTINA

Throughout most of Italy, crostini means any toast or buttered bread presented at the beginning of a meal. But in Florence, crostini is bread spread with this liver pâté. Serve it warm or cold, as a snack or appetizer.

For another delicious variation, float the crostini in bowls of hot broth.

1	large onion, finely chopped
1	stalk celery, finely chopped
1	large carrot, finely chopped
½	cup olive oil
1	pound chicken livers or calf liver (trimmed of tough membrane)
¼	cup butter or margarine
1	tablespoon chopped canned anchovy fillets
2	tablespoons finely chopped capers
	Pepper
	Broth or consommé (optional)
	Minced fresh parsley and whole capers
	Thinly sliced French rolls, toast, or crisp crackers

Combine onion, celery, and carrot with olive oil in a wide frying pan over medium heat; cook, stirring for about 15 minutes or until vegetables are quite soft but not browned. Add liver (if using calf liver, cut it into chunks) and cook over medium heat, stirring, for about 5 minutes or until firm and slightly pink in center (cut a gash to test). Stir in butter until melted, then add chopped anchovy. In a blender or food processor, whirl mixture (a portion at a time, if necessary) to make a coarse purée. Stir in capers and season to taste with pepper.

Serve warm or cold. (If serving cold, cover and refrigerate; thin to a spreading consistency by stirring in broth, a little at a time. To reheat, place in top of double boiler over simmering water, stirring occasionally until warm.)

Mound warm or cold pâté in a small dish and garnish with parsley and whole capers. Spread generously on sliced rolls, toast, or crackers. Makes about 2½ cups.

FRIED SQUID
FRITTO DI CALAMARI

Squid is a delicious seafood bargain. Its fine-textured, snowy flesh has a flavor and tenderness much like that

(Continued on page 11)

of abalone—at a fraction of the cost. Mediterranean cooks have long made calamari the focus of many tantalizing recipes. Here squid is lightly seasoned and quickly fried in golden ringlets and curlicues for a hot appetizer course.

1	to 2 pounds fresh or frozen and thawed squid
	Garlic salt
½	cup each fine dry bread crumbs and all-purpose flour for each 1 pound squid
	Salad oil

Holding squid under running water, peel off and discard all of the transparent, speckled membrane from hood, exposing pure white meat of hood. Carefully pull and discard long, transparent, sword-shaped shell from inside hood. Gently separate body from hood.

Strip off and discard all material that easily comes free from body, including ink sac. (If sac breaks, rinse body to remove ink.) Spread tentacles open to expose center. Squeeze gently to pop out hard, parrotlike beak from between tentacles.

Squeeze out and discard contents of hood; rinse inside. Slice hood crosswise into strips ¼ to ½ inch wide, forming rings.

Drain cleaned squid, then sprinkle with garlic salt. Coat with mixture of crumbs and flour; shake off excess.

In a medium-size deep pan or wok, pour oil to a depth of 1½ inches and heat to 375° on a deep-frying thermometer. Have a lid handy to cover pan loosely, as legs tend to spatter fat. Lower a slotted spoonful of coated squid into hot oil and cook for only about 30 seconds or until lightly browned (squid becomes very

---

Attenzione! Trimmed artichokes stand at attention, stems in the air, for the classic Roman Artichoke Platter (page 17). The artichokes, moistened with a light dressing, can be served as a salad or vegetable dish. In the background, you see Fennel Bread Sticks (page 90), a crunchy contrast for the artichokes.

---

tough if overcooked). Lift from oil with slotted spoon and drain on paper towels; keep warm.

Repeat process with remaining squid, always allowing oil to return to 375° before each addition. Serve hot. One pound of squid makes 6 appetizer servings or 2 or 3 main-dish servings.

HAM & CHEESE APPETIZER SANDWICHES
SPIEDINI ALLA ROMANA

Crisply batter-fried, these hot little ham and cheese sandwiches are a favorite cocktail-hour nibble in fashionable Italian restaurants. The buttery anchovy sauce can be omitted if you prefer to serve the sandwiches as finger food, rather than with a knife and fork.

8	thin slices French or Italian bread, trimmed of crusts
4	sandwich-size slices mozzarella cheese
8	thin slices prosciutto
¾	cup milk
⅓	cup all-purpose flour
2	eggs, lightly beaten
⅓	cup olive oil or salad oil
2	tablespoons butter or margarine
2	teaspoons lemon juice
1	teaspoon anchovy paste

Make sandwiches, using 2 slices bread, 1 slice cheese, and 2 slices prosciutto for each sandwich. Cut each sandwich into quarters and fasten each quarter with a wooden pick. Place milk, flour, and beaten eggs in 3 separate dishes.

Heat oil in a medium-size frying pan over medium heat until oil sputters when a drop of milk is added. Lightly dip each quarter sandwich, on both sides, in milk, then in flour, and finally in egg. Brown sandwiches, a few at a time, turning once, until crusty and golden; remove to a warm plate and keep warm.

In a small frying pan, melt butter over medium-high heat until foamy; mix in lemon juice and anchovy paste until well blended. Drizzle

---

sauce over sandwiches and serve hot. Makes 16 appetizers.

ARTICHOKES CELLINI
CARCIOFI CELLINI

Two cheeses flavor the golden crust that forms on these delicate artichokes as they bake.

12	to 16 small artichokes, 2½ inches or less in diameter, or 1 package (9 oz.) frozen artichoke hearts
	Acid water (1 tablespoon vinegar to each 1 quart water)
	Salted water
1	small package (3 oz.) cream cheese
¼	cup chopped chives, fresh, frozen, or freeze-dried
¼	cup butter or margarine, softened
	Salt and pepper
½	cup shredded Parmesan cheese

Cut off and discard top third of each fresh artichoke, peel off outer leaves down to pale green inner ones, peel stem, and cut in half lengthwise; immerse in acid water until all are prepared.

In a 2 to 3-quart pan, cover fresh artichokes with boiling salted water and cook, with lid on, for about 15 minutes or until artichokes are easily pierced. (If using frozen artichokes, cook according to package directions.) Drain well. In a buttered shallow baking dish (one you can serve from), arrange artichokes close together in a single layer.

Blend cream cheese with chives and butter. Sprinkle artichokes with salt and pepper, dot them evenly with cheese mixture, then sprinkle evenly with Parmesan cheese. (At this point you may cover and refrigerate, if made ahead.)

Bake, uncovered, in a 375° oven for 20 to 25 minutes or until topping is golden. Serve on small plates, with forks. Makes 24 to 32 fresh artichoke appetizers (12 to 16 if you use frozen artichoke hearts).

BAKED MUSHROOMS
FUNGHI RIPIENI

Stuffed with garlic, crumbs, parsley, and their own chopped stems, and topped with Parmesan cheese, these mushroom caps are a favorite Italian hot appetizer or first course.

1	**pound (18 to 20) medium-size mushrooms**
2	**tablespoons butter or margarine**
2	**tablespoons olive oil**
1	**clove garlic, minced or pressed**
2	**tablespoons chopped fresh parsley**
½	**teaspoon salt**
⅛	**teaspoon** each **thyme leaves and oregano leaves**
	Dash each **pepper and ground nutmeg**
¼	**cup** each **soft bread crumbs and shredded Parmesan cheese**

Carefully remove stems from mushrooms; reserve caps and chop stems finely. In a medium-size frying pan, over medium heat, place butter and oil. When butter is melted, add chopped mushroom stems and cook, stirring, until juices have evaporated and mushrooms are lightly browned. Mix in garlic, parsley, salt, herbs, pepper, nutmeg, and crumbs; remove from heat. Mound equal amounts of cooked mixture into mushroom caps, and sprinkle evenly with Parmesan cheese.

Place caps in a greased shallow baking pan. Bake, uncovered, in a

400° oven for 20 to 25 minutes or until cheese is lightly browned. Makes 18 to 20 appetizers.

STUFFED CLAMS
VONGOLE OREGANATE AL FORNO

Patterned after baked clams served in Naples, this appetizer makes an interesting beginning for a meal.

You can also prepare fresh mussels this way to make another popular Italian seafood dish, called cozze gratinate.

2	**dozen small hard-shell clams in shell, well scrubbed**
2	**tablespoons water**
¼	**cup butter or margarine, softened**
1	**large clove garlic, minced or pressed**
2	**tablespoons finely chopped fresh parsley**
¼	**teaspoon oregano leaves**
3	**tablespoons soft bread crumbs**
	Lemon wedges

Place clams and water in a large heavy pan over medium heat. Cover and simmer just until clams open (5 to 10 minutes). When cool enough to handle, remove clams from shells; save half the shells.

In a small bowl, stir together butter, garlic, parsley, oregano, and bread crumbs. Set each clam back into a half shell and spread with about 1 teaspoon of the butter mixture. Arrange filled shells, side by side, in a shallow baking pan. (At this point you may cover, and refrigerate, if made ahead.)

Broil clams 4 inches from heat until lightly browned (3 to 4 minutes). Serve with lemon wedges. Makes 2 dozen appetizers.

CARPACCIO
CARNE AL CARPACCIO

A comparatively recent creation, Carpaccio is usually traced to Harry's

Bar in Venice in the early 1960s. The dish, named for a 15th century Venetian painter, exemplifies elegant simplicity. It consists of paper-thin slices of uncooked beef—a sort of gossamer beef tartare—usually served with a dollop of mustard or mayonnaise (or a combination) and a lemon or lime wedge. Other possible adornments are olive oil, capers, and very finely chopped sweet onion.

In Italy one may order it as a main dish, enhanced by slivered Parmesan cheese, artichokes, sliced raw or marinated mushrooms, or even white truffles. Though often served as a first course, it does make a fine lunch or supper with a salad.

The selection of beef is of first importance when a dish needs so little preparation. Use a very lean, compact, boneless cut, trimmed of any surface fat. We find that first-cut top round meets these requirements.

Slicing the beef paper-thin is easier if you freeze it slightly first. Use a food slicer adjusted to slice very thinly, or a very sharp knife (in combination with a mallet for light pounding).

1	**pound first-cut top round, trimmed of fat, if necessary**
½	**cup mayonnaise**
6	**tablespoons Dijon or tarragon-flavored Dijon mustard**
2	**teaspoons lemon juice**
	Lemon or lime wedges

Wrap meat lightly and freeze just until firm but not hard (1 to 2 hours). Meanwhile, combine mayonnaise, mustard, and lemon juice; mix until smooth, then cover and refrigerate. Using a food slicer, cut frozen beef, across the grain, paper-thin; or using a very sharp knife, slice beef as thin as possible, then place slices, a few at a time (allow room for expansion), between pieces of plastic wrap and pound with the flat side of a mallet until slices are paper-thin. As meat is sliced, or sliced and pounded, carefully arrange slices, slightly overlapping, on individual plates or on a large platter. Serve with sauce and garnish with lemon. Makes 8 to 10 servings.

A wedge of juicy, ripe melon draped with a see-through slice of coral prosciutto—what a beautiful way to begin a meal!

If anyone asks where you found the idea for such a cool, refreshing starter, say you came across it while browsing through a 15th century Italian cook book. There is, indeed, such a book, and it was Renaissance Italians who began the tradition of melon and meat starters. Pears and figs combine deliciously with meat, too.

You can give this Renaissance idea a renaissance by choosing meats that are non-Italian, such as Canadian bacon, Westphalian ham, tongue, corned beef, smoked thuringer, or whatever strikes your fancy at the delicatessen. As long as the meat is cut in very thin slices, it's probably a good candidate to try with melon, figs, or pears.

If you're a purist, though, you can visit an Italian deli and select one or more of the following cold cuts.

Prosciutto. The best of this salted, dried ham comes from the Parma region of Italy, where it dries slowly to perfection in the fresh mountain air. While other imported or locally made prosciutto can be a worthy substitute, you might want to treat yourself to real Parma prosciutto at least once so you'll know how tender and sweet this treasure of a ham is. Prosciutto di San Daniele is an equally famous, though less exported, prosciutto.

Coppa. In American delicatessens, coppa is usually a moderate-size cylinder of dried, processed pork shoulder. Coppa is marbled with fat and often comes in both sweet (nonspicy) and hot (spicy) versions.

Salami. You can find tasty domestic as well as imported dry salami. It usually combines beef and pork, and is flavored with pepper, garlic, or wine. Genoa salami has more pork than other salami and is flavored with garlic.

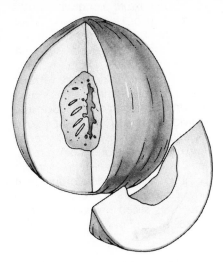

Cacciatore. Sometimes called salametti, this is a small salami of pork and beef spiced with pepper. It was just the right size for a hunter (cacciatore) to tuck into his pocket for lunch—hence the name.

Mortadella. The original bologna from Bologna, mortadella is finely ground pork and beef subtly seasoned (but not bland) and studded with whole peppercorns or pistachio nuts. It is usually the largest round cold cut in the deli case.

Galantina. A mildly spiced combination of coarsely minced veal and pork, sometimes with pistachio nuts, it is held together by gelatin—like head cheese.

MELONS FOR MEATS

Here's a list of our favorite melon and meat duos—some traditional, some innovative. To make each first-course serving, place a wedge of seeded melon on a plate and accompany it with 1 or more thin slices of one of the meats suggested.

If you prefer, you can cut melon into peeled crescents, cubes, or balls and roll a thin slice of meat around each piece. Or you could arrange wedges of several kinds of melons and several kinds of meats on a tray and let guests select their own combinations.

Crenshaw. Juicy and faintly spicy, this red gold melon is exceptional with baked ham, prosciutto, galantina, and coppa.

Cantaloupe. Its easygoing flavor matches readily with coppa, Genoa or dry salami, cacciatore, prosciutto, galantina, and mortadella.

Casaba. The cucumberlike, almost neutral flavor of the casaba is delightfully refreshing with prosciutto or dry salami.

Honeydew. There's a hint of honey in the white to green flesh of this rich melon, and it is best with highly flavored meats. Prosciutto is its most famous companion; vying for equal billing are coppa, Genoa salami, dry salami, and cacciatore.

Persian. It's as versatile as cantaloupe and goes well with the same meats (see cantaloupe).

FIGS WITH MEAT

Dark or light fresh figs are superb with dry salami, coppa (especially the hotly seasoned version), and prosciutto. For each first-course serving, place 1 or 2 figs on a plate with several slices of meat alongside.

PEARS WITH MEAT

In late summer or fall, use buttery-textured Bartlett pears in combination with meats; during the winter select juicy ripe Anjou, Comice, or Bosc pears.

Pears with Prosciutto. For each first-course serving, place ½ a cored pear (peeled, if desired) on a plate; drizzle pear with lemon juice to preserve color. Alongside the pear place 3 or 4 paper-thin slices prosciutto, rolled, or rippled onto the plate. Grind a light sprinkling of black pepper over all.

Pears with Salami. Cut pears in sections and accompany with thick or thin slices of salami. Allow ½ pear for a first-course serving.

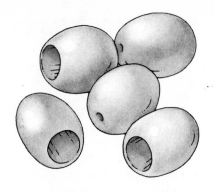

ANTIPASTO PLATTER
ANTIPASTO MISTO

Vegetables and tuna simmer in a tomato-based cooking sauce to make this handsome appetizer platter. You can vary the vegetables: other choices are artichoke hearts, tiny onions, and green beans.

1	cup each **catsup, chili sauce, and water**
½	cup each **olive oil, tarragon wine vinegar, and lemon juice**
1	**clove garlic, minced or pressed**
2	**tablespoons brown sugar**
1	**tablespoon each Worcestershire and prepared horseradish**
	Dash of ground red pepper (cayenne)
	Salt
1	**very small cauliflower**
3	**medium-size carrots**
2	**stalks celery**
½	**pound small whole mushrooms**
1	**jar (8 oz.) peperoncini (small pickled Italian-style peppers)**
2	**cans (7 oz.** each**) solid pack tuna**
1	**can (2 oz.) rolled anchovies with capers**
	Pimento-stuffed olives, sliced
	Fresh parsley

In a 4 to 5-quart pan, combine catsup, chili sauce, water, oil, vinegar, lemon juice, garlic, brown sugar, Worcestershire, horseradish, red pepper, and salt to taste. Bring to a boil, then reduce heat and simmer, uncovered, for a few minutes. Break cauliflower into flowerets; slice carrots ¼ inch thick (use a ruffle-edged cutter if you have one); slice celery diagonally into 1½-inch lengths. Add cauliflowerets, carrots, and celery to catsup mixture along with mushrooms and pickled peppers. Cover, reduce heat, and simmer slowly until tender-crisp when pierced with a fork (about 20 minutes). Drain tuna and add to mixture, taking care to keep pieces whole; simmer, uncovered, just until heated through. Spoon into individual serving dishes or into a divided serving dish, keeping each kind of vegetable and the fish separated. Cool and then chill. (At this point you may refrigerate until next day, if made ahead.) Garnish with anchovies, sliced olives, and parsley. Makes 10 to 12 appetizer servings.

PICKLED VEGETABLES
GIARDINIERA

Specialty food shops and Italian delicatessens usually carry the brightly colored vegetable mixture known as giardiniera. The truth is, these pickled vegetables are easy to make at home. They're delicious as appetizers or with cold meats, and a small jar of giardiniera makes an attractive gift.

12	to 18 **small carrots (about ¾ inch in diameter at top)**
1	**small bunch celery**
2	**large red or green bell peppers**
1	**large (about 2 lbs.) cauliflower**
1	**cup salt**
4	**quarts cold water**
1	**pound pickling or tiny white boiling onions, peeled**
2	**quarts white vinegar**
¼	**cup mustard seeds**
2	**tablespoons celery seeds**
1	**small dried hot red chile**
2½	**cups sugar**

Peel carrots; cut in half lengthwise and then into 1½-inch lengths; measure 4 cups. Remove strings from celery; slice lengthwise and then into 1½-inch lengths; measure 3 cups. Remove seeds and stems from peppers and cut into 1-inch-wide strips. Break cauliflower into 1½-inch-thick flowerets and trim stems.

Stir salt into the cold water until dissolved. Add measured carrots and celery, peppers, cauliflowerets, and onions. Let stand, covered, in refrigerator for 12 to 18 hours (overnight); then drain, rinse in cold water, and drain again.

In a 6-quart stainless steel or enamel pan, combine vinegar, mustard seeds, celery seeds, chile, and sugar; bring to a boil and continue to boil for 3 minutes. Add vegetables and boil until vegetables are almost tender (10 minutes); discard chile.

Have ready 6 hot sterilized pint jars (to sterilize, immerse in boiling water for 15 minutes) and scalded self-sealing lids and bands (pour boiling water over them). Remove 1 jar at a time from boiling water and pack with boiling vegetables. Run a spatula around inside of jar to release any air bubbles.

Stir boiling vinegar mixture to blend seasonings, then pour into jar, filling jar to within ½ inch of rim. Wipe rim with a damp cloth. Place lid on jar, and screw on ring band as tightly as you comfortably can. Set jar on a folded towel away from drafts. Repeat until all jars are filled.

Leave on ring bands until jars are cool. Test seal by pressing lid with your finger. If it stays down when pressed, jar is sealed. If it pops back up, it's not sealed. Store any unsealed jars in refrigerator and use within a month. Store sealed jars in a cool, dry place. Makes 6 pints.

An Italian deli delight, our display of meats to mix and match with melons (or figs or pears) includes (clockwise from top right), cornucopias of dry salami on cantaloupe, whole cacciatore, galantina with pistachio nuts, dry salami, prosciutto, three-in-one meat (salami, coppa, and mortadella), sliced coppa, whole coppa, folded mortadella slices, and prosciutto draped over honeydew melon. A squeeze of lime enhances the melon.
See Classic Antipasto: Melon and Meat (page 13).

Vineyards account for much of the patchwork of the hilly Italian countryside. Grapes from these vineyards produce wines that are a natural complement to Italian food and are known throughout the world. Italy's huge selection of wines—over 200 varieties with legally protected names of origin—rates high in the United States, one of Italy's good customers. Here is a brief survey of some of Italy's popular wines.

WHITE WINE

Soave is dry and pale—maybe Italy's best-known white wine. It comes from a district east of Verona and is delicious with seafood or light pasta dishes.

Verdicchio, a dry, medium-bodied wine, can be recognized by its distinctive amphora-shaped bottle. It originates in the Adriatic coastal region of the Marches and goes well with seafood.

Orvieto is an Umbrian wine that is made both dry (secco) and semi-sweet (abboccato). The dry version complements poultry or fish; the semisweet Orvieto goes well with dessert cheeses.

Frascati, dry and light-bodied, is popular with dishes native to Rome, as it is produced in the Alban hills

just southeast of the city. Chicken, pasta, or fish go well with this wine.

Corvo, both white and velvety red versions, comes from near Palermo in Sicily. Serve either of them with veal, chicken, or pasta dishes.

RED WINE

Chianti may be the first wine you think of when ordering Italian food. Tuscany's pride, it is always red and is made principally from the Sangiovese grape that is grown in a well-defined area between Florence and Siena. At the heart of this region is the 100-square-mile area from which Chianti Classico comes. Young Chianti is fresh and light; when aged, it becomes richer, warmer, and more complex. Serve Chianti with meats and pasta.

Barolo, one of several respected, long-lived red wines from the Piedmont region, is a full-bodied, mellow wine made from the Nebbiolo grape. Best when moderately aged, Barolo goes well with red meats and game.

Barbera comes from another grape grown in Piedmont. It makes a wine that ranges from light and fruity to a full-bodied version that can be served with spicy meats and game. Several California winemakers also produce Barbera.

Grignolino, a dry, light-bodied red wine, is another Piedmontese wine with a California counterpart. You'll enjoy it with almost any meat dish or pasta.

SPARKLING WINE

Asti Spumante, made from the Moscato grape, is aromatic and delicately sweet. It comes from Piedmont and has several California cousins in the Muscat family. It's a good wine to serve with dessert.

SWEET WINE

Marsala is a fortified dessert wine from Sicily that is indispensable as an ingredient in many Italian dishes.

ARTICHOKES VINAIGRETTE
CARCIOFI ALL'ACETO

Italians have been cooking artichokes for centuries. They boil them, fry them, bake them, and even put them in sauce for pasta.

In this recipe, they are presented as a first course, simply marinated in a tart, slightly sweet dressing with red and green bits. You can use frozen artichoke hearts or fresh ones. Since they're served cool, you can prepare them well ahead.

1	package (9 oz.) frozen artichoke hearts, or 12 to 16 small artichokes, 2½ inches or less in diameter
6	tablespoons olive oil
2	tablespoons red wine vinegar
3	tablespoons minced sweet pickle
1	tablespoon sweet pickle liquid
2	tablespoons each minced fresh parsley and canned pimento

Cook frozen artichokes according to package directions. (If using fresh

artichokes, prepare and cook them according to directions in Artichokes Cellini, page 11.) Drain and place in a small deep bowl. Pour olive oil and vinegar over artichokes. Gently mix in pickle, pickle liquid, parsley, and pimento. Cover and chill for at least 4 hours or until next day.

Lift artichokes from marinade and arrange 6 to 8 halves on each individual plate. With a slotted spoon, remove some of the minced ingredients from marinade and spoon them over artichokes. Makes 4 servings.

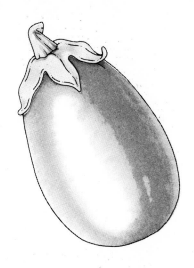

EGGPLANT RELISH
CAPONATA

Caponata is a thick piquant mixture based on cooked eggplant; this version is Sicilian. You can serve it as a first course or as part of an antipasto presentation. It also makes an excellent vegetable relish with meats such as barbecued beef or lamb.

½	cup olive oil or salad oil
2	cups diced celery
1	large eggplant (unpeeled), cut into ¾-inch cubes
1	large onion, chopped
⅓	cup wine vinegar
1	teaspoon sugar
2	large ripe tomatoes, peeled, seeded, and diced
1	cup water
1	tablespoon capers, drained
¼	cup sliced pimento-stuffed olives
1	can (2¼ oz.) sliced ripe olives, drained
2	tablespoons minced fresh parsley
	Salt
	Assorted crackers
	Crisp lettuce leaves

Heat oil in a wide frying pan over medium-high heat. Add celery and cook, stirring often, until tender. With a slotted spoon, remove celery from pan and reserve.

Place eggplant in pan, reduce heat to medium, and cook, stirring, until eggplant is lightly browned and tender. Add onion and continue cooking and stirring until onion is soft but not browned. Using a slotted spoon, remove eggplant and onion from pan and add to reserved celery.

Place vinegar, sugar, tomatoes, and water in pan; cook over medium heat, stirring, for 5 minutes. Return celery, eggplant, and onion to pan. Stir in capers, stuffed olives, ripe olives, and parsley; reduce heat and simmer, uncovered, for about 20 minutes more. Taste and add salt, if needed. Remove from heat; cool, cover, and refrigerate until needed. Serve at room temperature, spread on crackers or spooned onto crisp lettuce leaves. Makes 6 to 8 servings.

SEAFOOD SALAD
INSALATA DI MARE

Lemony squid salad is a first-course favorite. Scoglio di Frisio, a Roman restaurant specializing in Neapolitan dishes, inspired the recipe for this version.

	Water
1	pound fresh or frozen and thawed squid, cleaned as directed for Fried Squid (page 9)
1	can (10 oz.) whole clams
	Zest (colored part of peel) from 1 small lemon, cut into very thin strips
¼	cup lemon juice
⅓	cup olive oil
2	tablespoons finely chopped fresh parsley
	Salt and pepper

In a deep pan over high heat, bring a large quantity of water (enough to cover squid) to a boil. Drop in squid and cook just until edges begin to curl (about as long as it takes for boiling to resume). Drain and set aside.

Drain liquid from clams into another pan. Add lemon zest and bring to a boil; remove from heat and stir in clams and cooked squid; cover and chill.

Stir in lemon juice, olive oil, and parsley. Add salt and pepper to taste. Serve cool but not ice cold. Makes 6 first-course servings.

ROMAN ARTICHOKE PLATTER
CARCIOFI ALLA ROMANA
(Pictured on page 10)

Diners in Rome are accustomed to the rakish look of trimmed artichokes, up-ended with stems in the air. Drenched with a minted dressing, the artichokes are served as a first course or vegetable side dish.

10	to 12 medium-size artichokes, 2½ to 3 inches in diameter
	Acid water (1 tablespoon vinegar to each 1 quart water)
2	tablespoons each lemon juice and red wine vinegar
1	tablespoon chopped fresh mint leaves or ¾ teaspoon dry mint
¼	teaspoon each salt and oregano leaves
½	teaspoon grated lemon peel
⅛	teaspoon freshly ground black pepper
¾	cup olive oil

Cut off and discard top third of each artichoke. Peel off outer leaves of artichokes down to pale green inner ones. Peel green surface from base and stem, and trim stem end. Immerse in acid water until all are prepared. Boil according to directions in Artichokes Cellini (page 11), allowing 25 to 35 minutes.

Drain cooked artichokes well; gently arrange in a single layer in a shallow dish. In a small bowl, combine lemon juice, vinegar, mint, salt, oregano, lemon peel, and pepper. Using a whisk or fork, gradually beat in olive oil until well blended. Pour dressing over artichokes. Cover lightly and let stand, turning occasionally in dressing, until artichokes have cooled to room temperature.

Serve at room temperature, standing artichokes up on cut leaves in a flat platter. Eat with a knife and fork, scooping out fuzzy choke when it is exposed. Makes 5 or 6 servings.

3

FETTUCCINE, SPAGHETTI, LINGUINE, MOSTACCIOLI, ZITI—

PASTA, GNOCCHI

ALL WITH SUPERB SAUCES; HOMEMADE RAVIOLI. LASAGNE,

& RISOTTO

CANNELLONI; ITALIAN-STYLE RICE AND MORE

THIN NOODLES & TINY SHRIMP

TAGLIATELLE CON GAMBERETTI

In seafood-loving Venice we found this zesty combination—homemade noodles in a quick, puréed tomato sauce with thumbnail-size shrimp. You might serve it with one of the dry white wines of the area, such as a Soave or Tocai, and follow it with an entrée of simple grilled chicken or fish.

⅓	cup olive oil
1	small onion, finely chopped
1	clove garlic, minced or pressed
1	can (14½ oz.) Italian-style tomatoes
⅓	cup dry white wine
½	teaspoon salt
	Dash of crushed red pepper (cayenne)
1	recipe Egg Pasta or Pasta Verde (page 34), cut into thin noodles about 10 inches long, or 8 ounces packaged thin noodles
	Salted water
¼	cup finely chopped fresh parsley
½	pound cooked small shrimp

The very first Italian word you ever learned may have been "spaghetti," or perhaps "macaroni." While the debate goes on as to who invented pasta, there is no doubt that Italian cooking has made it famous.

Many a good Italian cook makes tender egg noodles at home, and may make such close relatives as gnocchi, risotto, and polenta, too. That same Italian cook probably buys dried pasta (known generically as macaroni) as well, and in a variety of shapes and forms.

Our recipe for Egg Pasta is on page 34. It can be cut into noodles of any width, including lasagne strips and cannelloni squares. But whether you make your own noodles or use the packaged kind, success depends on skillful cooking. And the secret is to use plenty of water. For a half pound of pasta—enough for four servings—use at least 3 quarts salted water. Bring it to a full boil in a large kettle, and boil rapidly, uncovered, until pasta reaches the stage Italians call al dente ("to the tooth")— tender but firm. Then drain well and serve at once.

The name says it: this is Pasta Rapido (page 19), rapid pasta. The sauce takes so little time that you should bring the pasta water to a boil before starting the sauce of dried hot chiles, olive oil, garlic, and parsley. Here the sauce is shown on homemade whole wheat pasta cut medium-wide.

Heat oil in a medium-size frying pan over medium heat; add onion and cook, stirring occasionally, until soft. Mix in garlic, tomatoes (break up with a spoon) and their liquid, wine, salt, and red pepper. Adjust heat so mixture boils gently and cook, uncovered, stirring occasionally, for 10 minutes. Transfer half the sauce to a blender or food processor and purée it. Return puréed sauce to pan with remaining sauce.

Cook noodles in a large kettle of boiling salted water until al dente (1 to 2 minutes for fresh noodles, or follow package directions). Drain well and place on a warm platter. Add parsley and shrimp to sauce and stir for a few minutes over medium heat until shrimp is hot. Spoon sauce over pasta. Makes 4 first-course servings.

PEPPERY PASTA

PASTA RAPIDO

(Pictured on page 18)

This really is "rapid pasta." It's the kind of pasta dish that requires boiling the pasta water before you even begin making the sauce. Despite the simple ingredients, it's a spicy favorite with Italians and one of the popular

PASTA, GNOCCHI & RISOTTO **19**

items on the menu at the Grand Hotel in Rome.

⅓	cup olive oil
2	small, dried hot red chiles, each broken into 3 pieces
2	cloves garlic, minced or pressed
½	teaspoon salt
½	cup chopped fresh parsley
1	recipe Egg Pasta (page 34) made with 1 cup all-purpose flour and 1 cup whole wheat flour, cut into medium-wide noodles about 10 inches long, or 8 ounces packaged medium-wide noodles
	Salted water

Heat olive oil in a small pan over low heat. Add chiles and cook until they begin to brown. Add garlic and cook for about 30 seconds more or just until limp (do not brown). Add salt and parsley and cook, stirring occasionally, for 1 minute more. Remove from heat.

Cook noodles in a large kettle of boiling salted water until al dente (2 to 3 minutes for fresh noodles, or follow package directions). Drain well and place on a warm platter. Spoon hot sauce over noodles. Lift and mix gently, then serve. Makes 4 to 6 servings.

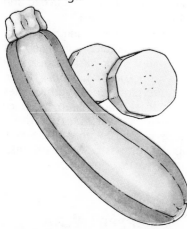

SPRINGTIME NOODLES
TAGLIARINI PRIMAVERA
(Pictured on page 26)

Before you begin cooking this colorful pasta dish, have all the vegetables cut and ready to use—the sauce cooks quickly and is ready to serve in minutes.

½	pound asparagus
½	pound mushrooms, sliced
¼	cup slivered prosciutto or baked ham (optional)
¼	cup butter or margarine
1	medium-size carrot, thinly sliced
1	medium-size zucchini, diced
1	recipe Egg Pasta (page 34), cut into thin noodles about 10 inches long, or 8 ounces packaged thin noodles
	Salted water
3	green onions (including tops), sliced
½	cup frozen tiny peas, thawed
1	teaspoon dry basil
½	teaspoon salt
	Dash each ground nutmeg and white pepper
½	pint (1 cup) whipping cream
¼	cup freshly grated Parmesan cheese
	Chopped fresh parsley
	Additional grated Parmesan cheese

Snap off and discard white fibrous ends of asparagus. Cut spears diagonally into 1-inch lengths, but leave tips whole.

In a wide frying pan over medium-high heat, melt butter. Add mushrooms, prosciutto (if used), asparagus, carrot, and zucchini; cook, stirring occasionally, for 3 minutes. Cover pan and cook for 1 more minute.

Meanwhile, cook noodles in a large kettle of boiling salted water until al dente (1 to 2 minutes for fresh noodles, or follow package directions); drain well.

To vegetable mixture add green onions, peas, basil, salt, nutmeg, pepper, and cream. Increase heat to high and cook until liquid boils all over and forms large shiny bubbles. Return drained noodles to kettle in which they were cooked, pour vegetable sauce over noodles, and lift and mix gently so noodles are thoroughly coated. Add the ¼ cup Parmesan cheese and mix again.

Turn into a warm bowl, sprinkle with parsley, and serve at once with additional Parmesan cheese. Makes 4 to 6 servings.

FETTUCCINE WITH MINTED TOMATO SAUCE
FETTUCCINE NOVECENTO QUATTRO

Tomatoes—fresh or canned—with mint and toasted walnuts make an easy and very quick sauce for fresh fettuccine.

½	cup coarsely chopped walnuts
2	large, ripe tomatoes or 1 can (14½ oz.) Italian-style tomatoes
¼	cup dry white wine or water
1	teaspoon dry basil
¼	cup chopped fresh mint leaves or 1 tablespoon dry mint
¾	teaspoon salt
	Dash of pepper
⅓	cup olive oil or salad oil
1	small onion, finely chopped
1	clove garlic, minced or pressed
1	recipe Egg Pasta (page 34), cut into medium-wide noodles about 10 inches long, or 8 ounces packaged medium-wide noodles
	Salted water
	Grated Parmesan cheese

Spread walnuts in a shallow pan and toast in a 350° oven for 10 to 12 minutes or until browned. Meanwhile, peel, seed, and coarsely chop tomatoes. If using canned tomatoes, break up with a spoon and use liquid. In a medium-size bowl, combine tomatoes, wine (omit if using canned tomatoes), basil, mint, salt, and pepper; set aside.

Heat oil in a medium-size frying pan over medium heat. Add onion and cook until soft; stir in garlic and tomato mixture. Adjust heat so that mixture boils gently; cook, uncovered, stirring occasionally, for 5 minutes.

Meanwhile, cook noodles in a large kettle of boiling salted water until al dente (1 to 2 minutes for fresh noodles, or follow package directions). Drain well and place in a warm serving bowl. Spoon hot sauce over noodles. Lift and mix pasta gently, then sprinkle with walnuts. Serve with Parmesan cheese. Makes 4 to 6 servings.

follow package directions). Drain well and place on a warm platter; keep warm.

Meanwhile, in a wide frying pan over medium heat, place butter and oil. When butter is melted, add green onions, garlic, tomatoes, and wine. Cook, stirring, until mixture boils. Adjust heat so mixture boils gently, and cook for 2 minutes. Mix in lemon juice, crab, and parsley. Cook, stirring, just until crab is heated through. Season to taste with salt and pepper. Spoon sauce over pasta. Lift and mix pasta gently, then serve. Makes 4 servings.

GREEN FETTUCCINE WITH MASCARPONE
FETTUCCINE VERDE CON MASCARPONE

Mascarpone is a deliciously rich, faintly tart Italian cream cheese. In this recipe it serves as a sauce, melting around each strand of buttery homemade green noodles mixed with basil and pine nuts. Look for mascarpone in cheese stores, or make your own following the directions for Fresh Cheese on page 57.

¼	cup butter or margarine
½	cup pine nuts (pignoli)
1	small clove garlic, minced or pressed
1	recipe Pasta Verde (page 34), cut into medium-wide noodles about 10 inches long, or 8 ounces packaged medium-wide green noodles
	Salted water
½	cup mascarpone, or Fresh Cheese made with whipping cream (page 57)
3	tablespoons chopped fresh basil leaves
	Freshly grated Parmesan cheese

Melt butter in a small pan over low heat. Add pine nuts and garlic and cook, stirring frequently, just until nuts are lightly browned.

Meanwhile, cook noodles in a large kettle of boiling salted water until al dente (1 to 2 minutes for fresh noodles, or follow package directions).

Drain well and place in a warm serving bowl. Spoon mascarpone over noodles, about 1 heaping tablespoon at a time, and mix lightly. Stir basil into pine nut mixture; pour over noodles and lift and mix pasta gently before serving. Serve with Parmesan cheese to add to each serving. Makes 4 first-course servings.

FRESH PASTA WITH CREAM
FETTUCCINE ALFREDO

This is the famed rich fettuccine dish immortalized by Alfredo's restaurant in Rome. You'll have to serve this dish as soon as the last bit of cream is tossed with the noodles, because noodles are like sponges and they rapidly soak up the cream if allowed to stand. One way to make sure the fettuccine won't have to wait for your guests is to compose it in a chafing dish at the table.

1	recipe Egg Pasta (page 34), cut into medium-wide noodles about 10 inches long, or 8 ounces packaged medium-wide noodles
	Salted water
6	tablespoons butter or margarine
1½	cups whipping cream
1	cup (3 oz.) grated Parmesan cheese
	Salt and pepper
	Freshly grated or ground nutmeg

Cook noodles in a large kettle of boiling salted water until al dente (1 to 2 minutes for fresh noodles, or follow package directions). Drain well.

Meanwhile, melt butter in a wide frying pan (or chafing dish, if you plan to assemble this at the table) over high heat until butter is lightly browned. Add ½ cup of the cream and boil rapidly until slightly thickened. Reduce heat to medium, add noodles, and mix gently. Then add half the cheese and ½ cup of remaining cream. Lift and mix pasta gently. Repeat with remaining cheese and cream; mix again. Sea-

ANGEL HAIR PASTA WITH CRAB
CAPELLI D'ANGELI CON GRANCHIO

The very names of some pastas are so irresistible that one gives in to them, untasted and unseen. Capelli d'angeli (angel hair) casts such a spell, and in this recipe—with fresh crab, white wine, lemon, and tomato—the initial enthusiasm is completely justified. What's more, this lunch or supper dish is quick to cook.

1	recipe Egg Pasta (page 34), cut into very thin noodles about 10 inches long, or 8 ounces packaged capelli d'angeli or capellini
	Salted water
2	tablespoons butter or margarine
¼	cup olive oil or salad oil
½	cup sliced green onions
1	clove garlic, minced or pressed
2	medium-size ripe tomatoes, peeled, seeded, and chopped
¼	cup dry white wine
1	tablespoon lemon juice
½	pound cooked crab, flaked
¼	cup chopped fresh parsley
	Salt and pepper

Cook noodles in a large kettle of boiling salted water until al dente (1 to 2 minutes for fresh noodles, or

son with salt and pepper to taste and generously sprinkle with nutmeg. Serve immediately Makes 4 to 6 first-course servings.

PASTA WITH PEAS
TORTELLINI CON PISELLI

Green peas, filled pasta, cream, and cheese combine for a delicate Roman dish. You might serve it as a first course for a meal featuring a simple roast, or it can be the entrée for supper or lunch. You can use either filled tortellini or small ravioli, called raviolini.

1	package (12 oz.) freshly made or frozen tortellini or other small filled pasta such as raviolini
	Salted water
3	cups freshly shelled peas (about 3 lbs. peas in shells), or frozen petite peas, thawed
2	tablespoons butter or margarine
1/8	teaspoon freshly grated nutmeg
1 1/2	to 2 cups whipping cream
1	egg, beaten
1	cup freshly grated or shredded Parmesan cheese
	Additional grated or shredded Parmesan cheese and grated nutmeg

Drop tortellini into a large kettle of rapidly boiling salted water. When water returns to a boil, cook pasta for 10 minutes, then add fresh peas and cook for 5 minutes more, until pasta is al dente (if using frozen peas, cook pasta for 13 minutes, add frozen peas, and cook for 2 minutes more). Drain peas and pasta.

In a wide frying pan over medium heat melt butter. Add nutmeg and 1 1/2 cups of the cream along with peas and pasta. Increase heat to high and cook until liquid boils all over.

Remove pan from heat and stir in egg evenly; mix in the 1 cup cheese. If mixture is a little thick, add more cream to smooth sauce. Sprinkle with additional cheese and a little nutmeg. Serve at once. Makes 4 main-dish or 6 first-course servings.

OLD-FASHIONED RAVIOLI
(Pictured on facing page)

Yes, making ravioli the old-fashioned way takes time and effort. And yes, the results are well worth it!

The procedure isn't overwhelming if you space the preparation for these meat-filled and meat-sauced pasta squares over two or three days. Mix the filling one day (but stop before the cheese and eggs are added) and refrigerate it. The next day, mix in the cheese and eggs, fill the ravioli, and freeze them until needed. You can make the sauce on another day and freeze it, too, until you need it.

We give directions for rolling out the dough by hand or with a pasta machine. After the dough is filled, our directions call for using a ravioli pin to shape and seal the plump squares of dough and filling. Then we give directions for using a pastry wheel to cut the ravioli apart. The photograph on page 23 shows a 24-inch ravioli rolling pin that makes 1-inch ravioli. If you can't find a ravioli rolling pin in a gourmet specialty shop, you can cut the filled dough into squares by using just the fluted pastry wheel, but the seal won't be as good.

FILLING

2/3	pound pork chops, cut 1/2 inch thick
1/2	pound boneless beef chuck, cut 1/2 inch thick
1	tablespoon olive oil
2	cloves garlic
3	sprigs fresh parsley
1/4	teaspoon each dry rosemary, thyme leaves, and salt
	Dash of pepper
1	large bunch fresh spinach (about 1 lb.) or 1 package (10 or 12 oz.) frozen chopped spinach
2	tablespoons butter or margarine
1	or 2 eggs
2	tablespoons grated Romano or Parmesan cheese

PASTA

1	recipe Egg Pasta (page 34)
	Salted water

SAUCE

1	poun
2	table
1	large
4	clove press
1	cup li fresh
1	teasp
1/2	teasp thyme
1	teasp
1	can (a
1	large tomat
1	cup w

TOPPING

Grated Romano or Parmesan cheese

To make filling, cut pork from bones; reserve bones for sauce. Trim excess fat and any gristle from pork and beef. Cut meat into 2-inch squares. Heat oil in a wide frying pan over medium-high heat. Add meat and cook until browned on all sides. Add garlic, parsley, rosemary, thyme, salt, and pepper. Reduce heat to low and cook, uncovered, stirring occasionally, until pork is no longer pink when slashed (about 10 minutes).

Meanwhile, wash fresh spinach, drain, and discard stems and coarse leaves. Cook in a large pan with 1/2 inch of boiling water for 5 minutes (if using frozen spinach, cook according to package directions); drain. When

(Continued on page 24)

Rave reviews for ravioli! Especially homemade Old-fashioned Ravioli (page 22) stuffed with a mixture of spinach, pork, beef, and herbs, then topped with a robust meat sauce and Parmesan cheese. Clockwise from top left you see the main stages of ravioli making: eggs broken into a well of flour and ready for mixing, then kneading; a well-kneaded ball of pasta dough ready to be rolled out and filled; filled ravioli sectioned off by the ravioli rolling pin, and ready to be cut apart by the fluted pastry wheel, then plopped into a kettle of boiling water.

cool enough to handle, squeeze spinach with your hands to remove as much moisture as possible.

Melt butter in a frying pan over medium heat. Add spinach and cook, stirring, for 3 minutes.

Using a food processor or the finest blade of a meat grinder, very finely chop meat mixture. Finely chop spinach as well, but do not purée. In a bowl, combine meat and spinach. (At this point you may cover and refrigerate until next day if made ahead. Let mixture come to room temperature before continuing.) Beat 1 egg and stir into meat mixture along with cheese. If mixture seems stiff, beat another egg and stir into mixture. Set aside.

To prepare ravioli, divide Egg Pasta dough into 4 equal portions. Keeping unrolled portions covered, roll out 1 portion at a time, either by hand or with a pasta machine, according to directions that follow.

After ravioli have been filled and cut, you can cook them immediately; or transfer ravioli to floured baking sheets, freeze until firm, then transfer to plastic bags for longer storage in freezer.

To make sauce, cook meat in 1 tablespoon of the oil in a wide frying pan over medium-high heat until crumbly and browned. Transfer meat to a Dutch oven. Add remaining 1 tablespoon oil to frying pan. Add onion, garlic, and bones (reserved when making filling). Cook, stirring, until onion is limp. Add parsley, basil, rosemary, thyme, pepper, and salt; cook for 1 minute. Spoon onion mixture over meat in Dutch oven. Add tomato purée to meat. Strain liquid from tomatoes to remove seeds; add liquid to meat. Slit tomatoes and squeeze out seeds; chop tomatoes and add to meat. Stir in water. Bring sauce to a boil, then cover, reduce heat, and simmer, stirring occasionally, until sauce is thickened (2 hours). Remove bones. At this point you may cool, cover, and refrigerate, if made ahead; or freeze for longer storage.

To cook ravioli, drop freshly made or frozen ravioli into a large kettle of boiling salted water. When water

returns to a boil, cook pasta gently, stirring occasionally, until tender (10 to 12 minutes); drain well. While ravioli are cooking, heat sauce; allow ¾ to 1 cup sauce for every 50 ravioli. Ladle ravioli into a warm serving bowl. Spoon hot sauce over ravioli and sprinkle with Romano cheese. Makes about 200 one-inch ravioli.

To roll ravioli by hand. On a floured work surface, roll out 1 portion of dough into a rectangle or square about 1/16 inch thick for bottom layer. Spread filling about ¼ inch thick over bottom layer; be sure filling extends almost to edge of dough. For top layer, roll out another portion of dough to same size and thickness as bottom layer; place on top of filled layer and stretch it to cover bottom layer completely. Since it's hard to spread filling smoothly, without lumps or air pockets, it's a good idea to run a standard rolling pin very lightly over top layer of dough, just to even it out. Next run ravioli rolling pin slowly across top layer, pressing down firmly to seal dough layers and enclose filling in ravioli squares.

Finally, with a floured, fluted pastry wheel, cut filled squares apart along imprinted lines. Also run pastry wheel around outer edges to seal any half-formed ravioli (you can use these irregular ravioli for soup). With a spatula, transfer ravioli to a floured baking sheet. Repeat entire procedure with remaining dough and filling. Cook or freeze according to recipe directions.

To roll ravioli with a pasta machine. Roll out one portion of dough by machine to the third from the last setting. Do not let rolled strip dry. Immediately spread filling, about ¼ inch thick, over half the length of strip. Fold unfilled half of strip back over filled portion. Even out filling by lightly rolling a standard rolling pin across top. Then, with ravioli rolling pin, start rolling from widest side. Roll slowly, pressing firmly.

With a floured, fluted pastry wheel, cut filled squares apart along imprinted lines. Also run pastry wheel around outer edges to seal any half-formed ravioli (you can use these

irregular ravioli for soup). With a spatula, transfer ravioli to a floured baking sheet. Repeat entire procedure with remaining dough and filling. Cook or freeze according to recipe directions.

MEATBALLS & SPAGHETTI AMERICAN-STYLE

A steaming mound of spaghetti cloaked in a robust herby tomato sauce and topped by plump meatballs—this is Italian-American hearty dining at its most satisfying. It's a large recipe, and if you don't serve it all at once, you can freeze leftover meatballs and sauce. For variety, the meatballs can later be used in sandwiches and the sauce on another pasta.

	Tomato Sauce (recipe follows)
5	slices day-old sweet French bread, crusts removed
2	pounds ground lean beef
1	cup (3 oz.) grated Parmesan cheese
1	large onion, finely chopped
½	cup chopped fresh parsley
1	teaspoon *each* oregano leaves and salt
½	teaspoon pepper
2	teaspoons dry basil
3	cloves garlic, minced or pressed
3	eggs
3	tablespoons olive oil or salad oil
2	to 3 ounces spaghetti per person
	Salted water
	Additional grated Parmesan cheese

Combine ingredients for Tomato Sauce and set aside.

In a food processor or blender, whirl bread to make crumbs (you should have 2 cups lightly packed crumbs). In a large bowl, mix together crumbs, ground beef, the 1 cup Parmesan cheese, onion, parsley, oregano, salt, pepper, basil, garlic, and eggs until well blended. Form mixture into 1½-inch meatballs.

Heat olive oil in a wide frying pan

over medium heat. Add meatballs and brown on all sides, shaking pan frequently so balls keep their round shape. Drain briefly on paper towels. Add meatballs to sauce. Bring to a boil, then reduce heat; cover and simmer for 45 minutes.

Cook spaghetti in a large kettle of boiling salted water according to package directions until al dente. Drain well and place spaghetti on a warm platter. Spoon sauce with meatballs over spaghetti. Serve with additional Parmesan cheese. Makes about 4 dozen meatballs and 2½ quarts sauce.

Tomato Sauce. In a large kettle or Dutch oven, combine 2 cans (1 lb. 12 oz. each) tomato purée, 2 cloves **garlic** (minced or pressed), ½ cup chopped fresh **parsley**, ½ pound **mushrooms** (sliced), 1 stalk **celery** (finely chopped), 1 medium-size **carrot** (chopped), ¾ cup **dry red wine**, 2 tablespoons dry **basil**, 1 tablespoon **oregano leaves**, 2 teaspoons **salt**, 1 teaspoon **sugar**, ½ teaspoon **pepper**, and 1½ cups **water**.

SPAGHETTI WITH TOMATO SAUCE
SPAGHETTI AL POMODORO

You can make this rich, red sauce with or without ground beef. Either way, it is excellent with spaghetti or with such thinner varieties as spaghettini or vermicelli. If you wish, the recipe can be doubled to make 10 to 12 cups sauce.

½	cup dried Italian mushrooms
	Hot water
2	tablespoons olive oil or salad oil
½	cup chopped fresh parsley
1	stalk celery, finely chopped
1	medium-size onion, finely chopped
1	clove garlic, minced or pressed
1	-inch sprig fresh rosemary or ¼ teaspoon dry rosemary
1	small fresh sage leaf or ¼ teaspoon crumbled dry sage leaves
2	cans (8 oz. each) tomato sauce
1	can (1 lb.) tomatoes
½	small dried hot red chile (optional)
	Salt
1	pound spaghetti
	Salted water
	Grated Parmesan cheese

Place mushrooms in a small bowl and barely cover with hot water; set aside. In a large pan, heat oil over medium heat and add parsley, celery, onion, garlic, rosemary, and sage. Cook, stirring, until vegetables are soft. Stir in tomato sauce, tomatoes (break up with a spoon) and their liquid, and chile (if used). Pour in all of the mushroom soaking liquid but the last bit (containing residue). Chop mushrooms and add to pan. Bring to a boil; then cover, reduce heat, and simmer, stirring occasionally, until sauce is reduced to about 5 cups (about 2 hours). Taste and add salt, if needed. Remove chile, if used.

Cook spaghetti in a large kettle of boiling salted water according to package directions until al dente. Drain well and place on a warm serving platter. Spoon hot sauce over spaghetti. Serve with Parmesan cheese to add to each serving. Makes 6 to 8 servings.

Meat Sauce (Salsa alla Bolognese). Follow directions for tomato sauce (preceding), but first brown 1 pound **ground lean beef** (crumbled) in the oil, then add vegetables and continue as directed. Makes about 6 cups sauce.

LINGUINE WITH WHITE CLAM SAUCE
LINGUINE ALLE VONGOLE

Reserve a few clams in their shells to garnish this appealing pasta and seafood dish. It makes a fine, quick lunch or supper dish. You'll notice the recipe doesn't include grated Parmesan cheese—that's because Italians do not generally serve it with seafood pastas.

3	to 4 dozen small hard-shell clams in shell, well scrubbed
½	pound linguine or spaghetti
	Salted water
2	tablespoons butter or margarine
2	tablespoons olive oil
1	small onion, finely chopped
3	cloves garlic, minced or pressed
½	cup dry white wine
	Salt and pepper
½	cup chopped fresh parsley

Place clams and ¼ cup water in a large heavy pan. Cover and simmer just until clams pop open (5 to 10 minutes). When cool enough to handle, remove clams from shells and set aside (save a few clams in shells for garnish, if you wish). Strain clam broth through a piece of dampened muslin to remove grit; reserve broth.

Cook linguine in a large kettle of boiling salted water according to package directions until al dente; drain well.

While linguine cooks, place butter and oil in a wide frying pan over medium heat. When butter is melted, add onion and cook, stirring often, until soft.

Mix in garlic, wine, and strained clam broth. Bring to a boil, stirring occasionally, and cook until liquid is reduced by about half. Add clams, season with salt and pepper to taste, and stir in parsley.

Arrange linguine on a warm serving platter. Spoon hot sauce over linguine. Garnish with reserved clams in shells, if you wish. Makes 4 servings.

SPAGHETTI CARBONARA

Beaten raw egg is the secret of this delicate and delicious spaghetti dish. The egg coats the pasta and causes the bits of sausage, prosciutto, and cheese to cling evenly.

A less expensive but equally delicious variation is made with ground beef, onion, and fennel seeds.

¼	pound mild Italian sausages
¼	pound thinly sliced prosciutto or cooked ham
4	tablespoons butter
½	cup chopped fresh parsley
3	eggs, well beaten
½	cup grated Parmesan cheese
	Freshly ground black pepper
½	pound spaghetti
	Salted water
	Additional grated Parmesan cheese

Remove casings from sausages and crumble meat. Finely chop prosciutto. In a wide frying pan over medium-low heat, melt 2 tablespoons of the butter. Add sausage and half the prosciutto to pan and cook, stirring, until sausage is lightly browned and prosciutto is curled (about 10 minutes). Stir in remaining prosciutto.

If you wish to complete the preparation at the table, have ready in separate containers the remaining 2 tablespoons butter, parsley, eggs, the ½ cup Parmesan cheese, and pepper.

Cook spaghetti in a large kettle of boiling salted water according to package directions until al dente. Drain well and add to hot meat mixture. At the table (if you wish), add

butter and parsley to spaghetti mixture; mix quickly to blend. At once pour in eggs and quickly lift and mix spaghetti to coat well with egg. Sprinkle in the ½ cup cheese and a dash of pepper; mix again. Serve with additional Parmesan cheese. Makes 4 servings.

Ground Beef Carbonara Sauce. Follow directions for Carbonara Sauce (preceding), but omit sausage and prosciutto. Instead brown ½ to ¾ pound **ground lean beef** (crumbled) with ¼ teaspoon **fennel seeds** (coarsely crushed), 1 small **onion** (finely chopped), and 1 clove **garlic** (minced or pressed). Continue to cook until onion is soft. Beat eggs with ¼ teaspoon **salt**.

SPAGHETTINI WITH ANCHOVY SAUCE
SPAGHETTINI ALLA PUTTANESCA

If the Italians aren't naming their dishes for saints, they're naming them for sinners—translated literally, this is "harlot's spaghetti." Dried red chile gives zest to this assertive Neapolitan sauce, which is quick to put together for an impromptu first course or supper.

¼	cup olive oil
1	medium-size onion, finely chopped
½	small dried hot red chile, crushed
1	clove garlic, minced or pressed
1	can (14½ oz.) Italian-style tomatoes
1	can (8 oz.) tomato sauce
⅓	cup slivered ripe olives
1	tablespoon capers
¼	teaspoon oregano leaves
½	pound spaghettini
	Salted water
1	can (2 oz.) anchovies, drained and chopped
¼	cup chopped fresh parsley

Heat olive oil in a wide frying pan over medium heat. Add onion and chile and cook until onion is soft; mix in garlic, tomatoes (break up with

a spoon) and their liquid, tomato sauce, olives, capers, and oregano. Adjust heat so that mixture boils gently and cook, uncovered, stirring occasionally, until sauce is slightly thickened (15 to 20 minutes).

Meanwhile, cook spaghettini in a large kettle of boiling salted water according to package directions until al dente. Drain well and place on a warm platter. Mix anchovies and parsley into sauce; spoon hot sauce over spaghettini. Makes 4 to 6 first-course servings, or 2 or 3 main-course servings.

BUCATINI, AMATRICE-STYLE
BUCATINI ALL' AMATRICIANA

Amatrice, a small town north of Rome, gives its name to this favorite Roman pasta combination made with bucatini, a thin spaghetti with a hole through the middle. You might also use perciatelle, a plumper variety that is also pierced.

Part of the flavor of the zesty sauce comes from pancetta, often found among the cold meats in Italian delicatessens. Pancetta resembles a salami-shaped roll of bacon (with a higher proportion of lean to fat) and has a flavor similar to a prosciutto. Unlike bacon, pancetta is not usually smoked.

¼	pound sliced pancetta or bacon
	Olive oil
1	medium-size onion, finely chopped
½	teaspoon crushed dried hot red chile
1	clove garlic, minced or pressed
1	can (14½ oz.) Italian-style tomatoes
⅓	cup dry white wine
2	tablespoons chopped fresh parsley
½	pound bucatini, perciatelle, or spaghetti
	Salted water
	Salt (optional)
	Grated Parmesan cheese

(Continued on next page)

Rumor has it that Tagliarini Primavera (page 20) is the dish Botticelli's models dined on after posing for his famous portrait of spring, "Primavera." Thin strands of tagliarini combine with asparagus, carrots, mushrooms, peas, zucchini, green onions, prosciutto, a touch of cream, and a grating of Parmesan cheese—truly a springtime celebration.

Pesto is the word for "pounded." The Genoese originators of pesto sauce used a mortar and pestle to pound fresh basil, Parmesan cheese, oil, and garlic to a smooth green paste. Today a blender or food processor eases the making of this superb sauce.

Pesto is best known as a sauce for pasta, but it's delicious served atop hot buttered vegetables such as artichokes, green beans, broccoli, carrots, cauliflower, eggplant, potatoes, peas, spinach, tomatoes, or zucchini.

You can spread pesto on fresh tomato halves, too, then sprinkle them with grated Parmesan cheese and broil until they're heated and the topping is browned. Delicious!

Versatile pesto can also be used as a seasoning to give a tomato-based sauce or homemade mayonnaise an instant Italian accent. It can even perk up a homemade or canned soup; just stir in Basic Pesto to taste.

Following the recipe for Basic Pesto, we present some additional serving ideas, but you'll probably begin inventing your own pesto-sauced recipes when you see how easy it is to make—and how marvelous it is to eat.

BASIC PESTO

Our basic pesto recipe has garlic as an option but you could use pine nuts or a little lemon instead. Look for fresh basil at the supermarket in summer and early fall.

2	cups lightly packed fresh basil leaves, washed and thoroughly dried
1	cup (3 oz.) freshly grated Parmesan cheese
½	cup olive oil
1	or 2 cloves minced garlic (optional)

Place basil, Parmesan, oil, and garlic in a blender or food processor. Process until basil is finely chopped. Use pesto at once, or place in small jars and add a thin layer of olive oil to each jar to keep pesto from darkening. Refrigerate for up to a week, or freeze for longer storage. Makes about 1 ⅓ cups.

Pasta with Pesto. To 4 cups hot, cooked, drained **fettuccine, spaghetti,** or similar **pasta,** add 6 tablespoons **Basic Pesto** and 4 tablespoons softened **butter** or margarine; toss gently. Add 1 cup grated **Parmesan cheese** and mix. Serve additional Parmesan cheese and pesto to be added to taste. Makes 4 to 6 servings.

Pesto Butter. Blend 3 tablespoons **Basic Pesto** with ½ cup soft **butter.** Spoon over hot vegetables, use with breadsticks, or spread on Italian or French bread. Makes ⅔ cup.

Pesto Dressing. Blend 6 tablespoons **Basic Pesto** with ⅓ cup **wine vinegar,** ⅔ cup **olive oil,** and 1 minced or pressed **garlic clove** (optional). Use on salad greens or your favorite seafood salad, or as a marinade for cold cooked vegetables. Makes 1 ⅓ cups.

...Bucatini, Amatrice-style (cont'd.)

Cut pancetta or bacon into ½ by 1-inch strips. In a wide frying pan over medium heat, cook pancetta, stirring frequently, until crisp and lightly browned; remove with a slotted spoon and set aside. Measure fat in pan and add enough oil to make a total of ¼ cup. To pan, add onion and chile and cook, stirring often, until onion is soft. Mix in garlic, tomatoes (break up with a spoon) and their liquid, wine, and parsley. Adjust heat so mixture boils gently; cook, uncovered, stirring occasionally, until sauce is slightly thickened (10 to 15 minutes).

Meanwhile, cook bucatini in a large kettle of boiling salted water according to package directions until al dente. Drain well and place on a warm platter. Mix pancetta into sauce; taste and add salt, if needed. Spoon sauce over bucatini. Serve with Parmesan cheese to add to each serving. Makes 4 first-course servings.

RIGATONI WITH CREAMY TOMATO SAUCE
RIGATONI ALLA BAGUTTA

The fat, ridged macaroni tubes called rigatoni are good with bold, chunky sauces, such as this Milanese tomato-cream sauce with sausage and peas.

¼	pound mild Italian sausages
2	tablespoons butter or margarine
1	small onion, finely chopped
1	clove garlic, minced or pressed
2	medium-size ripe tomatoes, peeled, seeded, and chopped
½	cup each canned tomato sauce and dry white wine
¼	teaspoon salt
½	pound (about 2½ cups) rigatoni or mostaccioli
	Salted water
¼	cup fresh or frozen peas
½	cup whipping cream
	Grated Parmesan cheese

Remove casings from sausages; crumble meat. In a deep, heavy frying pan over medium-low heat, melt butter. Add sausage and onion and cook slowly, stirring occasionally, until sausage is lightly browned. Mix in garlic, tomatoes, tomato sauce, wine, and salt; increase heat to medium and bring mixture to a boil. Cover, reduce heat, and simmer for 15 minutes.

Meanwhile, cook rigatoni in boiling salted water according to package directions until al dente. Drain well and place in a warm serving bowl. Keep warm.

Mix peas and cream into sausage sauce. Increase heat to medium-high and cook, stirring, until sauce boils all over in large shiny bubbles and is slightly thickened. Spoon over rigatoni and mix lightly. Serve with Parmesan cheese to add to each serving. Makes 4 first-course servings.

RIGATONI WITH SAUSAGE SAUCE
RIGATONI LE VELETTE

Italian sausage flavors this simple Umbrian cream-and-white-wine sauce for plump rigatoni. Rigatoni are large pasta tubes with ridges; you can substitute thinner tubes called mostaccioli (mustaches).

½	**pound mild Italian sausages**
¼	**cup butter or margarine**
½	**pound (about 2½ cups) rigatoni or mostaccioli**
	Salted water
¾	**cup whipping cream**
¼	**cup** each **dry white wine and grated Parmesan cheese**
	Grated nutmeg
	Additional grated Parmesan cheese

Remove casings from sausages; crumble meat. In a deep, heavy frying pan over medium-low heat, melt butter. Add sausage and cook slowly, stirring occasionally, until sausage is lightly browned. Meanwhile, cook rigatoni in boiling salted water according to package directions until al dente; drain well.

Add cream and wine to sausage; increase heat to medium-high and bring to a boil. Adjust heat so mixture boils gently; cook, stirring occasionally, until sauce is slightly thickened (about 5 minutes). Mix in drained rigatoni and the ¼ cup cheese. Sprinkle lightly with nutmeg. Serve at once with additional grated Parmesan cheese. Makes 4 to 6 first-course servings.

PASTA TWISTS WITH TOMATO & MOZZARELLA
FUSILLI ALLA VESUVIANA

Cheese-tossed noodle twists are topped with a quick-cooking tomato and basil sauce to make a favorite Neapolitan dish. For this recipe use short, corkscrew-shaped fusilli, not the long, twisty strands that go by the same name.

¼	**cup olive oil**
3	**cloves garlic, cut in halves**
1	**can (14½ oz.) Italian-style tomatoes**
¼	**teaspoon oregano leaves**
¼	**cup dry red wine**
½	**teaspoon salt**
⅛	**teaspoon pepper**
¼	**cup lightly packed fresh basil leaves or 1 tablespoon dry basil**
½	**pound (2½ to 3 cups) fusilli or rotelle**
	Salted water
1	**cup shredded mozzarella cheese**
	Grated Parmesan cheese

Heat oil in a medium-size frying pan over medium heat. Add garlic and cook, stirring, until it turns a pale golden brown; remove and discard garlic. Add to pan tomatoes (break up with a spoon) and their liquid, oregano, wine, salt, pepper, and basil. Adjust heat so mixture boils gently; cook, uncovered, stirring occasionally, until sauce is slightly thickened (15 to 20 minutes).

Meanwhile, cook fusilli in a large kettle of boiling salted water according to package directions until al dente. Drain well and place in a

warm serving bowl. Mix hot fusilli gently with mozzarella cheese. Spoon tomato sauce over all. Serve with Parmesan cheese to add to each serving. Makes 4 to 6 first-course servings.

ORECCHIETTE WITH SAUSAGE SAUCE
ORECCHIETTE AL POMODORO

A specialty of Apulia and Basilicata in southeastern Italy, orecchiette—as their Italian name suggests—are shaped like tiny ears. The less anatomically minded might liken their shape to that of the round-crowned, wide-brimmed hats worn by Italian priests. However you perceive them, they taste delicious with a tomato-and-sausage sauce.

½	**pound mild Italian sausages**
2	**tablespoons olive oil**
1	**medium-size onion, finely chopped**
1	**clove garlic, minced or pressed**
1	**can (1 lb.) tomatoes**
¼	**cup tomato paste**
1	**teaspoon dry basil**
½	**teaspoon salt**
⅛	**teaspoon pepper**
½	**pound (about 2½ cups) orecchiette or medium-size macaroni shells**
	Salted water
¼	**cup chopped fresh parsley**
	Grated dry jack or Parmesan cheese

Remove casings from sausages; crumble meat. Heat oil in a wide frying pan over medium heat. Add sausage and onion and cook, stirring often, until sausage is lightly browned. Mix in garlic, tomatoes (break up with a spoon) and their liquid, tomato paste, basil, salt, and pepper; bring to a boil. Cover, reduce heat, and simmer for 15 minutes. Uncover and adjust heat so sauce boils gently; cook, stirring occasionally, until sauce is slightly thickened (about 5 minutes).

Meanwhile, cook orecchiette in a

large kettle of boiling salted water according to package directions until al dente. Drain well and place in a warm serving bowl. Mix parsley into sausage sauce; spoon hot sauce over orecchiette and mix lightly. Serve with grated cheese to add to each serving. Makes 4 to 6 first-course servings.

MALLOREDDUS WITH LAMB RIBLETS
MALLOREDDUS A LA CANTINELLA

A Sardinian restaurant in Rome features this unusual pasta. Homemade malloreddus are like tiny, ridged gnocchi. In packaged form they can be found in stores carrying a wide variety of pasta imported from Italy. If you can't find malloreddus, you can use cavatelli or medium-size shells instead.

Lamb spareribs, though not very meaty, give the sauce flavor and body. When you purchase them, have each side of ribs cut in half across the bones.

2	pounds lamb spareribs, cut across bones in about 2-inch lengths
	Salt
2	tablespoons olive oil
1	medium-size onion, finely chopped
2	cloves garlic, minced or pressed
¾	teaspoon ground cinnamon
½	small dried hot red chile, crushed
1	can (1 lb.) tomatoes
¼	cup each tomato paste, water, and chopped fresh parsley
½	pound (about 1¾ cups) malloreddus, cavatelli, or medium-size macaroni shells
	Salted water
	Grated Parmesan cheese

Cut lamb between bones to make small square pieces. Sprinkle with salt. Heat oil in a deep, heavy frying pan over medium heat. Brown lamb pieces, about half at a time. Remove when browned and set aside.

When all lamb is browned, pour off and discard all but 1 tablespoon of the pan drippings; add onion to remaining drippings and cook until onion is soft. Mix in garlic, then return lamb to pan. Sprinkle with cinnamon and chile. Add tomatoes (break up with a spoon) and their liquid, tomato paste, water, and parsley; bring to a boil. Cover, reduce heat, and simmer until lamb is tender (about 1 hour). Skim and discard fat, then continue cooking, uncovered, until sauce is thickened (5 to 10 minutes).

Meanwhile, cook malloreddus in a large kettle of boiling salted water according to package directions until al dente. Drain well and arrange in a warm serving bowl. Spoon hot lamb sauce over malloreddus. Serve with Parmesan cheese to add to each serving. Makes 6 first-course servings or 3 or 4 main-dish servings.

VEAL & CHICKEN CANNELLONI
CANNELLONI ALLA BONA
(Pictured on the cover)

Legendary cannelloni such as these are not achieved without some effort. At least a day ahead, though, you can separately prepare each of the four main elements: the veal, ricotta, and chicken filling; the fresh pasta in which it is wrapped; the sauce in which the cannelloni rest; and the cheese that swathes and coats the filled noodles as they bake.

The results are well worth the work. The recipe is named for its creator, a California restaurateur who introduced many to the grandeur of Italian cooking at its finest.

FILLING

¼	cup butter or margarine
1	large onion, finely chopped
1	small clove garlic
1½	pounds chicken thighs, boned and skinned
½	pound boneless veal
1	cup (8 oz.) ricotta cheese
½	cup freshly grated Parmesan cheese
2	egg yolks
¾	teaspoon salt
⅛	teaspoon ground nutmeg

SAUCE

1½	tablespoons butter or margarine
2	tablespoons chopped shallots or green onions (white part only)
5	medium-size ripe tomatoes, peeled, seeded, and diced
½	cup chicken broth
½	teaspoon each salt and dry basil
¼	cup butter or margarine
1½	tablespoons all-purpose flour
1	cup milk
1	can (14½ oz.) regular-strength chicken broth, or 1½ cups Brown Stock (page 38)

½	recipe Egg Pasta (page 34)
	Salted water
1	tablespoon olive oil or salad oil

(Continued on page 32)

It was Roman soldier food: polenta. One of many Italian dishes dating back to antiquity, polenta made with millet and wheat was the staple food of the Roman army. Since the introduction of corn from the New World, though, polenta has been made with cornmeal. Simple peasant food, it provides the perfect foil for spicy dishes. The recipe for Polenta is on page 33.

TOPPING

About 1½ pounds teleme cheese

To make filling, melt butter in a medium-size frying pan over medium heat; add onion and garlic and cook until soft; do not brown. Cut chicken and veal into 2-inch-square pieces and place in a shallow baking pan just large enough to hold them in a single layer. Spoon cooked onion mixture evenly over meat.

. Bake, uncovered, in a 350° oven for 35 minutes; cool slightly. Transfer to a food processor and process until meats are finely ground. Add ricotta cheese, Parmesan cheese, egg yolks, salt, and nutmeg; process until smoothly blended. (Or, using finest blade of a food chopper, grind cooked meat mixture with ricotta, passing some of the ground mixture through a second time to clear the chopper of solid pieces. Transfer to a bowl and add Parmesan cheese, egg yolks, salt and nutmeg; stir to blend thoroughly.) At this point you may cover and refrigerate for up to 48 hours, if made ahead.

To make sauce, melt the 1½ tablespoons butter in a medium-size pan over medium heat. Add shallots and cook until soft. Add tomatoes, the ½ cup chicken broth, salt, and basil; bring to a boil. Reduce heat and simmer, uncovered, stirring occasionally, until mixture is reduced to about 2 cups (about 40 minutes).

Meanwhile, melt the ¼ cup butter in a large pan over medium heat; blend in flour and cook, stirring, until golden. Gradually stir in milk and the 1 can chicken broth. Adjust heat so mixture boils gently; cook, uncovered, stirring occasionally, until liquid is reduced to about 2 cups (about 25 minutes). Stir in tomato mixture and simmer gently for about 15 minutes more; set aside. (At this point you may cover and refrigerate for up to 3 days, if you wish. Reheat when ready to assemble cannelloni.)

To prepare pasta, divide Egg Pasta dough into 2 equal portions. Roll out each portion, by hand or machine, to a strip about 4 inches by 40 inches.

Cut each strip into 4-by-5 inch rectangles; you should have 16 rectangles. In a wide shallow pan, bring about ½ inch salted water to a boil; add oil. Place noodles, about 4 at a time, in water without crowding or overlapping. Cook each batch of noodles until al dente, but not soft (about 2 minutes). With a slotted spatula, lift noodles from water and drain flat on a clean towel. Mound about 3 tablespoons filling evenly along a 5-inch side of each cooked pasta rectangle; roll to enclose filling.

To assemble, pour heated sauce into a shallow container about 12 by 15 inches, or two 6 by 15-inch baking dishes, or 8 individual baking dishes (each about 3 by 6 inches). Set cannelloni into sauce, spacing them ½ to ¾ inches apart. Top each cannelloni with a slice of cheese just slightly larger in length and width than the top of each noodle.

Bake, uncovered, in a 425° oven for 10 to 15 minutes or until heated through. Makes 8 main-dish servings of 2 cannelloni each.

BAKED ZITI
ZITI AL FORNO

The large, tubular macaroni known as ziti makes an abundant casserole when baked with tiny meatballs in tomato sauce and topped with mozzarella cheese.

SAUCE

2	tablespoons butter or margarine
2	tablespoons olive oil
1	large onion, finely chopped
¼	pound mushrooms, thinly sliced
2	cloves garlic, minced or pressed
1	can (about 1 lb.) tomato purée
1	large can (1 lb. 12 oz.) Italian-style tomatoes
½	cup dry red wine
1	teaspoon salt
1	bay leaf
½	teaspoon oregano leaves
¼	teaspoon pepper
¼	cup chopped fresh parsley

MEATBALLS

2	tablespoons butter or margarine
1	tablespoon olive oil or salad oil
1	medium onion, finely chopped
1	egg
¾	cup soft bread crumbs
1½	teaspoons salt
	Dash each pepper and ground nutmeg
½	cup sauce (preceding)
1½	pounds ground lean beef

PASTA

1	package (1 lb.) ziti or mostaccioli
	Salted water
1	pound mozzarella cheese, thinly sliced
½	cup grated Parmesan cheese

To make sauce, place butter and oil in a 5 to 6-quart pan over medium heat. When butter is melted, add onion and mushrooms and cook until onion is soft. Mix in garlic, tomato purée, tomatoes (break up with a spoon) and their liquid, wine, salt, bay leaf, oregano, pepper, and parsley; bring to a boil. Cover, reduce heat, and simmer until sauce is reduced to about 5 cups (about 1½ hours). Remove bay leaf.

To make meatballs, place ½ tablespoon **each** of the butter and oil in a large frying pan over medium heat. When butter is melted, add onion and cook until onion is lightly browned; transfer to a mixing bowl and cool slightly. Beat in egg, bread crumbs, salt, pepper, nutmeg, and the ½ cup sauce. Add ground beef and mix lightly to blend well. Shape into 1-inch meatballs. In same pan in which onions were cooked, heat remaining 1½ tablespoons butter and ½ tablespoon oil over medium heat. When butter is melted, brown meatballs, about half at a time. Remove when browned and add to sauce.

Cook ziti in a large kettle of boiling salted water according to package directions until al dente. Drain well and combine with meatball mixture. Spread mixture in a shallow 4-quart casserole. Cover evenly with mozzarella cheese, then sprinkle evenly with Parmesan cheese. Bake, uncovered, in a 350° oven for 30 to 35 minutes or until top is golden brown. Makes 8 to 10 servings.

CREAMY BAKED LASAGNE
LASAGNE AL FORNO

Homemade green pasta makes this Bologna-style lasagne special. With packaged noodles it will be good, but somewhat less delicate.

¾	pound mild Italian sausages
1½	pounds ground lean beef, crumbled
1	large onion, finely chopped
2	stalks celery, finely chopped
2	medium-size carrots, shredded
1	can (6 oz.) tomato paste
1	can (14½ oz.) regular-strength beef broth
1½	teaspoons dry basil
½	teaspoon dry rosemary
½	recipe Pasta Verde (page 34), cut into wide strips about 12 inches long, or 12 to 16 packaged lasagne noodles
	Salted water
	Cheese Sauce (recipe follows)
1	cup (4 oz.) shredded fontina or Jack cheese
1	cup grated Parmesan cheese

Remove casings from sausages; crumble meat. In a wide frying pan or Dutch oven, combine sausage, ground beef, onion, celery, and carrots; cook over high heat, stirring, until meat is lightly browned and juices have evaporated. Spoon off excess fat, if necessary. Stir in tomato paste, broth, basil, and rosemary. Reduce heat to medium-high and cook, stirring often, until mixture is very thick; set aside.

Cook pasta in a large kettle of boiling salted water until al dente (3 to 4 minutes for fresh noodles, or follow package directions). Drain, rinse with cold water, and drain again. Arrange a fourth of the lasagne noodles in a shallow 3-quart baking dish. Spread with a fourth of the meat mixture, then with a fourth of the Cheese Sauce. Repeat this layering 3 more times, ending with Cheese Sauce. Sprinkle evenly with fontina and Parmesan cheeses. If made ahead, cover and refrigerate.

Bake, uncovered, in a 375° oven for 25 to 35 minutes or until hot and bubbly. Cut into squares to serve. Makes 8 servings.

Cheese Sauce. In a medium-size pan over medium heat, melt ¼ cup **butter** or margarine. Add 1 large **onion** (finely chopped) and cook, stirring, until onion is soft. Blend in ¼ cup **all-purpose flour** and ⅛ teaspoon **ground nutmeg**. Cook, stirring, until bubbly. Gradually stir in 1 can (14½ oz.) regular-strength **beef broth** and 1 cup **milk**. Cook, stirring, until sauce boils and thickens slightly. Stir in 2 cups (8 oz.) shredded **fontina** or jack cheese, stirring until cheese melts.

POLENTA
(Pictured on page 31)

If you're in the mood for traditional, simple Italian food, polenta is a good choice to serve with Sweet-Sour Ribs (page 69) and Venetian Liver (page 76). One of many Italian dishes dating back to antiquity, a version of polenta nourished soldiers of the Roman Army.

A coarsely ground cornmeal, as well as the mush it makes when cooked with water, polenta is a staple in certain areas of northern Italy, particularly around Venice and Florence. The mush is considered properly made when boiled in a brass pot that tapers from a flaring rim to a narrow base; it is stirred with a wooden spoon or stick until the polenta is so thick it pulls from the sides of the pan and the stick can stand upright without aid.

Traditionally, too, polenta is cut into slices with a tautly held string. It is then served freshly made and hot; or it is cooled and the slices may be grilled. Both may be topped with butter and cheese, or a sauce.

6	cups water
	About 1 teaspoon salt
2	cups polenta
	About 3 tablespoons butter (optional)
	Grated or shredded cheese such as Parmesan, Romano, fontina, or Jack
	Sauce (optional)

In a large deep pan over high heat, bring water and 1 teaspoon salt to a boil; gradually stir in polenta. Reduce heat and simmer gently, stirring frequently to prevent sticking, until mixture is very thick (about 30 minutes); use a long-handled spoon because mixture pops and bubbles and can burn you. Stir in 3 tablespoons butter, if you wish, and add salt, if needed.

Butter a deep medium-size bowl. Spoon polenta into bowl and let set for 10 minutes. Invert onto a flat plate; mixture will unmold and hold shape of bowl. Cut polenta into thick slices and serve hot, topped with more butter and cheese, or any meat or tomato sauce in this chapter that is intended to spoon onto pastas. Makes 8 to 10 servings.

Grilled Polenta Slices. Cut cold polenta in slices about ¾ inch thick. Brush lightly on all sides with olive oil or melted butter and place on a grill about 4 or 5 inches over an even bed of medium-hot coals. Cook 6 to 7 minutes on each side, or until lightly toasted and heated throughout.

EGG PASTA
PASTA ALL'UOVO

Tender, springy, fresh pasta dough is perfect for noodles of all sizes, and also for ravioli (page 22). The Pasta Verde (Green Pasta) variation can be used whenever you want a touch of color. For further variations you can substitute whole wheat flour or semolina flour for up to half of the all-purpose flour.

The amount of liquid that any flour can absorb varies with the moisture already in the flour, and with the temperature and humidity in your kitchen. Indeed, there's really no way to tell how much water you'll need until you start working with the dough.

2 **cups all-purpose flour**
2 **large eggs**
3 **to 6 tablespoons water**
Additional all-purpose flour for kneading, rolling, and cutting

Mound flour on a work surface or in a large bowl and make a deep well in center. Break eggs into well. With a fork, beat eggs lightly and stir in 2 tablespoons of the water. Using a circular motion, begin to draw flour from sides of well. Add 1 more tablespoon of the water and continue mixing until flour is moistened. If necessary, add more water, a tablespoon at a time. When dough becomes stiff, use your hands to finish mixing. Pat dough into a ball and knead a few times to help flour absorb liquid. Then clean and lightly flour the work surface.

If you plan to use a pasta machine (manual or electric), first knead dough by hand, sprinkling with flour if needed, for 3 or 4 minutes or until dough is no longer sticky. Then proceed with pasta machine.

If you plan to use a rolling pin, knead dough by hand, sprinkling with flour if needed, for 10 minutes or until dough is smooth and elastic. Cover and let dough rest for 20 minutes. Then proceed with rolling pin.

With pasta machine or rolling pin, roll out a fourth of the dough at a time to desired thinness. Keep unrolled portion covered. When all dough is rolled, cut strips into desired shapes by machine or by hand. Machine-rolled dough makes about 4 cups cooked pasta when machine-cut into medium-wide noodles, or about 32 pieces lasagne. Yield of hand-rolled noodles may vary.

Pasta Verde (Green Pasta). Cook ½ package (10-oz. size) **frozen chopped spinach** according to package directions. Let spinach cool, then squeeze out as much liquid as possible. Mince finely; you should have ¼ cup spinach. Make **Egg Pasta,** substituting the spinach for the water. Add a few drops **water** only if dough is very dry.

FOOD PROCESSOR PASTA

The action of a food processor in making pasta reduces mixing time to seconds and kneading time from 10 minutes to 2 or 3—truly pasta presto!

2 **cups all-purpose flour**
2 **large eggs**
4 **tablespoons water**
Additional all-purpose flour for kneading, rolling, and cutting

Using metal blade, process flour and eggs for 5 seconds or until mixture looks like cornmeal. With motor running, pour 4 tablespoons water down feed tube and process until dough forms a ball. Dough should be well blended, but not sticky. If it feels sticky, add a little flour as it mixes and the dough takes shape. If dough looks crumbly, add another teaspoon or two of water to form dough. If food processor begins to slow down or stop—a good indication that dough is properly mixed—turn off motor and proceed to next step.

Turn dough onto a floured work surface and knead until smooth and elastic.

If you plan to use a pasta machine (manual or electric), you can roll dough out immediately. If you plan to use a rolling pin, cover dough and let it rest for 20 minutes.

With pasta machine or rolling pin, roll out a fourth of the dough at a time to desired thinness. Keep unrolled portion covered. When all dough is rolled, cut strips into desired shapes by machine or by hand. Machine-rolled dough makes about 4 cups cooked pasta when machine-cut into medium-wide noodles, or about 32 pieces lasagne. Yield of hand-rolled noodles may vary.

Processor Pasta Verde. Cook ½ package (10-oz. size) **frozen chopped spinach** according to package directions. Let spinach cool, then squeeze out as much liquid as possible. Process spinach (you should have ¼ cup) with 2 **large eggs** until spinach is finely chopped. Add 2 cups **all-purpose flour** and process until dough forms a ball. Add a few drops **water** only if dough is very dry.

PASTA BY MACHINE

The following directions apply to both manual and electric pasta machines. The directions are general, though, since brands of pasta machines differ slightly in size and function.

Kneading and rolling. Flatten a fourth of the dough slightly; flour it, then feed it through the widest roller setting. Fold the dough into thirds and feed it through the rollers again. Repeat the folding and rolling process 8 to 10 times or until the dough is elastic. If the dough feels at all damp or sticky, flour both sides each time it's rolled.

When the dough is smooth and pliable, set the rollers one notch closer together and feed the dough through. Flour the dough if it's damp or sticky. Repeat the rolling, setting the rollers closer each time, until the dough is a long strip as thin as you want it.

Cut the strip in half crosswise for easy handling. Place the strip halves on a floured cloth or sheet and leave uncovered while you roll the remaining portions. Let each strip dry for 5 to 10 minutes until it feels leathery but pliable.

Cutting. Feed each strip through the medium-wide blades for fettuccine or through the narrow blades for thin noodles (tagliarini). Some machines have attachments for wide and narrow lasagne, but lasagne can also be cut easily by hand, as can ravioli (page 22).

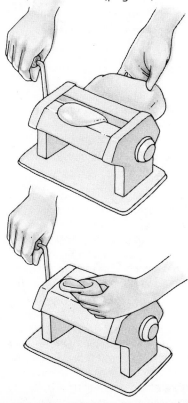

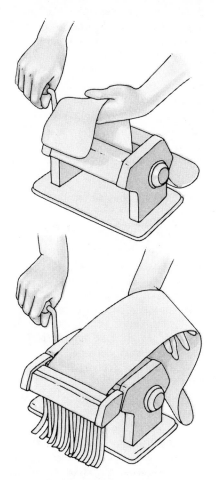

Lightly flour the cut noodles to keep the strands separate. Once cut, the noodles can be handled in either of two ways: you can toss them in a loose pile, or you can carefully gather the strands as they emerge from the machine (or have someone else gather them) and lay them in neat rows.

It's best to cook the noodles right away. After all, the point of making your own pasta is to enjoy the wonderful taste of freshly made noodles.

If you make more noodles than you need, you can let them dry for 30 minutes to an hour until they're dry but still pliable. Then place them in a plastic bag and refrigerate for as long as 2 days, or freeze for longer storage (up to 2 months). Do not thaw before cooking.

PASTA BY HAND

Once your pasta dough is mixed, a few minutes of friendly kneading will make it tender, elastic, and springy.

Kneading. Flatten the dough ball slightly, then fold the farthest edge toward you. With your finger tips or the heel of your palm, press and push the dough away from you, sealing the fold. Rotate the dough a quarter-turn and continue the folding-pushing motion, making a turn each time. Knead with a gentle, rhythmic motion until the dough is smooth and elastic.

To reduce elasticity so dough will be easier to shape, cover the dough and let it rest for about 20 minutes.

Rolling. With a rolling pin, roll out a fourth of the dough into a rectangle about 1/16 inch thick. If the dough is sticky, turn and flour both sides as you roll. Transfer the rolled strip to a lightly floured surface or cloth and leave uncovered while you roll out the remaining portions. Let each strip dry for 5 to 10 minutes until it feels flexible like a chamois cloth.

Cutting. Place a strip of rolled pasta dough on a lightly floured cutting board and sprinkle with flour. Starting at narrow end, roll up jelly roll fashion and cut into slices as wide as you want the noodle. Fettuccine is usually about 1/4 inch wide and tagliarini about 1/8 inch; lasagne is about 2 inches wide.

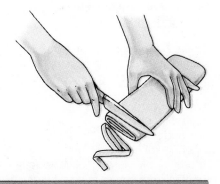

RISOTTO

Risotto is rice cooked to develop a creamy, flowing consistency. Even in its plainest form—seasoned only with a little onion, garlic, broth, and cheese—risotto is distinctive and worthy of presentation as a first-course dish, or as a course to follow antipasto. It is also an elegant companion for simply roasted or grilled meats.

The amount of cooking liquid you'll need, as well as the cooking time, will vary with the rice you use and the pan in which you cook it. Short-grain rice, for example, usually cooks a little faster.

Parmesan is typically the cheese used in risotto, but Asiago or Romano make interesting substitutions. The flavor of imported Romano is much sharper than the domestic version, so if you use imported Romano, use only half the amount called for in the recipe; you can add more to taste when the risotto is served.

3	tablespoons butter or margarine
2	tablespoons olive oil
1	small onion, finely chopped
1	small clove garlic, minced or pressed
1	cup imported Italian rice, short-grain (pearl) rice, or long-grain rice
2	cans (14½ oz. each) regular-strength chicken or beef broth, or about 3½ cups Brown Stock (page 38)
½	cup freshly shredded or grated Parmesan cheese
	Salt (optional)
	Additional shredded or grated Parmesan cheese

Place 2 tablespoons of the butter with olive oil in a heavy 2-quart pan or deep 10-inch frying pan over medium heat. When butter is melted, add onion and cook, stirring, until soft and golden. Add garlic and rice and stir until rice looks milky and opaque (about 3 minutes). Mix in broth; cook, stirring occasionally, until mixture comes to a boil. Adjust heat so rice boils gently; cook, un-covered, stirring occasionally, until rice is tender and most of the liquid has been absorbed (20 to 25 minutes). Toward end of cooking time, stir rice often to prevent sticking. Remove from heat and add half the Parmesan cheese and remaining 1 tablespoon butter; mix gently. Taste and add salt, if needed.

Turn into a warm serving bowl and top with remaining cheese. Pass additional cheese at the table. Makes 4 to 6 first-course servings.

Creamy Risotto. Prepare basic Risotto, but decrease broth to about 3 cups. When rice is almost tender, stir in ½ cup whipping cream.

Risotto with White Truffles. Prepare basic Risotto, using Italian or pearl rice, but omit garlic and cook onion in 3 tablespoons butter (omit olive oil). Use only 3 cups chicken broth, adding to it the juice drained from 1 can (1 oz.) white truffles. When rice is almost tender, stir in ½ cup whipping cream. Slice truffles paper thin.

When you stir in the last 1 tablespoon butter, add ¾ cup freshly grated Parmesan cheese and about half the truffles. Turn into a warm serving dish and top with the remaining truffles and ¼ cup more Parmesan cheese.

Risotto alla Milanese. Prepare basic Risotto, using Italian or pearl rice with chicken broth as the liquid. About 10 minutes before rice is done, stir in ¼ teaspoon saffron (ground or threads) dissolved or steeped in ¼ cup hot chicken broth or white wine.

Asparagus Risotto. Prepare basic Risotto, but decrease broth to about 3 cups and add ⅛ teaspoon white pepper. While risotto is cooking, snap off tough ends of ½ pound asparagus. Cut stems diagonally into ½-inch slices; set tips aside. About 10 minutes before rice is done, mix in sliced asparagus stems; about 5 minutes later, mix in tips. When rice is almost tender, stir in ½ cup whipping cream.

Risotto with Four Cheeses. Prepare basic Risotto, using Italian or pearl rice; omit garlic. Use about 3 cups chicken broth as the liquid. While rice is cooking, shred ¼ cup each fontina and Bel Paese cheese; crumble ¼ cup Gorgonzola or other blue-veined cheese. When rice is almost tender, stir in ¼ cup whipping cream, a dash of ground nutmeg, and fontina, Bel Paese, and Gorgonzola cheeses; stir until cheese melts. Add Parmesan cheese as directed in recipe for basic Risotto. Omit last 1 tablespoon butter.

BAKED SEMOLINA GNOCCHI
GNOCCHI ALLA ROMANA

Semolina is finely milled durum wheat. Look for it—often with the Italian spelling, semolino—in Italian specialty food stores and some gourmet stores. If you prefer, you can chill the cooked semolina overnight before shaping and baking it.

Serve the gnocchi, sizzling from the oven, as a first course or as a side dish with meat in a sauce.

3	cups milk
¼	teaspoon ground nutmeg
2	cloves garlic, minced or pressed
	Dash of pepper
1	cup semolina
2	eggs
1	cup freshly grated Parmesan cheese
	All-purpose flour
¼	cup butter or margarine, melted

Pour milk into a 3-quart pan and place over medium heat. Stir in nutmeg, garlic, and pepper. Bring mixture just to a boil, then add semolina in a fine stream, stirring constantly; cook, stirring, until mixture is very thick (about 5 minutes). Remove from heat.

In a large bowl, beat together eggs and ¾ cup of the Parmesan cheese. Add hot semolina mixture, a little at a time, mixing in well. Spread out on a lightly buttered baking sheet until cool. (At this point you may cover and refrigerate until next day.)

Shape into 1½-inch balls; coat lightly with flour, then flatten slightly.

Arrange, overlapping slightly, in rows in a lightly buttered shallow 2-quart baking dish. Drizzle with butter and sprinkle evenly with remaining ¼ cup cheese.

Bake in a 425° oven for 15 to 20 minutes or until edges are lightly tinged with brown. Makes 6 servings.

POTATO GNOCCHI
GNOCCHI DI PATATE

Gnocchi may be easier to make than pronounce. The word means "lumps" and describes the gnocchi's shape. Like polenta and pasta, it's a centuries-old Italian staple. Originally gnocchi were made with flour and water, but potato gnocchi quickly followed the arrival of the potato in the Old World. Here, little potato-based gnocchi are served with a fine veal sauce.

For peak flavor, it's best to make the mashed potatoes from scratch. Also, the dough should be used as soon as it's prepared, otherwise it becomes too soft to handle easily. Cooked gnocchi, however, can be kept warm for up to 3 hours before serving, and the sauce can be made days ahead.

Veal Sauce (recipe follows)
3 cups hot, finely mashed, unseasoned russet potatoes
About 1½ cups all-purpose flour
1½ teaspoons salt
1 tablespoon olive oil or salad oil
2 eggs
Salted water
2 to 3 tablespoons melted butter
1½ cups grated Parmesan cheese or shredded Jack cheese, or ¾ pound teleme cheese, thinly sliced

Make Veal Sauce. While sauce is simmering, make gnocchi.

In a bowl, combine hot mashed potatoes, 1½ cups flour, salt, and oil; blend with a fork. Add eggs and mix thoroughly into potato mixture. Turn potato dough out onto a well-floured board and knead gently about 15 times. If dough is soft, work in a

An American attempting to describe the white truffle—the culinary jewel of Alba—invariably compares it to a potato. It is with appearance, though, that the similarity of these two products from beneath the soil ends.

The white truffle is a lesser-known member of the fungus family to which the black truffles of France belong, and it is distinguished by its incredibly pervasive, unique aroma.

White truffles exquisitely complement the flavors of such foods as cheese, eggs, creamy sauces, and delicate meats. When the fall harvest is in full sway, the Italians sliver the raw truffle into thin brown flakes and use them with abandon in their finest dishes, such as Risotto with White Truffles (page 36) and Fonduta (page 54).

Outside of Italy, though, fresh white truffles are rare. A fine food merchant might fly in a few specimens for favored clientele, but ordinarily you will need to search for canned white truffles in fancy food shops dealing in Italian imports. The truffles are costly, but you may find the extravagance worthwhile for special occasions.

little more flour. Shape into a fat loaf and set on a floured area to prevent sticking.

Cut off one piece of dough (about ½ cup) at a time and roll on a very lightly floured board into a ⅜-inch-thick cord. Cut cord into 1¼-inch lengths and roll each length in the center lightly under your forefinger to give the piece a bow shape. Arrange shaped gnocchi, slightly apart, on a lightly floured baking sheet.

Cook, dropping about 20 gnocchi at a time into a large kettle of boiling salted water. When gnocchi return to surface of water (stir gently if they haven't popped up in about 1 minute), adjust heat so water boils gently. Cook for 5 minutes (6 minutes, if frozen).

Remove cooked gnocchi from water with a slotted spoon; drain well and place in a shallow, rimmed pan. Mix gnocchi gently with melted butter. Cover tightly and place in a warm oven (150°) while you cook remaining gnocchi. They will keep for as long as 3 hours if they are well covered to retain moisture. Flavor is best if they don't cool after cooking.

Arrange half the gnocchi in a layer in a wide, rimmed, ovenproof serving dish and top with half the hot Veal Sauce and half the cheese. Top with remaining gnocchi, sauce, and cheese. Heat in a 375° oven for about 10 minutes or until cheese melts and gnocchi are very hot. Broil top lightly if desired. Makes 6 main-dish servings or about 8 first-course servings.

Veal Sauce. In a bowl, pour warm water over ½ cup **dried Italian mushrooms**; let stand for 30 minutes. Meanwhile, heat 3 tablespoons **olive oil** in a wide frying pan over medium heat. Add ¼ cup minced **bacon** and cook until bacon is limp. Add ¾ pound **ground veal**, 1 medium-size **onion** (finely chopped), 1 **carrot** (finely chopped), and 2 stalks **celery** (finely chopped). Cook, stirring, until veal is browned and vegetables are soft.

Squeeze water from mushrooms, finely chop, and add to meat mixture along with 1 can (1 lb.) **tomatoes** (break up with a spoon) and their liquid, 1 can (8 oz.) **tomato sauce**, 1 cup **dry red wine**, 1½ teaspoons **salt**, ⅛ teaspoon **pepper**, and ¼ teaspoon **ground allspice**. Adjust heat so mixture boils gently; cook, uncovered, stirring occasionally, until sauce is thickened and reduced to about 4 cups (about 2 hours). Cool, cover, and refrigerate, if made ahead.

4

SOUPS, SALADS

& VEGETABLES

Italian soups range from the light and delicate—sometimes simply a richly flavored homemade brown stock—to rib-sticking minestrone. And since you might want to combine a soup and salad, or soup and vegetable, to make a simple meal with freshly baked bread or rolls, we've grouped soups, salads, and vegetable side dishes in this chapter.

Of course, a soup or salad can open a meal, too, or a vegetable dish can complement the main dish. Indeed, a salad often follows the main course of an Italian meal.

Italians enjoy salads of vegetables both cruda (raw) and cotta (cooked). Sometimes elements of both are combined. What makes Italian salads so special? The answer lies in the freshness and flavor of the olive oils and vinegars that dress them.

Like salads, cooked vegetable dishes in Italy display a respect for the seasonal freshness of their skillfully prepared vegetables— especially eggplant, tomatoes, beans, spinach, Swiss chard, artichokes, peppers, and peas.

WEDDING SOUP
ZUPPA MARITATA

There's potential showmanship in the making of this rich, elegant soup, since you can complete the last step at the table. Have the hot broth with cooked pasta ready in a chafing dish over direct flame. Add some of the broth to the mixture of butter, cheese, and cream that gives the soup its unique, velvety quality; then return the mixture to the chafing dish.

6	cups Brown Stock (recipe follows) or 3 cans (14½ oz. each) regular strength chicken or beef broth
2	ounces vermicelli, or ½ cup tiny soup pasta (pastina)
½	cup (¼ lb.) butter (use sweet butter if you use canned broth), softened
1	cup freshly grated Parmesan cheese
4	egg yolks
⅛	teaspoon ground nutmeg
1	cup whipping cream
	Salt

In a large deep pan over high heat, bring broth to a boil. Break vermicelli into shorter lengths, if you wish; add vermicelli or other noodles to boiling broth. Reduce heat to medium and simmer, uncovered, for 5 to 8 minutes or until noodles are tender to bite.

In a medium-size bowl, combine butter, cheese, egg yolks, and nutmeg until smooth, then gradually stir in cream. Spoon a small amount of the simmering broth into cream mixture and stir to blend, then return all to the soup, stirring constantly. At once, remove soup from heat. Salt to taste, and ladle into serving bowls. Makes 4 to 6 main-dish servings or 8 to 10 first-course portions.

Brown Stock. Place 3 to 4 pounds **meaty beef bones** in a shallow baking pan large enough to hold them in a single layer. Sprinkle with 1 large **onion** (chopped) and 1 medium-size **carrot** (sliced). Bake, uncovered, in a 450° oven for about 25 minutes or until meat and bones are well browned.

Transfer browned beef bones and vegetables to a 12-quart or larger kettle. Add a little water to pan in which bones baked and scrape brown particles free from pan; add to kettle. Also add to kettle 2 large **onions** (chopped), 4 medium-size **carrots** (sliced), 1 small **turnip** (chopped), 2 stalks **celery** and their leaves (chopped), 3 to 4 pounds bony chicken pieces (necks, backs, wings), about 3 pounds **veal shank bones** (if not available, increase beef and chicken bones by a total of about 3 lbs.), 6 sprigs **fresh parsley,** ½ teaspoon **black peppercorns,** 2 **bay leaves,** and 4 quarts **water.** Bring to a boil over moderately high heat; cover, reduce heat, and simmer for 4 to 6 hours.

Strain stock to remove bones and vegetables. Taste, and add **salt,** if you wish. Cover and refrigerate stock for several hours or overnight. Lift off and discard fat from surface. Cover and refrigerate stock for up to 4 to 5 days or freeze in 1 to 1½-quart containers. Makes about 4 quarts stock.

ESCAROLE SOUP
ZUPPA DI SCAROLA

Use the tender inside leaves of escarole (the salad green that is also called broad-leaf endive) to make this soup.

1	head escarole
¼	cup shell or elbow macaroni
	Boiling salted water
2	tablespoons butter or margarine
2	tablespoons finely chopped onion
4	cups Brown Stock (page 38) or 2 cans (14½ oz. each) regular-strength chicken broth
⅛	teaspoon ground nutmeg
¼	teaspoon thyme leaves, crumbled
	Salt and pepper
	Grated Parmesan cheese

Discard coarse outer leaves of escarole. Wash, drain, and stack tender green leaves and cut into strips about ¼ inch wide (you should have about 6 cups, lightly packed); set aside.

Cook macaroni in boiling salted water according to package directions until just tender; drain and set aside. In a 2-quart pan over medium heat, melt butter. Add onion and escarole, and cook, stirring, for about 3 minutes. Add broth, nutmeg, and thyme; bring to a boil. Add cooked

macaroni and salt and pepper to taste. Cook for about 1 minute longer. Serve with Parmesan cheese to add to each serving. Makes 4 to 6 first-course servings.

HARRY'S CHICKEN SOUP

Harry's Bar in Venice may have been Ernest Hemingway's great favorite, but Harry's Bar in Florence is the one that makes the smooth and elegant soup that inspired this one.

Home cooks will find it easy to make. Use the bony parts of a cut-up chicken to make a flavorsome broth, add the best portions of the meat to make it substantial, then blend in eggs, cheese, and cream to make it velvety.

3	to 3½-pound broiler-fryer chicken, cut up
10	cups water
4	chicken bouillon cubes
8	to 10 sprigs parsley
2	stalks celery, cut into chunks
2	carrots, cut into chunks
	Parmesan Cream (directions follow)
2	tablespoons cornstarch blended with 2 tablespoons water
	Finely chopped fresh parsley
	Freshly grated Parmesan cheese

In a 5 to 6-quart kettle or Dutch oven, place giblets (save liver for other uses) and bony parts of chicken (neck, back, wings); set aside thighs, drumsticks, and breast. Add water, bouillon cubes, parsley sprigs, celery, and carrots. Bring to a boil over high heat; cover, reduce heat, and simmer for 30 minutes. Add drumsticks and thighs and continue simmering, covered, for another 30 minutes. Add breast and simmer, covered, for 15 minutes more; total cooking time for soup is 1 hour and 15 minutes.

Strain and reserve broth. Pull skin and meat from bones of thighs, drumsticks, and breast. Cut meat into bite-size chunks; discard skin, bones, remaining chicken parts, and vegetables. Measure broth; you should have 6 cups. If not, add water to make this amount, or boil to reduce to this amount.

Prepare Parmesan Cream; set aside. Stir cornstarch mixture into broth; bring to a boil, stirring. Stir several cups of the hot broth into Parmesan Cream, then return all to pan. Add reserved chicken meat, and cook, stirring, over low heat until slightly thickened; do not boil or soup will curdle. (At this point you may cover and refrigerate, if made ahead. Reheat, stirring, in a double boiler over simmering water.)

Pour soup into a tureen or ladle directly into individual bowls and sprinkle lightly with chopped parsley. Serve with Parmesan cheese to add to each serving. Makes 4 main-dish or 8 first-course servings.

Parmesan Cream. In a medium-size bowl beat 6 **egg yolks** until blended, then stir in 1 cup (3 oz.) **grated Parmesan cheese** and ½ cup **whipping cream.**

ROMAN EGG SOUP
STRACCIATELLA

Technique is simple but important in the preparation of Rome's famous scrambled egg soup. After you bring the stock to a full rolling boil, you pour in a mixture of beaten eggs and Parmesan cheese, then remove soup from the heat.

(Continued on next page)

4 to 6 cups Brown Stock (page 38) or 3 cans (14½ oz. each) regular-strength chicken or beef broth

2 eggs

¼ cup shredded Parmesan cheese

2 tablespoons minced fresh parsley

Additional shredded Parmesan cheese

In a 2 to 3-quart pan over high heat, bring stock to a full rolling boil. In a small bowl beat eggs to blend with the ¼ cup cheese and parsley. Pour mixture into boiling liquid and **immediately** remove from heat; **do not stir.** Ladle into bowls; serve with additional Parmesan cheese. Makes 4 to 6 first-course servings.

ITALIAN EGG SOUP
ZUPPA PAVESE

A golden egg yolk floating on a toast raft characterizes this quick soup. It is originally from Pavia, in Lombardy.

Butter or margarine

4 slices French or Italian bread

¼ cup freshly grated Parmesan cheese

4 cups Brown Stock (page 38) or 2 cans (14½ oz. each) regular-strength chicken broth

4 egg yolks

Additional grated Parmesan cheese

Generously butter one side of each bread slice. Place slices, buttered side up, on a baking sheet. Bake in a 350° oven for 15 to 20 minutes or until toasted golden and crusty. Sprinkle each slice with 1 tablespoon of the cheese and broil until cheese is lightly browned.

Meanwhile, in a medium-size pan over high heat, bring stock or broth to a boil and ladle into 4 soup bowls. Float a slice of the hot toast in each and let stand until edges curl up slightly (2 to 3 minutes). Then carefully slip a raw egg yolk on top of the toast in each bowl.

Serve with additional Parmesan cheese. Makes 4 first-course servings.

IDA'S MINESTRONE

Minestrone (the word means "big soup") changes from region to region, from household to household, and from season to season. This version originated near the old walled town of Lucca and, like many minestrones, it starts with a bean-stock base. In fall or winter, you might include only carrots, potatoes, onions, and leeks; in spring and summer you could add peas, zucchini, green beans, or other fresh vegetables.

You'll have to ask at a delicatessen to have the prosciutto bone saved for you.

BASIC STOCK

1 pound (about 2 cups) dried pinto, pink, or cranberry beans, rinsed and drained

3½ to 4 quarts Brown Stock (page 38) or water

1 teaspoon salt

10 or 12-inch-long prosciutto bone; or ½ pound salt pork, cut into thick slices

½ cup canned tomato sauce

¼ teaspoon ground allspice

Salt and pepper

VEGETABLES

1 cup each of 6 of the following:

Carrots, cut in small pieces

Thick-skinned potatoes, peeled and diced

Thin-skinned potatoes, diced

Curly cabbage, coarsely chopped

Leeks, coarsely chopped

Onions, coarsely chopped

Zucchini, cut in small pieces

Green beans, cut in small pieces

Wax beans, cut in small pieces

Peas, fresh or frozen

TOPPING

Grated or shredded Parmesan cheese

In a large kettle, combine dried beans with stock and bring to a boil. Continue to boil for 2 minutes, then remove from heat and covered, for 1 hour. Add prosciutto bone and bring cover and simmer for 1½ or until beans are tender. save stock; discard bone half the beans, as well as if used. Force remaining beans through a wire s whirl in a blender or food with some of the stock).

In same kettle, combine reserved beans, salt po stock, tomato sauce, a additional salt and pepp Add vegetables and brin cover and simmer for 1½

Serve hot with Parmes Makes 6½ quarts or about 25 first-course servings or about 10 main-dish servings.

NORTH BEACH MINESTRONE

Italian families who settled in the North Beach district of San Francisco made this kind of thick minestrone.

1 pound (about 2 cups) dried cranberry or pink beans, rinsed and drained

4 quarts water or Brown Stock (page 38)

4 beef marrow bones, each 3 inches long

4 slices meaty beef shanks (each 1 inch thick)

Cooked Vegetables (directions follow)

2 or 3 large potatoes, peeled and diced

½ pound green beans, strings and ends removed and cut into 2-inch lengths

4 small zucchini, sliced

3 cups shredded cabbage

½ cup salad macaroni (ditalini)

About 2 teaspoons salt

Green Sauce (recipe follows)

Grated Parmesan cheese

In a large kettle, combine dried beans with water and bring to a boil. Continue to boil for 2 minutes, then remove from heat and let stand, covered, for 1 hour (or, if you prefer, cover beans with the water and let stand overnight; if using Brown Stock, do not soak overnight).

Add beef bones and shanks to kettle and bring to a boil; cover, reduce heat, and simmer for 2 hours. Let cool; remove meat and bones. Force half the beans through a wire strainer (or whirl, in a blender or food processor with some of the stock). Return to soup, along with lean meat. Scoop marrow from bones and add to soup; discard bones. Add Cooked Vegetables to soup and bring to a boil; reduce heat and simmer for 30 minutes.

Then add potatoes and green beans and simmer, uncovered, for 10 minutes; next add zucchini, cabbage and macaroni. Season to taste with salt. Simmer, uncovered, for 5 minutes more. Stir in Green Sauce. Ladle soup into bowls. Serve with Parmesan cheese to add to each serving. Makes about 6½ quarts soup or about 25 first-course servings or about 10 main-course servings.

Cooked Vegetables. Heat ¼ cup **olive oil** or salad oil in a wide frying pan over medium heat. Add 2 large **onions** (diced) and cook until soft. Then add 2 cups **each** diced **carrots, celery,** and **leeks**; cook, stirring occasionally, for 5 minutes. Mix in 1 can (1 lb.) **tomatoes** (break up with a spoon) and their liquid; adjust heat so that mixture boils gently and cook, uncovered, for 10 minutes or until most of the liquid has evaporated.

Green Sauce. Heat 2 tablespoons **olive oil** in a small frying pan over medium heat. Add ½ cup lightly packed chopped fresh **parsley,** 1 clove **garlic** (minced or pressed), and 2 tablespoons crumbled **dry basil** and cook until parsley is bright green. Use at once.

GREEN MINESTRONE
MINESTRONE ALLA GENOVESE
(Pictured on page 42)

Genoa is the home town of this delicate minestrone. Instead of a bean base, it uses a meat stock in which you cook bright green vegetables and macaroni. To each serving you add a spoonful of pesto.

4	**quarts water**
1	**pound** each **ham and bony chicken parts (wings, backs, necks)**
¼	**pound sliced prosciutto or bacon**
2	**cups** each **diced potato and sliced celery**
4	**small zucchini, sliced in ½-inch pieces**
	About 1½ cups sliced leeks
1	**pound Italian green beans, cut into 2 to 3-inch lengths**
½	**cup salad macaroni (ditalini)**
1	**cup freshly shelled peas (about 1 lb. peas in shells)**
3	**to 4 cups shredded cabbage**
	About 2 teaspoons salt
	About 1 cup Basic Pesto (page 28)

In a large kettle combine water, ham, chicken, and prosciutto; set on high heat and bring to a boil. Reduce heat; cover and simmer for 2 hours. Strain and reserve stock; discard meat and bones. Bring stock to a boil. Add potatoes and reduce heat; cover and simmer for 10 minutes. Remove cover and add celery, zucchini, leeks, green beans, and macaroni; simmer, uncovered, for 5 minutes. Stir in peas and cabbage and cook, uncovered, for 4 or 5 minutes more. Salt to taste. Ladle soup at once into bowls and spoon in pesto to taste. Makes 6 to 7 quarts or 10 to 12 main-dish servings.

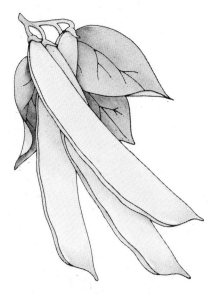

PASTA & BEAN SOUP
PASTA E FAGIOLI

Here's a whole-meal soup that draws its hearty peasant flavor from beans, onion, carrots, ham, and tiny pasta. Lightly cooked minced garlic floating on the soup seasons each serving.

1	**pound (about 2 cups) dried small red beans or cranberry beans, rinsed and drained**
8	**cups water**
3	**cloves garlic**
1	**large onion, chopped**
1½	**cups shredded carrots**
1	**cup finely chopped celery**
1	**can (14½ oz.) Italian-style tomatoes**
	About 3 pounds shank-end, bone-in, fully cooked ham
¼	**cup tiny soup pasta (pastina)**
2	**tablespoons olive oil**
2	**tablespoons minced fresh parsley**
	Grated Parmesan cheese

In a 6-quart pan, combine dried beans and water; bring to a boil. Continue to boil for 2 minutes, then remove from heat. Cover and let stand for 1 hour (or, if you prefer, cover beans with the water and let stand overnight).

Mince or press 1 clove of the garlic; add to bean mixture, along with onion, carrots, celery, tomatoes (break up with a spoon) and their liquid, and ham. Bring to a boil, then reduce heat and simmer, covered, until beans are tender (2 to 2½ hours).

Lift out ham and discard bone; coarsely chop ham. In a blender or food processor, whirl about half the soup until smooth; return to pan. Add pasta and chopped ham and cook, stirring, over medium heat for 5 minutes or until pasta is tender.

Finely chop remaining 2 cloves garlic. In a small frying pan, cook garlic in oil until lightly browned. Pour soup into a tureen. Spoon oil and garlic mixture into center of soup and sprinkle parsley around mixture. Serve with Parmesan cheese. Makes 8 to 10 servings.

COUNTRY VEGETABLE SOUP
ZUPPA ALLA PAESANA

Less complex than a minestrone, this rustic white bean and cabbage soup from Tuscany makes a satisfying first course, lunch, or supper with bread and cheese.

½	cup dried small white beans, rinsed and drained
2	cups water
2	tablespoons *each* butter or margarine and olive oil
1	medium-size onion, finely chopped
2	stalks celery, finely chopped
3	medium-size carrots, shredded
½	cup chopped fresh parsley
1	clove garlic, minced or pressed
½	teaspoon rubbed sage
¼	teaspoon pepper
1½	quarts chicken broth or Brown Stock (page 38)
1	can (1 lb.) tomatoes
2	cups shredded cabbage
	Salt
	Grated Parmesan cheese

In a medium-size pan, bring beans and water to a boil; continue to boil briskly for 2 minutes. Remove from heat; cover and let stand for 1 hour (or if you prefer, cover beans with the water and let stand overnight).

In a 4 to 5-quart pan or Dutch oven, melt butter with oil over medium heat. Add onion, celery, and carrots; cook, stirring occasionally, until onion is soft. Mix in parsley, garlic, sage, pepper, broth, and beans (with their liquid). Bring to a boil, cover, reduce heat, and simmer for about 2 hours or until beans are nearly tender.

Add tomatoes (break up with a spoon) and their liquid. Continue to simmer, covered, until beans are very tender (30 to 45 minutes). With a slotted spoon, remove about 1 cup of the cooked vegetables. Place in a blender or food processor with about ½ cup of the broth and whirl or process until smoothly puréed. Return purée to soup. Mix in cabbage and cook over medium heat, uncovered, until wilted and bright green (3 to 5 minutes). Taste and add salt, if needed. Serve with Parmesan cheese to add to each serving. Makes about 2 quarts or 4 to 6 servings.

Green minestrone? It must be Irish! No, it's a time-honored, basic form of minestrone from Genoa. In fact, Christopher Columbus probably was welcomed home with such a soup. It captures the sunny spring of the Ligurian countryside and the simple comforts of home. The recipe for Green Minestrone is on page 41.

MOZZARELLA, TOMATO & BASIL SALAD
INSALATA CAPRESE

One of the most stylish and colorful of Italian salads is this red, white, and green arrangement of tomato, cheese, and fresh basil. If you are unable to find genuine water-buffalo-milk mozzarella imported from Italy, or domestic fresh mozzarella packed in water, choose from several good alternatives.

2	large tomatoes, peeled
2	slices, each ¼-inch-thick (about 4 oz. total) mozzarella di bufalo, mozzarella, smoked mozzarella, teleme, or provolone cheese
8	fresh basil leaves
	Olive oil
	Red wine vinegar
	Salt and freshly ground black pepper

Cut each tomato crosswise, making 4 pretty slices; discard stem and bottom ends. Place 2 tomato slices side by side on each of 4 individual salad plates. Cut each cheese slice into quarters that are more or less triangular. Put a triangle of cheese on each tomato slice. Top with basil leaves. Drizzle with olive oil and sprinkle lightly with vinegar. Serve with salt and pepper. Makes 4 servings.

VEGETABLE DIPPING SALAD
VERDURE MISTE IN PINZIMONIO

An oil-and-vinegar dressing into which you dip bits of crisp, raw vegetables: this is one of the most basic types of Italian salad. A fine Italian olive oil (page 44) or a flavorful vinegar will give the dip distinction. Balsamic vinegar, an excellent choice for this salad, is an aged-in-wood wine vinegar with a fruity flavor all its own; it comes from Modena.

	Raw vegetables: Fennel or celery sticks, red or green bell pepper strips, radishes, thin carrot sticks, tender inner romaine leaves
2	tablespoons balsamic or red wine vinegar
1	clove garlic, minced or pressed (optional)
¼	teaspoon salt
	Dash of pepper
⅓	cup olive oil

Arrange vegetables attractively on a serving platter or small tray. Allow ½ to ¾ cup vegetables per person. In a small bowl, mix vinegar, garlic (if used), salt, pepper, and oil until well blended.

Place bowl of dressing in center of vegetables to use as a dip. Makes about ½ cup dressing.

SICILIAN GREEN SALAD
INSALATA VERDE ALLA SICILIANA

As salad mates, oranges and olives blend compatibly with romaine.

1	head romaine, washed, drained, and chilled
1	can (2¼ oz.) sliced ripe olives, well drained
2	oranges, peeled, white membrane removed, and thinly sliced crosswise
¼	cup orange juice
2	teaspoons red wine vinegar
½	teaspoon salt
¼	teaspoon paprika
¼	cup olive oil or salad oil

(Continued on next page)

A display of olive oil cans in an Italian delicatessen is a wonderful sight. It's a pleasure to see the pink and gold cans with ornate pictures of tigers, the olive green cans with their stylish silver lettering announcing their contents, and the variety of cans with pictures of everything from roosters to saints. There are even glass bottles of **olio extra vergine di oliva** (extra virgin olive oil) with hand-numbered labels. We were admiring one such bottle—sealed, corked, and labeled like a fine wine (and more expensive than many wines)—when the delicatessen's proprietor picked it up and cradled it reverently. Turning to us he sighed nostalgically, "This is what I gave my wife on our fortieth wedding anniversary."

It's true. Some olive oils are precious enough for anniversary presents, and others are more suitable for ordinary occasions. But how do you determine which to buy? They're all so attractive, it would be hard to decide by packaging alone. If you look closely at those elaborate labels, though, you'll find some helpful clues—key words to the grade of the oil.

The finest grade is "extra virgin"; it comes from the first mechanical pressing of high-quality, ripe, undamaged olives. This grade of olive oil is usually a light gold-green and is slightly cloudy. The opacity indicates low acid and high quality. This kind of oil has a pronounced fruity flavor—like ripe olives. It is best in dishes where such intense flavor can be appreciated without masking other flavors. Green salads dressed with extra virgin olive oil are simply splendid.

For most ordinary cooking, though, "virgin" grade is very acceptable and much more practical. It, too, comes from the first mechanical pressing of the olives, but the olives are not as ripe or unblemished as those destined for "extra virginity." A still lower grade is labeled "pure" olive oil, meaning it's a mixture of the lower-quality virgin olive oil and oil pressed from virgin olive oil's residual pulp. The second pressing, done with hot water, has a higher acid content. It's further refined to remove acid, color, and odor. Pure olive oil is usually a clear gold color. It, too, is quite adequate and very practical for ordinary cooking.

Lucca, in Tuscany, and the region near Lake Trasimeno in Umbria are two areas famous for their olive oils. Some of their most expensive and delicious olive oils are still pressed by hand-drawn or mule-drawn Roman presses. There is something rather romantic about such products. We hope you'll splurge at least once and treat yourself to a salad dressed with "extra virgin" olive oil.

...Sicilian Green Salad (cont'd.)

Break lettuce into bite-size pieces (you should have 7 to 8 cups) and place in a large salad bowl. Top with olives and orange slices. In a small bowl, mix orange juice, vinegar, salt, paprika, and oil. Pour over salad and mix lightly to serve. Makes 4 to 6 servings.

SPINACH SALAD WITH PINE NUT DRESSING
INSALATA DI SPINACI

You can make this salad with spinach or with a combination of spinach and butter lettuce.

6 to 8 cups spinach leaves, or half spinach leaves and half torn butter lettuce
¼ cup toasted pine nuts (pignoli)
2 tablespoons tarragon wine vinegar
¼ teaspoon each grated lemon peel and salt
Ground nutmeg
⅓ cup olive oil or salad oil

Wash greens well; drain and chill.

In a small frying pan over medium heat, stir nuts until lightly browned (6 to 8 minutes); set aside. Place spinach in a salad bowl.

In a small bowl mix vinegar, lemon peel, salt, dash of nutmeg, and oil. Mix in pine nuts. Pour dressing over spinach and mix lightly. Sprinkle lightly with additional nutmeg. Makes 4 to 6 servings.

GREEN SALAD WITH MINT & BACON
INSALATA AL LARDO

You can substitute fresh spinach leaves or tender dandelion greens for part of the romaine in this salad if you wish. What makes the salad special is its hot bacon dressing.

1	head romaine, washed, drained and chilled
½	pound thick-sliced bacon, diced
1	large clove garlic, minced or pressed
¼	cup firmly packed, finely chopped fresh mint
2	tablespoons red wine vinegar
	Freshly ground pepper
	Salt

Break lettuce into bite-size pieces (you should have 7 to 8 cups) and place in a large salad bowl; cover and refrigerate if done ahead. In a wide frying pan over low heat, cook bacon until just barely crisp; remove with a slotted spoon and drain. To the drippings, add garlic and cook slowly until soft but not browned. Stir in mint, drained bacon, and vinegar.

Pour at once over salad greens and mix lightly to serve. Season with pepper and salt to taste and serve at once. Makes 4 to 6 servings.

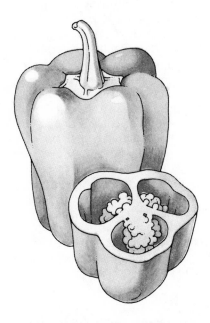

ROAST PEPPER SALAD
INSALATA DI PEPERONI

Roast peppers, with the easy addition of tomato and anchovies, make a colorful summer salad.

6	medium-size green or red bell peppers, roasted (see preceding recipe)
1	large tomato, sliced
8	to 10 canned anchovies, drained
	Garlic salt and pepper
½	teaspoon crumbled oregano leaves
2	tablespoons olive oil

Place peppers on a shallow rimmed plate. Layer tomato and anchovies over peppers. Sprinkle lightly with garlic salt and pepper, then with oregano. Drizzle with olive oil. Makes 2 to 3 servings.

ROASTED SWEET PEPPER & EGGPLANT SALAD
INSALATA DI PEPERONI E MELANZANE

The mellow, flavor and tender texture of roasted peppers add interest to this handsome salad. Use red or green peppers or a combination of the two.

6	large green or red bell peppers, roasted (directions follow)
1	medium-size (about 1 lb.) eggplant
6	tablespoons olive oil
3	medium-size onions
2	tablespoons red wine vinegar or lemon juice
1	teaspoon salt
	Pepper
1	or 2 large tomatoes, cut in wedges

Cut peppers crosswise into ½-inch strips; place in a large bowl and set aside. Peel eggplant, if desired. Slice eggplant into ½-inch-thick slices. Using about 2 tablespoons of the olive oil, lightly brush both sides of each eggplant slice, then cut into ½-inch-thick strips. Set strips on a baking sheet and broil, turning frequently, about 4 inches from heat until very soft and well browned on all sides (about 20 minutes). Add eggplant to peppers.

Meanwhile, cut onions in half vertically, then lengthwise in thin slices. Heat remaining 4 tablespoons olive oil in a wide frying pan over medium heat. Add onions and cook, stirring, until soft and golden (about 20 minutes); add to pepper mixture. Add vinegar, salt, and pepper to taste; mix lightly. Serve, or cover and let stand at room temperature for as long as 4 hours. Garnish with tomato wedges. Makes 4 to 8 servings.

To roast peppers: Place peppers in a single layer in a broiler pan and broil, turning frequently, about 1 inch from heat until peppers are blistered and charred on all sides. Then place in a paper or plastic bag and let them sweat for 15 to 20 minutes. Strip off skin. Cut peppers lengthwise into 4 pieces and remove and discard stems and seeds. If made ahead, cool, wrap airtight, and refrigerate for 1 to 2 days. Freeze for longer storage.

GREEN BEAN & POTATO SALAD
INSALATA DI PATATE E FAGIOLINI

(Pictured on page 47)

Diced, cooked potatoes marinated in oil and vinegar combine with green beans for this Genoese salad. It's delicious with steaks or hamburgers.

1	pound small, thin-skinned potatoes
	Salted water
¼	cup olive oil
1	tablespoon white wine vinegar
	Salt
	Pepper or seasoned pepper
½	pound small, slender green beans, ends and strings removed, and cut into 1-inch lengths; or 1 package (9 oz.) frozen French-cut green beans
2	tablespoons minced onion
	Canned anchovy fillets and capers (optional)

In a pan, cover potatoes with boiling, salted water and cook just until tender to pierce (about 25 minutes); drain. When cool enough to touch, peel and dice. Mix with oil, vinegar, and salt and pepper to taste. Set aside to cool.

In a pan, cover beans with boiling water and cook, uncovered, just until barely tender (or cook frozen beans according to package directions). Drain and at once immerse in cold water to cool; drain again. Mix beans with potatoes and onion and chill until ready to serve. Garnish, if desired, with anchovies and capers. Makes 6 servings.

ROMAN CAULIFLOWER
CAVOLFIORI ALLA ROMANA

A richly flavored light sauce of vegetables distinguishes this treatment of cauliflower. Both sauce and vegetable can be cooked separately early in the day, then combined and reheated to serve.

¼	cup olive oil
1	carrot, finely chopped
1	large onion, finely chopped
1	clove garlic
2	mild Italian sausages (about ¼ lb.), casings removed and meat crumbled (optional)
1	stalk celery, finely chopped
1	bay leaf
1	tablespoon tomato paste or catsup
1	large cauliflower (about 2 lbs.)
2	quarts salted water
	Salt

Heat oil in a wide frying pan over low heat; add carrot, onion, garlic, and sausage and cook slowly, stirring occasionally, until onion is soft but not browned. Add celery, bay leaf, and tomato paste and continue to cook, stirring occasionally, until carrot is soft. (At this point you may cover and set aside, if made ahead.)

Separate cauliflower into large flowerets; discard outer leaves. In a 3 to 4-quart pan, bring salted water to a boil over high heat and add cauliflower. Cook, uncovered, for 6 minutes after boil resumes; drain. (If cooked ahead, immediately immerse cauliflower in cold water. Drain when cool; cover and refrigerate.)

To serve, add 3 tablespoons water to onion mixture and stir over medium heat until mixture begins to bubble. Add cauliflower and continue to cook, stirring gently, until cauliflower is heated through. Salt to taste; discard garlic, if you wish. Makes 4 to 6 servings.

ITALIAN BEANS IN A MIST
FAGIOLINI IN UMIDO

The wide, quick-cooking Italian green beans would lose their bright color if prepared in the Old-World way of simmering slowly in this sauce.

Here, though, the sauce is seasoned by a little meat or mushrooms and prepared first. The beans are cooked briefly in water and then mixed with the sauce just long enough for flavors to meld.

¼	cup olive oil
1	large onion, finely chopped
1	large clove garlic
¼	pound finely chopped baked ham (about ⅔ cup) or thinly sliced mushrooms
2	quarts salted water
1	pound Italian or regular green beans, ends and strings removed (if necessary)
	Salt

Heat oil in a wide frying pan over low heat, add onion, garlic, and ham and cook slowly, stirring occasionally, until vegetables are soft. (At this point you may set aside, if made ahead.)

In a 3 to 4-quart pan bring salted water to a boil over high heat and add beans, pushing them down. Cook, uncovered, for 3 minutes after boil resumes (about 6 minutes, if using standard green beans); drain well. (If cooked ahead, immediately immerse beans in cold water. Drain when cool; cover and refrigerate.)

To serve, add 3 tablespoons water to onion mixture and stir over medium heat until mixture begins to bubble. Add beans and continue to cook, stirring gently, until beans are heated through. Salt to taste; discard garlic, if you wish. Makes 4 to 6 servings.

PEAS WITH PIMENTOS
PISELLI CON PEPERONI ROSSI

Fresh shelled peas are the base of this colorful dish. If they are not in season, use frozen tiny or petite peas, heating them only with the sauce.

3	tablespoons olive oil
1	mild Italian sausage (about 2 oz.), casing removed and meat crumbled (optional)
1	large onion, finely chopped
1	clove garlic
1	small jar (2 oz.) diced pimentos, drained
1	quart salted water
4	cups freshly shelled peas (about 3 lbs. in pods) or 1 large package (1 lb.) frozen tiny peas, thawed
	Salt

Heat oil in a wide frying pan over low heat; add sausage, onion, and garlic and cook slowly, stirring occasionally, until onion is soft but not browned (about 15 minutes). Stir in pimento. (At this point you may cover and set aside, if made ahead.)

In a 3 to 4-quart pan bring salted water to a boil over high heat. Add peas and cook, uncovered, until a rolling boil resumes (about 3 minutes); drain. (If cooked ahead, immediately immerse peas in cold water. Drain when cool; cover and refrigerate.)

To serve, add 3 tablespoons water to onion mixture and stir over medium heat until mixture begins to bubble. Add peas and continue to cook, stirring gently, until peas are heated through. Salt to taste; discard garlic, if you wish. Makes 6 to 8 servings.

Here's a salad with a difference. No lettuce or tomatoes—Just pretty potato cubes contrasting with Julienne green beans. The cooked vegetable salad chills in a light dressing until serving time. Dry salami and Pine Nut Sticks (page 89) complement our Green Bean & Potato Salad (page 45).

SAVORY ARTICHOKES
CARCIOFI IN UMIDO

When very small artichokes are trimmed down to their pale green leaves, they can be cooked so tenderly that they are entirely edible.

This dish, with tomatoes, onions, and basil, or the variation with prosciutto or ham, can be served as a vegetable side dish or as a first course.

24	small artichokes, 2½ inches or less in diameter
	Acid water (1 tablespoon vinegar to each 1 quart water)
2	tablespoons olive oil
1	large onion, chopped
2	medium-size tomatoes, peeled and chopped
1	clove garlic, minced or pressed
½	teaspoon dry basil
¾	teaspoon salt
¼	teaspoon pepper
½	cup water
	Grated Parmesan cheese

Cut off and discard top third of each artichoke, peel off outer leaves down to pale green inner ones, and peel stem; place immediately in acid water.

Heat oil in a large frying pan over medium heat; add onion, tomatoes, garlic, basil, salt, pepper, water, and drained artichokes. Cover and simmer until artichokes are easily pierced (about 15 minutes). Sprinkle with Parmesan cheese. Makes 6 servings.

Artichokes with Prosciutto. Prepare artichokes as above. Increase olive oil to ¼ cup. Add 1 large onion (finely chopped), ½ cup (2 oz.) finely chopped prosciutto or baked ham, 1 large clove garlic, artichokes, and ½ cup water. Cook as above until artichokes are very tender.

Season with salt to taste. Discard garlic, if you wish. Before serving, sprinkle with 2 tablespoons finely chopped fresh parsley. Makes 6 servings.

FRIED GREEN PEPPERS
PEPERONI IN PADELLA

Sautéed peppers have a full rich sweetness that is a complement to grilled meats or chicken.

2	tablespoons each olive oil and butter or margarine
4	large green peppers, seeded and cut lengthwise into 1½-inch-wide strips
1	clove garlic, minced or pressed
⅛	teaspoon pepper
1	teaspoon oregano
	Salt

In a wide frying pan over medium heat, combine oil and butter. When butter is melted, add peppers and garlic; cook, stirring occasionally, until lightly browned. Sprinkle with pepper and oregano. Cover and cook over low heat just until limp and tender (about 15 minutes). Salt to taste. Serve hot or warm. Makes 4 to 5 servings.

SWISS CHARD BUNDLES
BIETOLE

Little bundles of fresh chard, all cooked, assembled, and ready to serve straight from the market, are one of the conveniences Italian shoppers enjoy. But no matter—they're simple to prepare at home, and delicious to serve warm or at room temperature with a sprinkling of good olive oil (see page 44).

1	bunch (about 1 lb.) Swiss chard
	Salted water
	Lemon wedges
	Olive oil
	Salt and pepper

Remove and discard large, coarse stem ends of chard. In a large kettle, bring an ample amount of salted water to a boil over high heat. Add chard and cook, uncovered, until leaves are limp (2 to 3 minutes). Drain well. Select and set aside 6 to 8 perfect leaves. Stack remaining leaves and chop coarsely. Divide chopped chard into 6 to 8 portions.

On each whole leaf, arrange a portion of the chopped chard. Fold in sides, then roll up from stem end to make a neat packet. Arrange in a shallow serving dish. Garnish with lemon wedges. Accompany with olive oil, salt, and pepper to add to taste. Makes 4 to 6 servings.

ROAST POTATOES & ARTICHOKES
PATATE ARROSTE E CARCIOFI

As served in Milan, this vegetable combination is a splendid complement to Veal Chops with Sage (page 65).

1½	quarts salted water
4	small artichokes, trimmed well, or 1 package (9 oz.) frozen artichokes
⅓	cup lemon juice
¼	cup butter or margarine
2	tablespoons olive oil
2	cloves garlic, slivered
½	teaspoon dry rosemary
4 to 6	small thin-skinned potatoes
2	medium-size onions, cut in sixths
½	teaspoon grated lemon peel

In a large pan, bring salted water to a boil over high heat. If using fresh artichokes, add ¼ cup of the lemon juice to boiling water, add artichokes, and cook until tender (20 to 25 minutes); drain well. (If using frozen artichokes, cook, according to package directions; do not use the ¼ cup lemon juice.) Cut artichokes in halves; set aside.

In a 2 to 2½-quart baking pan, melt butter with oil in a 375° oven as it preheats. Remove pan from oven; swirl butter mixture with garlic, rosemary, and remaining 1⅓ tablespoons lemon juice. Peel a 1-inch-wide strip around center of each potato; add potatoes to butter mixture along with onions.

Cover and bake for 30 minutes; uncover and continue baking, turning potatoes and spooning butter mixture over them several times, for about 40 minutes more or until lightly browned and tender when pierced with a fork. Mix in artichokes and lemon peel. Continue baking for 5 to 10 minutes more or until artichokes are hot and potatoes and onions are well browned. Makes 4 to 6 servings.

ROAST POTATOES
PATATE ARROSTE

Slow cooking benefits this onion and potato combination. The dish bakes at meat-roasting temperature and can go in the same oven with a large roast.

	About 4 medium-size thick-skinned potatoes (2 lbs. total)
3	large onions, coarsely chopped
½	cup olive oil
1	teaspoon salt
¼	teaspoon pepper

Peel potatoes and cut into ½-inch cubes. Place potatoes and onions in a rimmed 10 by 15-inch baking pan and mix evenly with oil, salt, and pepper. Bake, uncovered, in a 325° oven, stirring occasionally, for 2 to 2½ hours or until vegetables are a light golden color and potatoes mash very easily. Makes 6 to 8 servings.

EGGPLANT GRATIN
MELANZANE AL GRATIN

Vegetables served at room temperature are popular in Italy, particularly in summer. Served neither hot nor cold, they display a delicious spectrum of flavors.

Three examples of this style of cooking share a zestfully seasoned crumb topping, which can be frozen if you prepare more than you need for a single dish.

	Seasoned Crumbs (recipe follows)
2	medium-size eggplants (about 1 lb. each)
	About ¾ cup olive oil

Prepare Seasoned Crumbs. Trim and discard stems from eggplants; cut unpeeled eggplants crosswise into 1-inch-thick slices. Pour ½ cup of the olive oil into a rimmed 10 by 15-inch baking pan. Turn eggplant slices in oil to coat them, then place side by side in pan. Top each slice with 1 to 2 tablespoons crumbs, patting firmly in place. Drizzle crumbs with 4 to 5 tablespoons more olive oil to moisten.

Bake, uncovered, in a 375° oven for 1½ hours or until interior of eggplant slices is very creamy. Cool to room temperature; serve within about 6 hours. Makes 6 to 8 servings.

Seasoned Crumbs. Cut end from a 1-pound loaf **sour or sweet French bread**. Slice and toast enough of the center portion (about half the loaf) to make 1½ cups coarse crumbs; whirl in blender or food processor until fine. Mix crumbs with ½ cup finely chopped **fresh parsley**, ¾ teaspoon **salt**, 1 clove **garlic** (minced or pressed), 1 teaspoon crumbled **dry basil**, ¼ teaspoon **each** crumbled **dry rosemary** and **rubbed sage,** and 6 tablespoons **olive oil**. Cover and refrigerate for up to 5 days. Makes about 1½ cups.

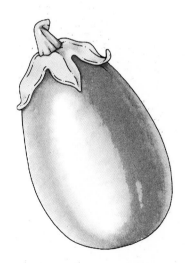

TOMATOES PARMESAN
POMODORI GRATINATI

Adding a quantity of Parmesan cheese to the basic crumb mixture gives baked tomatoes a golden crust. They can be served hot or at room temperature.

3	large, firm, ripe tomatoes (about 3-inch diameter)
½	cup Seasoned Crumbs (see recipe for Eggplant Gratin)
5	tablespoons olive oil
2	cloves garlic, minced or pressed
1½	teaspoons anchovy paste
1	cup grated Parmesan cheese

Peel tomatoes, cut out cores, and cut each in half crosswise. Gently squeeze out juice and seeds. In a bowl, stir together crumbs, 3 tablespoons of the oil, garlic, anchovy paste, and Parmesan cheese until blended. Pour remaining 2 tablespoons oil into a shallow baking pan; add tomatoes, cut side up. Distribute crumb mixture evenly among tomato halves, mounding it firmly in place.

Bake, uncovered, in a 375° oven for 15 minutes or until crumbs are well browned. Serve hot or at room temperature within 6 hours. Makes 6 servings.

BITTERSWEET ONIONS
CIPOLLE AGRODOLCE

These baked onions are also served at room temperature and are good as an antipasto dish or as a vegetable with meats or chicken.

4	large, flat, round onions
1	teaspoon sugar
1	tablespoon red wine vinegar
½	to 1 cup Seasoned Crumbs (see recipe for Eggplant Gratin)
¼	cup olive oil

Cut peeled onions in half crosswise. Set halves, cut side up, in a shallow baking pan just large enough to hold them in a single layer. Blend sugar and vinegar; drizzle evenly over onions. Pat 1 to 2 tablespoons of the crumb mixture over surface of each onion half. Drizzle evenly with olive oil.

Bake, uncovered, in a 375° oven for 45 minutes. Cool to room temperature; serve within 6 hours. Makes 8 servings.

5

EGGS &

CHEESE

Egg dishes are a quick and economical choice for many kinds of meals—a fact well appreciated in Italy. Good cooks throughout Italy have concocted ingenious ways of varying the forms and flavors of eggs to make omelets, frittatas, eggs poached in savory sauces, and a host of crisply crusted pies.

Green vegetables such as asparagus, spinach, Swiss chard, zucchini, and artichokes make colorful contributions to many Italian egg dishes.

Cheese is another important element in Italian egg dishes, and Italy produces a stunning variety of fresh and aged cheeses (see chart, page 61). You can even make your own Fresh Cheese, Italian-style, to serve at the table or to use in cooking and baking; the recipe is on page 57.

MILANESE ASPARAGUS
ASPARAGI ALLA MILANESE
(Pictured on page 50)

Fresh asparagus, butter-sautéed eggs, and Parmesan cheese combine pleasantly for a brunch or supper main dish with crusty bread and a dry white wine. It's a classic combination as a first course, too.

3	pounds asparagus
	Salted water
6	tablespoons butter or margarine
6	eggs
	Salt and pepper
½	cup shredded Parmesan cheese

Snap off and discard white fibrous ends of asparagus. Remove scales, if you wish. In a wide frying pan, bring 1½ inches of salted water to a rapid boil. Immerse spears in boiling water and cook, uncovered, until just tender when pierced (5 to 7 minutes). Drain well.

While asparagus cooks heat butter in another wide frying pan over medium-low heat. Break eggs into pan; cover and cook just until whites are set (yolks should still be quite

Milanese Asparagus (page 51) is a favorite light lunch of the Milanese business community, but you could serve this simple dish for brunch or as a first course. Just top tender-crisp asparagus with a butter-sautéed egg, drizzle extra butter from the pan over it, sprinkle with Parmesan cheese, and it's ready to serve.

liquid). Arrange hot asparagus in 6 warm serving dishes; sprinkle asparagus lightly with salt and pepper. Top each serving with an egg, spoon butter from pan over all, and sprinkle with cheese. Makes 6 servings.

TOMATOES & EGGS WITH MUSHROOMS
UOVA IN PURGATORIO
(Pictured on page 55)

Despite its interesting Italian name and fiery appearance, this dish isn't flavored with hot spices at all. It's an excellent choice for brunch with fresh figs, sliced coppa, toasted bread, and strong hot coffee blended with hot milk.

3 or 4	large tomatoes, peeled
3	tablespoons butter or olive oil
1	pound mushrooms, thinly sliced
6 to 8	eggs
	Salt and pepper
¾	cup (3 oz.) shredded Jack cheese
	Chopped fresh parsley

Cut tomatoes into cubes and drain in a colander for several minutes.

(Continued on next page)

Meanwhile, in a 10 to 11-inch frying pan over high heat, melt butter. Add mushrooms and cook, stirring, until they are soft and juices have evaporated. Add tomatoes and stir to heat through. With a spoon make 6 or 8 nest spaces and break an egg into each space. Sprinkle with salt and pepper and cover evenly with cheese. Cover pan and cook on low heat until eggs are set as you like. Garnish with parsley. Makes 3 or 4 servings.

PESTO OMELET
OMELETTE DI PESTO

All you need is a dollop of pesto to transform a simple omelet into an exceptional dish. It's worth reserving a few tablespoons of the suave fresh basil sauce the next time you make some for pasta.

2 or 3	eggs
1/4	teaspoon salt
	Dash each ground nutmeg and pepper
1	tablespoon water
1	teaspoon olive oil
2	teaspoons butter or margarine
1	tablespoon Basic Pesto (page 28)

Break eggs into a small bowl and add salt, nutmeg, pepper, and water. Beat with a whisk or fork for about 30 seconds. Heat oil and butter in a 7 to 8-inch omelet pan or a frying pan with sloping sides over medium-high heat until foamy. Tilt pan to coat sides and bottom. Pour in egg mixture and cook, gently lifting cooked portion to allow uncooked egg to flow underneath. Gently shake pan to keep omelet from sticking.

Continue to shake pan and lift omelet edges until there is no more liquid but top still looks moist and creamy. Spoon pesto down center of omelet, in line with pan handle.

Holding pan in your left hand, slide spatula under right edge of omelet, lift edge, and fold about a third of omelet over filling. Switch pan to your right hand and, tilting right end up and holding pan over a warm serving plate, gently shake pan to

slide unfolded edge of omelet just onto plate. Flick your wrist downward so that previously folded edge of omelet (guided by spatula) falls neatly over omelet edge on plate. Makes 1 serving.

PROVOLONE & PROSCIUTTO OMELET
OMELETTE AL FORMAGGIO E PROSCIUTTO

Individual omelets have a filling of sautéed onion and green pepper that is flavored with prosciutto and melting provolone cheese. These omelets make a delightful but quick brunch or supper.

8	eggs
3/4	teaspoon salt
1/8	teaspoon each ground nutmeg and pepper
2	tablespoons water
	About 2 tablespoons each olive oil and butter or margarine
1	small onion, cut vertically into slivers
1/4	cup finely chopped prosciutto or baked ham
1/4	cup slivered green pepper
1/2	cup shredded provolone cheese

Break eggs into a medium-size bowl and add salt, nutmeg, pepper, and water. With a whisk or fork, beat for about 30 seconds; set mixture aside. In a medium-size frying pan over medium heat, place 1 1/2 teaspoons **each** of the oil and butter. When butter is melted, add onion, prosciutto, and green pepper; cook, stirring, until onion is soft and lightly browned. Remove from heat and keep warm.

For each omelet, use a third or a fourth of the egg mixture. Heat 1 1/2 teaspoons **each** oil and butter in a 7 to 8-inch omelet pan and cook each omelet as directed for Pesto Omelet (this page).

Fill each with a third or a fourth of the onion mixture and shredded cheese, folding and turning out as in recipe for Pesto Omelet. Serve at once. Makes 3 or 4 servings.

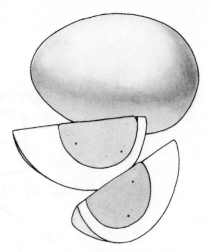

PESTO DEVILED EGGS
UOVA FARCITE

Deviled eggs have never tasted more flavorful than these—and all it takes is a touch of pesto. Perched on tomato slices, the eggs are perfect picnic fare; they're also fine as a first course.

6	eggs
2	tablespoons each Basic Pesto (page 28) and mayonnaise
	Salt
12	thin tomato slices

Place eggs in a straight-sided pan and fill pan with just enough cold water to cover eggs. Set pan, uncovered, over high heat and bring water to a simmer; reduce heat to medium so water remains at a gentle simmer, and cook for 12 to 15 minutes. Drain eggs and cover with cold water. When cool, crack and peel off shells. Cut eggs in half lengthwise and carefully remove yolks.

Mash yolks smoothly with pesto and mayonnaise; salt to taste. Fill each white with seasoned yolk mixture and place on a tomato slice. Makes 6 servings.

BAKED ARTICHOKE FRITTATA
TORTINO DI CARCIOFI

The Florentine way with a frittata is to bake it; as a result, it puffs almost as nicely as a soufflé. This supper dish or first course can be baked in a large casserole or in four shallow, individual baking pans (about 1½-cup size). The smaller ones will be done in about 25 minutes.

1	**package (9 oz.) frozen artichoke hearts**
6	**eggs**
½	**cup half-and-half (light cream)**
¼	**teaspoon salt**
⅛	**teaspoon** each **pepper and ground nutmeg**
1	**cup shredded fontina or Jack cheese**
½	**cup grated Parmesan cheese**

Cook artichoke hearts according to package directions; drain well. Spread artichokes evenly in a well greased, shallow 1½ to 2-quart baking pan (round or oval). Beat eggs with half-and-half, salt, pepper, and nutmeg. Stir in fontina cheese. Pour egg mixture over artichokes.

Bake, uncovered, in a 350° oven for 30 minutes. Sprinkle evenly with Parmesan cheese, return to oven, and bake for 5 to 8 minutes more or until frittata is puffed and lightly browned. Serve at once. Makes 4 servings.

SPINACH & ASPARAGUS FRITTATA
FRITTATA CON SPINACI E ASPARAGI

A frittata is a nonfolded omelet, cooked on both sides, with vegetables mixed right in with the eggs. It's cut into individual wedges and served hot or cool—an excellent choice for a luncheon main dish with salad or sliced tomatoes, or as a light snack. As with an omelet, you can vary the vegetables in a frittata to create interesting combinations. (A well-seasoned cast-iron pan or a nonstick frying pan is best for cooking.)

1	**pound spinach, stems discarded and leaves washed and drained**
1	**pound asparagus**
	Salted water
8	**eggs**
3	**tablespoons whipping cream or water**
¼	**teaspoon salt**
	Dash of pepper
2	**tablespoons shredded Parmesan or Romano cheese**
4	**tablespoons olive oil**
2	**cloves garlic, minced or pressed**

Place spinach in a pan over medium heat; cover and cook, stirring occasionally, until wilted (about 2 minutes). Turn into a colander and let drain; when cool, coarsely chop.

Snap off and discard white fibrous ends of asparagus. Cut spears into 1-inch lengths, but leave tips whole. In a wide frying pan, bring ½ inch of salted water to a rapid boil. Cook asparagus, uncovered, in boiling water until just tender when pierced (about 3 minutes). Drain and immerse in cold water to cool quickly (this preserves green color of asparagus), then drain again.

Beat eggs, cream, salt, pepper, and cheese just enough to evenly blend whites and yolks; set aside.

In a 10 to 11-inch frying pan with a nonstick fluorocarbon finish, combine 3 tablespoons of the oil with garlic. Place over medium heat and cook, stirring, until garlic is golden; **do not brown.** Add spinach and asparagus, distributing them evenly in pan; cook for about 2 minutes to heat through. Pour egg mixture over vegetables and cook, without stirring, until egg mixture is set about ¼ inch around outer edge. With a wide spatula, lift some of the egg mixture from sides of the pan, all the way around, tipping pan to let uncooked egg flow to pan bottom. Continue cooking until eggs are almost set but top of center is still moist and creamy.

Invert a large round flat plate (somewhat wider than frying pan) over frying pan. Holding pan and plate together, turn frittata out onto plate. Add the remaining 1 tablespoon oil to frying pan, then slide frittata from plate back into frying pan. Cook for about 2 minutes more to lightly brown bottom, then invert frittata, in the same manner as before, onto a serving plate. Cut into wedges and serve hot or at room temperature. Makes 3 or 4 servings.

Zucchini Frittata. Follow recipe for Spinach & Asparagus Frittata, but omit spinach and asparagus. Cook 1 pound fresh **zucchini** (thinly sliced) in about ½ inch boiling **salted water**, covered, until just tender (about 5 minutes). Turn into a colander, cool under cold running water, and drain. Combine zucchini; 1 can (2¼ oz.) **sliced ripe olives** (drained); ½ cup sliced **green onion** (including tops); and ¼ teaspoon **oregano leaves.** Add these vegetables to **olive oil** and **garlic,** distributing evenly in pan; cook for about 2 minutes. Add egg mixture; cook as directed.

Swiss Chard Frittata. Follow recipe for Spinach & Asparagus Frittata, but omit spinach and asparagus. Prepare egg mixture, and set aside. In nonstick 10 or 11-inch frying pan, heat 3 tablespoons **olive oil** over medium heat; add 1 medium-size **onion** (finely chopped) and 1 clove **garlic** (minced or pressed). Cook, stirring, until onion is soft. Add 1 package (12 oz.) **frozen Swiss chard** (thawed), or 2 cups packed chopped fresh Swiss chard; cook, stirring, until chard is limp and bright green and moisture has evaporated. Add egg mixture and cook as directed. Makes 3 or 4 servings.

Sicilian Ricotta Frittata. Follow recipe for Spinach & Asparagus Frittata, but omit spinach and asparagus. For egg mixture, place 1 cup **ricotta cheese** in a medium-size bowl. Beat in 6 **eggs,** one at a time. Stir in ⅓ cup grated **Parmesan cheese**, ¼ cup finely chopped fresh **parsley**, ¼ teaspoon **salt**, and a dash of **pepper**. Cook, as directed, in 2 tablespoons **butter** or margarine and 1 tablespoon **olive oil** combined with 1 clove **garlic** (minced or pressed); add another 1 tablespoon olive oil after turning frittata out of pan to brown other side. Makes 4 servings.

RICE & VEGETABLE CAKE
TORTA DI RISO

Custardlike rice and cheese squares, served warm or at room temperature, make a good accompaniment for a salad meal.

Serve the squares as you would a corn bread, to eat with your fingers or a fork.

1	**cup** each **water and milk**
3	**tablespoons butter**
1	**cup rice**
4	**green onions, thinly sliced**
1	**medium-size zucchini, shredded**
2	**tablespoons chopped fresh parsley**
1	**large clove garlic, minced or pressed**
4	**eggs**
½	**teaspoon thyme leaves**
½	**teaspoon salt**
⅛	**teaspoon** each **pepper and ground nutmeg**
½	**cup grated Parmesan cheese**
¼	**cup soft bread crumbs**

In a 3 to 4-quart pan, combine water, milk, and 1 tablespoon of the butter; bring to a boil over medium-high heat. Gradually mix in rice; then cover, reduce heat, and simmer until rice is nearly tender (about 15 minutes).

Meanwhile, in a medium-size frying pan, melt the remaining 2 tablespoons butter over medium heat. Add onions, zucchini, and parsley; cook, stirring, until most of the moisture from zucchini has evaporated. Remove from heat and mix in garlic.

In a large bowl, beat eggs with thyme, salt, pepper, and nutmeg. Add cooked rice mixture, zucchini

mixture, and cheese; mix lightly. Spread in a greased, shallow 2 or 2½-quart baking dish; sprinkle evenly with bread crumbs.

Bake, uncovered, in a 350° oven for 45 minutes or until edges are browned. Cut in squares or diamonds. Serve warm or at room temperature. Makes 6 to 8 servings.

PARMESAN & BASIL FRITTATA
FRITTATA ALLA PARMIGIANA

Unlike some frittatas, this one is finished by broiling, rather than browning both sides in the cooking pan. Under the broiler, the Parmesan cheese melts and the top of the frittata browns lightly. You might serve it for brunch, to accompany Italian Sausages with Peppers (page 69).

½	**cup sour cream**
8	**eggs**
¼	**teaspoon salt**
⅛	**teaspoon pepper**
2	**tablespoons finely chopped fresh basil or 1½ teaspoons dry basil**
2	**tablespoons** each **butter or margarine and olive oil**
⅓	**cup thinly sliced green onions**
½	**cup freshly grated Parmesan cheese**

Place sour cream in a medium-size bowl. Beat in eggs, to blend. Stir in salt, pepper, and basil.

In a 10 to 11-inch frying pan (with an ovenproof handle) over medium heat, place butter and oil. When butter is melted, add green onions and stir for 1 minute. Add egg mixture. As eggs set on bottom, lift cooked bottom portion of frittata with a spatula to allow uncooked egg to flow underneath. Continue cooking until eggs are softly set and top is still moist.

Remove from heat; sprinkle with cheese. Place pan 6 inches beneath heated broiler; broil just until cheese is melted and top is lightly browned (2 to 3 minutes). Cut into wedges and serve from pan. Makes 3 or 4 servings.

FONTINA SAUCE
FONDUTA
(Pictured on page 58)

This elegant cheese sauce of northern Italy is frequently served like the grand Swiss fondue—in a communally shared container with chunks of bread for dipping.

But Fonduta is considerably more versatile. Less rich and easier to make than fondue, it is basically a custard in which fontina cheese is melted.

An aromatic white truffle, shaved paper-thin, is the traditional—and extravagant—final addition to the sauce. But you can omit the truffle and still enjoy a taste that is much the same, though less assertive.

4	**egg yolks**
1	**cup milk**
3	**cups (about 12 oz.) finely shredded fontina cheese**
1	**can (½ oz.) white truffles (optional)**

In the top of a double boiler, stir egg yolks with milk until well blended. Place over slightly bubbling water (water should just touch bottom of the top unit). Cook, stirring constantly, for 7 to 8 minutes or until mixture is thickened enough to coat a metal spoon with a thick, velvety layer (if overcooked, the custard mixture first begins to look grainy, then separates).

Immediately stir in cheese, and continue to cook, stirring, until all but a few slivers of the cheese are smoothly melted. Remove double boiler from heat but leave Fonduta sauce over hot water for about 10 minutes, stirring occasionally. (At this point you may cover and refrigerate for as long as 5 days. To reheat,

(Continued on page 56)

These eggs, nestled in tomatoes and mushrooms and resting under a light topping of melted cheese, make a colorful brunch entrée. You might start with fresh fruit—melon, figs, or pears—and thin-sliced coppa (see page 13). Offer thick slices of buttered, and toasted Italian or French bread with these Tomatoes & Eggs with Mushrooms (page 51).

place over simmering water and stir until warm enough to serve.)

If truffles are used, drain their juice into the Fonduta. Cut truffles into paper-thin slices and stir most of the slices into the sauce; reserve a few for garnish. Makes about 2⅓ cups sauce.

Fonduta as an appetizer dip. Pour warm Fonduta into top unit of a chafing dish and set over hot water; keep warm. To eat, dip bite-size cubes of crusty bread (you'll need about half of a 1-lb. loaf) into the sauce. Makes 8 to 10 appetizer servings.

Fonduta with pasta. Spoon warm Fonduta onto hot, cooked, and drained pasta, such as fettuccine or tagliarini; allow about ½ cup Fonduta for each 1 cup pasta.

Fonduta with vegetables. Ladle warm Fonduta onto hot, cooked, and drained vegetables, such as broccoli, green beans, spinach, cauliflower, artichoke hearts or bottoms, asparagus, Italian green beans, celery, onions, leeks, or zucchini; or sautéed mushrooms, eggplant, or green or red bell peppers. Allow 2 to 3 tablespoons Fonduta for each ½ cup of vegetable.

Fonduta with veal or chicken. Prepare veal (chops, roasts, steaks) or chicken (breasts, legs, or the whole bird) by a simple method such as roasting, sautéing, or broiling, and serve with Fonduta as a sauce to ladle over individual portions of the hot meat. Allow about ¼ to ⅓ cup Fonduta for each serving (about ½ lb. boneless meat).

Fonduta with eggs. Spoon warm Fonduta over poached eggs; allow about 3 tablespoons Fonduta for each egg.

SPINACH & RICOTTA PIE
TORTA DI SPINACI E RICOTTA

Onion, oregano, and savory peperoni season a rich filling of mushrooms, spinach, and three kinds of cheese—ricotta, Swiss, and Parmesan—in this main-dish pie.

	Pastry for a 2-crust 9-inch pie
1	package (10 to 12 oz.) frozen chopped spinach, thawed
2	cups (1 lb.) ricotta cheese
¼	pound mushrooms, chopped
½	cup each shredded Swiss and Parmesan cheeses
¼	pound thinly sliced peperoni
¼	cup finely chopped onion
2	teaspoons prepared mustard
½	teaspoon oregano leaves
¼	teaspoon salt
	Dash of pepper
1	egg
	Tomato Sauce (recipe follows)

Prepare pastry. Drain spinach thoroughly; press out as much moisture as possible. In a bowl, combine spinach with ricotta cheese, mushrooms, Swiss cheese, Parmesan cheese, peperoni, onion, mustard, oregano, salt, and pepper; stir in egg. Roll out half the pastry on a floured board and use to line a 9-inch pie pan. Spread filling in pastry. Roll out remaining pastry for top crust; place on filling, seal, trim and flute edge, pricking top with a fork. Bake in a 425° oven for about 25 minutes or until crust is browned. Serve hot with Tomato Sauce. Makes 4 to 6 servings.

Tomato Sauce. In a small pan, heat 1 large can (15 oz.) **tomato sauce** with ½ teaspoon **garlic salt**, dash of **pepper,** and 1 teaspoon **Italian herb seasoning** or ¼ teaspoon **each** dry basil, oregano leaves, thyme leaves, and marjoram leaves.

EASTER TART
TORTA PASQUALINA

Italian cheese-and-vegetable tarts are at their best in Liguria, the coastal area that includes Genoa and Rapallo, the home of this version with Swiss chard. Though the name indicates it's an Easter specialty—and, indeed, it uses hard-cooked eggs—it can be served at other times, too.

The pie is generally served at room temperature. If you wish, you can make it ahead and refrigerate it overnight. Before serving, though, bake it (uncovered) in a 350° oven for about 10 minutes to crisp the crust.

1½	pounds Swiss chard
3	eggs
2	cups (1 lb.) ricotta cheese
½	cup fine dry bread crumbs
¾	cup grated Parmesan cheese
1	cup (4 oz.) shredded jack cheese
¼	cup each finely chopped onion and fresh parsley
¾	teaspoon salt
¼	teaspoon marjoram leaves
⅛	teaspoon each pepper and ground nutmeg
	Flour
1	package (10 oz.) frozen patty shells, thawed
6	hard-cooked eggs, peeled

Cut off white fibrous stem and center rib from chard leaves; discard. Rinse leaves, then shake off excess water and mince leaves.

In a large bowl, beat eggs lightly, then mix in chard. (Or, in a blender or food processor, whirl ⅓ of the chard with 1 of the eggs until puréed; repeat with remaining chard and eggs.) Stir in ricotta cheese, crumbs, Parmesan and jack cheeses, onion, parsley, salt, marjoram, pepper, and nutmeg.

On a lightly floured board, stack 4 of the patty shells; roll out and stretch with your hands into a 15-inch circle. Fit pastry in bottom and up sides of an 8-inch spring-form pan. Spoon in half the chard mixture, evenly space hard-cooked eggs on top, and cover with remaining chard mixture. Stack remaining patty shells and roll out into an 8-inch circle; place over filling and pinch pastry edges together to seal. Slash top in several places.

Place pan on a rimmed baking sheet. Bake in a 450° oven for 35 to 40 minutes or until a wooden pick inserted in center comes out clean. (If top pastry gets too brown, cover loosely with foil during last 10 minutes.) Uncover, cool on wire rack for 15 minutes, then remove pan sides and cool completely. Cut in thin wedges to serve. Makes 10 to 12 servings.

You really haven't tasted fresh cheese until you've made it yourself —or been to Italy. Homemade ricotta cheese, too, is a revelation in light texture and fresh flavor. And you'll be surprised at how easy it is to make.

Both ricotta and fresh cheese have numerous uses. Serve them plain or with fruit; use them in main dishes and desserts. You'll find suggestions with each recipe.

FRESH CHEESE

Whole milk produces a luscious light cheese that is the basis of the Summer Cheesecake on page 104 and the filling for the Baked Cheese Crêpes on page 59. The tangy flavor is ideal with a sprinkling of chopped chives or seasoned pepper on appetizer crackers, or with toast and berry jam for breakfast.

Whipping cream makes a velvety, cool-tasting cheese comparable to the Italian mascarpone. Serve it as you would the whole-milk cheese, or use it in the Summer Cheese Torte on page 103 or the Green Fettuccine with Mascarpone on page 21.

Both cheeses will keep in the refrigerator for as long as 5 days.

2	quarts whole milk or 1½ cups whipping cream
¼	cup buttermilk (for whole milk cheese) or 2 tablespoons buttermilk (for cream cheese)

In a pan over medium heat, warm milk or cream to lukewarm (90° to 100°) and pour into a bowl. Stir in buttermilk. Cover and let stand at room temperature for 24 to 48 hours until a soft curd is formed (mixture will look like soft yogurt).

Curd forms faster on hot days than cool ones.

Line a colander with a clean muslin cloth that has been dipped in cold water and wrung dry; set in sink. Pour curd into colander and drain for about 10 minutes. Fold cloth over curd. Set colander on a rack in a rimmed pan (for milk curd, leave at least 1 inch between rack and pan bottom to allow for drained liquid).

Make whole unit airtight, covering with clear plastic film, and refrigerate to drain for 36 to 48 hours. Makes 2 cups with milk, 1 cup with cream.

HOMEMADE RICOTTA CHEESE

You won't need much in the way of equipment to make ricotta: a large kettle, a candy or deep-frying thermometer, a colander, and some cheesecloth.

This recipe makes 1 quart (2 pounds) of ricotta, but you can freeze any that will not be used within a week. It does become a little granular when frozen, so it's best to beat it with a rotary mixer or whirl it in a food processor before serving. The recipe can be cut in half for a smaller quantity.

You can enjoy ricotta while it's still warm, sprinkled with salt, pepper, or sugar. Chilled, it's delicious with fruit, whether sweetened or plain. And, of course, homemade ricotta is perfect in any recipe—from Veal & Chicken Cannelloni (page 30) to Ricotta Crumb Cake (page 103)— that calls for purchased ricotta.

4	quarts whole milk
1	quart cultured buttermilk
	Salt, pepper, sugar (optional)

In a 6 to 8-quart kettle, combine milk and buttermilk. Place over medium heat and set a candy or deep-frying thermometer into milk. Heat until temperature reaches 180° (about 40 minutes, if milk was refrigerated). Reduce heat to low and watch temperature on thermometer; it can range from 185° to 200° (remove from heat if temperature goes above 200°). Cook for about 20 minutes more for a very soft-curd cheese or about 35 minutes more for a more firm-curd cheese (1 to 1¼ hours total). Do not stir while cooking —it breaks up curd excessively and produces poor yield and texture. A small scorched area will probably develop on pan bottom, but this is just part of the ricotta flavor. To test curd, use back of spoon to gently press top of clot that forms. Clot should feel like baked custard, and the clear whey will surround it.

Line a colander with 3 or 4 thicknesses of cheesecloth that have been dipped in cold water and wrung dry; let edges of cloth hang over sides of collander. Gently pour cheese into colander; do not scrape pan. Let cheese drain for 30 minutes or longer. Serve warm, sprinkled with salt, pepper, or sugar; or cover and refrigerate for as long as a week and use as you would purchased ricotta. Makes about 1 quart (2 pounds) cheese.

ARTICHOKE TART
TORTA PASQUALINA II

This meatless Easter pie hails from Genoa and features artichokes in a creamy cheese custard.

1	sheet (half of a 17¼-oz. pkg.) frozen puff pastry
	Flour
2	packages (9 oz. each) frozen artichoke hearts
	Salted water
1	tablespoon olive oil
1	bunch (about 8) green onions, thinly sliced (including tops)
2	cups (1 lb.) ricotta cheese
½	cup sour cream
4	eggs
¾	cup grated Parmesan cheese
1	cup (4 oz.) shredded fontina or Swiss cheese
½	teaspoon dry tarragon
¼	teaspoon ground nutmeg
1	to 2 tablespoons beaten egg

Velvety fonduta, northern Italy's eloquent answer to Swiss fondue, can be served as a sauce for sautéed chicken or veal, as well as a dip for cubes of crusty bread. You can add slivers of truffles to the sauce for an extravagant but traditional final touch. Here you see Fonduta (page 54) with chicken, garnished with fluted mushrooms and watercress.

Remove puff pastry from freezer and let stand on a floured board or pastry cloth for about 20 minutes while preparing filling. Cook artichoke hearts in boiling salted water according to package directions; drain well. Heat oil in small frying pan over medium heat. Add green onions and cook, stirring, until wilted and bright green; set aside.

In a large bowl, beat together ricotta cheese, sour cream, the 4 eggs, Parmesan cheese, fontina cheese, tarragon, and nutmeg, beating until smoothly blended. Mix in artichokes and onions.

Cut off and set aside a third of the puff pastry. Roll out large section to make a circle, 15 to 16 inches in diameter. Fit into a 9-inch springform pan. Pour in artichoke filling. Fold top edges of pastry down over filling.

Roll out remaining pastry to make a 9-inch-diameter circle. Brush edge with beaten egg and place circle over filling, pressing pastry edges together firmly to seal. Brush top with beaten egg; pierce in several places with a fork.

Bake in a 400° oven for 45 to 50 minutes or until pastry is well browned. Let cool on a rack. Serve warm or at room temperature; cut into wedges to serve. Makes 8 to 10 servings.

BAKED CHEESE CRÊPES
CRESPELLE AL FORNO

Four cheeses fill and gild these delicate Umbrian crêpes. You might serve them for brunch or as a first course with a dry white Orvieto wine. One of the cheeses in the filling is Fresh Cheese that you can make at home if you wish; purchased ricotta cheese can also be used, but it will have a less creamy consistency.

CRÊPES

¾	cup all-purpose flour
⅔	cup each water and milk
2	eggs
1	tablespoon salad oil
⅛	teaspoon salt

FILLING

1	cup Fresh Cheese (page 57), made with whole milk; or ricotta cheese (page 57) or purchased
½	cup each shredded Parmesan and provolone cheese
¼	cup slivered prosciutto or baked ham

TOPPING

2	tablespoons butter or margarine
1	cup (4 oz.) shredded fontina or jack cheese

To make crêpes, place in a blender or food processor the flour, water, milk, eggs, oil, and salt; whirl or process (stopping motor to scrape down sides of container once or twice) until smooth. Cover batter and let stand for 1 hour or more; stir well before using.

Into a well-oiled 6 to 7-inch crêpe pan or other flat bottom frying pan over medium heat, put 1½ to 2 tablespoons batter, quickly tilting pan so batter flows over entire flat surface. Cook until crêpe appears dry and edge is lightly browned. Turn once to brown lightly on both sides, then turn out onto a plate. Stack crêpes as they are completed. You should have 12 to 16 crêpes.

To make filling, combine Fresh Cheese, Parmesan cheese, provolone cheese, and prosciutto until well blended. Spoon an equal amount of mixture down center of each crêpe and roll to enclose. Place filled crêpes, side by side, in a greased shallow baking dish about 8 by 12 inches.

Dot with butter and sprinkle evenly with fontina cheese. Bake in a 350° oven for 25 to 30 minutes or until cheese topping is melted and lightly browned. Serve at once. Makes 6 servings.

GRILLED MOZZARELLA SANDWICHES
MOZZARELLA IN CARROZZA

One of the small triumphs of the Neapolitan kitchen is this sandwich —mozzarella in a carriage, literally translated. It makes a quick hot lunch with a salad.

8	**slices French or Italian bread, crusts removed**
4	**thick slices (about 4 oz. total) mozzarella cheese**
¾	**cup milk**
⅓	**cup all-purpose flour**
2	**eggs lightly beaten with 1 tablespoon water**
3	**tablespoons** *each* **olive oil and butter or margarine**
2	**tablespoons chopped canned anchovies**
1	**tablespoon lemon juice**

Make sandwiches, using 2 slices bread and 1 slice cheese for each. Have ready milk, flour, and egg mixture, each in a separate shallow dish. Heat oil and butter in a wide frying pan over medium heat until foamy. Lightly dip each sandwich, on both sides, coating all over, first in milk, then in flour, and finally in eggs. Place in pan and brown on both sides, turning once, until crusty and golden; remove to a warm plate.

To drippings in pan, add anchovies and lemon juice, stirring to combine well. Pour sauce over sandwiches. Cut sandwiches in half and serve hot, to eat with a knife and fork. Makes 4 servings.

GARLIC & CHEESE TOAST
CROSTINI DI FORMAGGIO

Cheese melts over tomato and garlic-rubbed toast to make an appealing Florentine lunch sandwich or snack.

4	**slices sweet or sour French bread, or whole wheat bread**
1	**large clove garlic**
4	**teaspoons olive oil**
4	**large thin tomato slices**
4	**to 8 thin slices mozzarella cheese**
	Crushed oregano leaves

Toast bread and arrange slices in a single layer on a baking sheet. Cut garlic in half and rub cut surface over toast. Using about 1 teaspoon for each slice, drizzle with olive oil. On each piece of toast, place 1 tomato slice, cover with 1 or 2 cheese slices, and sprinkle lightly with oregano. Watching closely, broil about 4 inches from heat just until cheese melts (1 to 2 minutes). Serve hot. Makes 4 servings.

MILANESE GRILLED SANDWICHES
TOSTAS

Grilled ham-and-cheese sandwiches with savory condiments tucked into them are popular in Milan. We recommend them for an informal supper or impromptu party. Let guests assemble their own sandwiches and cook them on an electric grill or in a frying pan.

Provide at least four of the suggested condiments in separate small dishes. The sandwiches tend to drip, so provide each guest with an individual plate. Serve with green salad and dry white wine. Finish with a basket of fresh fruit.

½	**to ¾ pound sliced fontina or tybo cheese**
½	**to ¾ pound chunk teleme or sliced Jack cheese (cut portions as needed)**
½	**to ¾ pound sliced cooked ham**
¼	**to ⅓ pound thinly sliced prosciutto (optional)**
1	**large loaf (1 lb.) sliced egg bread, or Italian or French bread, sliced**
	Condiments (recipes follow)

Have all ingredients assembled and close at hand. To make a tosta, place a slice or two of cheese and meat between slices of bread. Toast in a sandwich grill on medium or high heat (or in a frying pan with a lid on medium heat, turning tosta as needed) until browned and cheese is melted; **use no fat.** Open sandwich and add any or all of the condiments. Makes 6 servings.

Russian Dressing. Blend ⅔ cup mayonnaise with ¼ cup drained **sweet pickle relish** and 2 tablespoons **chili sauce**; keep cold and covered until time to serve.

Liver Pâté. Use 1 can (about 4¾ oz.).

Red Peppers. Seed and sliver 1 large red bell pepper. Heat 2 tablespoons olive oil in a small frying pan over moderately high heat. Add pepper and 2 tablespoons **water** and cook, covered, until liquid evaporates. Remove cover and stir in 1 tablespoon **red wine vinegar** and **salt** to taste. Serve at room temperature. (Or substitute one 8-ounce jar sweet fried pepper with onions.)

Onions. Cut 1 large **onion** vertically into slivers. In a wide frying pan over medium-high heat, combine onion with ¼ cup **water** and 2 tablespoons **white wine vinegar**; boil and stir until liquid evaporates and onions are soft. **Salt** to taste and serve at room temperature. (Or substitute one 6-ounce jar pickled onions, and slice thinly.)

Mushrooms. Thinly slice ½ pound **mushrooms.** Heat 2 tablespoons olive oil in a medium-size frying pan over medium heat. Add mushrooms and cook until limp; add 2 tablespoons **white wine vinegar** and cook until liquid evaporates. **Salt** to taste and serve at room temperature. (Or substitute one 5-ounce jar marinated mushrooms, and slice thinly.)

Artichokes. Use 2 jars (6 oz. **each**) marinated **artichoke hearts,** cut in thin slices.

Eggplant Caponata. Use 1 can (about 5 oz.) **eggplant caponata,** or 1 cup homemade Caponata (page 9).

Pickled Peppers. Use 1 jar (about 8 oz.) **Italian-style pickled peppers** (peperoncini).

"End your meal with cheese to make you strong!" That's what our Italian friends laughingly admonish as they serve pungent cheeses with bold character and aroma for dessert.

Of course the Italians don't withhold their love for cheese until the last course. They demonstrate their affection by grating cheese on pasta, rice, and soup, and by combining it with meats, vegetables, and eggs.

Quite often in Italy, cheese makes a course in itself, accompanied by a crusty piece of bread and a glass of wine. When complementary fruits like juicy pears, plump grapes, or golden-fleshed peaches are in season, then cheese and fruit would likely be savored together as dessert.

At breakfast, the addition of cheese is a favored Italian way to give more staying quality to a light meal —usually just coffee, milk, and some sort of bread. For a more substantial Italian-style breakfast, you can add a chunk of cheese and some fruit; or spread bread (or toast) with ricotta and sprinkle it with salt and pepper, or drizzle it with honey.

Here is a sampler of the best-known Italian cheeses commonly available in the United States, along with some serving suggestions. Table cheese—cheese that's served by itself rather than baked in or sprinkled on food—should be kept covered and served at room temperature.

Cheese	Personality profile	Serving suggestions
Asiago	Semisoft and buttery mild when aged for a few months; aged longer, it grows firmer and more assertive. Light yellow with a slightly grainy texture.	Serve as a table cheese when young; good with fruit for dessert. Use for grating when mature.
Bel Paese	A soft, delicately flavored cheese developed in the 1920s by an enterprising Italian cheesemaker.	Table cheese; good for snacking any time.
Fontina	A magnificent, firm cheese with a sweet, nutlike flavor. Originally from the Valle d'Aosta in northern Italy.	Table cheese; delicious for dessert. Also noted as a cooking cheese melted for Fonduta (page 54).
Gorgonzola	Wonderful blue-veined cheese named after its town of origin near Milan. Semisoft, it has a well-developed personality after a mere 3 months of aging; when aged up to a year, it's positively demanding.	Classic table cheese served for dessert. Try it with pears for a delicious duo.
Mozzarella	Often made from water buffalo milk in Italy, but the domestic version is made from cow's milk—usually partially skimmed. Italian imports are more tender, less rubbery than ordinary domestic types.	On pizza; in lasagne. Mellow buffalo-milk mozzarella (bufalo) can be served as a table cheese.
Parmesan	This hard grating cheese is the best known of Italy's grana (grainy) cheeses. Made from skim milk, it can vary widely in saltiness and quality. Parmigiano Reggiano, Italy's most famous grana cheese, is produced only in a small area in northern Italy. The grated Parmesan sold in cylindrical containers in the United States can't compare with a freshly cut or grated Parmesan.	Fine Parmesan that is freshly cut and not overly dried can be served as table cheese—for dessert with dried figs, for instance. Otherwise, freshly grated or shredded Parmesan is used in many Italian dishes, from pasta and rice to ravioli filling and minestrone.
Pecorino	Cheese from sheep's milk. See Romano.	
Provolone	A firm but delicate cheese when young; grows tangy with aging. Provolone is usually smoked. In Italy it's often formed into little pigs and other shapes.	Table cheese; also great in a salami sandwich.
Ricotta	Italian cottage cheese—but sweeter, more moist than domestic cottage cheese, and without well-defined curds. Cheesecake recipes using this fresh cheese date back to Roman times.	Filling for stuffed pasta; sweetened with Marsala for dessert; in cheesecakes.
Romano	Sharp, salty, hard cheese known as pecorino Romano in Italy. More pungent than Parmesan, Romano is made from sheep's milk.	On pasta; in cooking, wherever you would use Parmesan but want a little more emphasis. As with Parmesan, this cheese is best when freshly grated.
Taleggio	Aromatic, soft, creamy cheese with mild but distinctive flavor. Made from cow's milk.	Table cheese; good after salad, or with grapes for dessert.
Teleme	Semisoft to soft, versatile domestic cheese. Good substitute for fontina.	Table cheese; softens at room temperature to spreading consistency. Use in recipes that call for a mild, runny cheese.

6

THE ITALIAN TOUCH WITH MEATS IS DEFT AND SURE—GRILLED

MEAT, POULTRY

STEAK AND LAMB CHOPS, SAUTÉED VEAL, SWEET-SOUR RIBS,

& FISH

SAVORY SPICY SAUSAGES

BASIC VEAL SCALOPPINE
SCALOPPINE DI VITELLO

Say "veal" and the immediate association is "scaloppine." The scaloppine technique is popular throughout Italy, and it's really quite simple: a little trimming, a little pounding, and a short sauté in the frying pan. Once you've finished with the basic preparation, the possibilities for sauces, seasonings, and finishing touches are endless. You can even use the same technique for chicken or turkey.

⅓	pound boneless veal for each serving, prepared for cooking (directions follow)
	All-purpose flour
	Butter, margarine, olive oil, or salad oil
	Salt and pepper

Coat each piece of prepared veal with flour, shake off excess, and set aside until all are coated.

Allow 2 tablespoons butter for each pound of veal to be sautéed. (Butter and margarine add flavor and enhance browning, but burn easily; a combination of butter and oil is flavorful and doesn't burn as readily. For the sake of brevity, directions in

In Italy, steaks, chops, and roasts are served relatively unadorned from the grill, spit, oven, or frying pan. Exceptions abound, though, and in this chapter you'll find succulent simmers, stews, and casseroles.

Nothing compares with tender, young Italian veal, but you can do nearly as well with the more mature veal available in the United States if you prepare and cook it carefully.

Beef, pork, or lamb may also make up the main course of an Italian meal. In this chapter you'll learn how the Florentines prepare their prize steak (page 72). You'll also learn how to make an Italian Boiled Dinner (page 73), and even how to make your own sausage (page 72).

Blessed with an abundance of seafood from the Mediterranean and Adriatic seas, the Italians developed techniques with fish and shellfish that also make fine dining.

A sumptuous Italian banquet is the culinary counterpart of Italian grand opera. Tuscan Chicken & Stuffed Mushrooms (page 80) on a bed of thin pasta is the prima donna. The supporting cast includes Bagna Cauda (page 8), a bowl of bubbling butter and olive oil made bold by garlic and anchovies —in which you dip crisp fresh vegetables. The grand finale features Marengo Cavour (page 100), a Florentine Meringue with a coffee and chocolate-flavored cream filling.

this recipe call for butter, but you may take your choice).

Melt butter in a 10 to 12-inch frying pan over highest heat. Add veal without crowding, and cook until edges of veal turn white (about 1 minute); turn slices over and cook until lightly browned on other side (about 1 more minute). As meat shrinks, move pieces close together and add more veal, keeping pan full at all times. If pan appears dry, add butter, about 1 teaspoon at a time.

Transfer veal to a warm platter and keep warm. Season with salt and pepper to taste, and it's ready to serve.

To trim and pound veal: You can use the thin boneless pieces of veal called scallops (scaloppine) or any piece of veal from the leg, loin, rib, or shoulder that is cut like a steak or chop (⅓ to ½ inch thick). All will be of comparable tenderness. (Some of the recipes that follow specify steaks cut from the leg because of their large shape.) If the price per pound of bone-in chops is half that of a boneless cut (or a small round-bone leg steak), it is more economical to choose the chops.

Cut away any bone (reserve for soup stock). Following natural divi-

(Continued on page 64)

sions, separate large steaks into smaller pieces. Closely trim away fat and all silvery-colored connective tissue and membrane; it shrinks when heated and causes the meat to curl.

Place two or three pieces of veal at a time between two pieces of wax paper or plastic wrap large enough to accommodate the meat when it expands to almost three times its original surface area. Pound each piece gently but firmly with the flat side of a heavy mallet to flatten meat evenly to about 3/16-inch thickness (or thinner if recipes specify). Repeat until all meat is pounded.

Cook veal immediately; or separate with wax paper or plastic wrap, stack in layers, and wrap well; or place slices side by side on wax paper, roll, then wrap well. Refrigerate for up to 1 day.

Lemony Veal Scaloppine. Prepare 1⅓ pounds boneless veal according to Basic Veal Scaloppine, cooking veal in butter. When all meat is cooked and set aside, add to pan an additional 1 tablespoon **butter,** 1 teaspoon grated **lemon peel,** and juice of 1 **lemon.** Boil rapidly, scraping brown particles free from pan, until liquid is slightly reduced. Pour sauce over meat and garnish with minced **parsley** or capers and **lemon** wedges. Makes 4 servings.

Veal Scaloppine with Teleme. Prepare 2 pounds **boneless veal** according to Basic Veal Scaloppine. After dusting meat with **flour,** sprinkle with 1 teaspoon crumbled **oregano leaves;** then cook. As veal is cooked, arrange in overlapping slices on an ovenproof platter. On top of meat, arrange thin slices of **teleme cheese** (about 5 oz. total); if teleme is unavailable, you can substitute fontina or jack cheese. Sprinkle with ¼ cup freshly grated **Parmesan cheese.** Broil 2 to 3 inches from heat just until cheese melts and is bubbly. Makes 6 servings.

Marsala Veal Scaloppine. Thinly slice ½ pound **mushrooms.** In a wide frying pan over medium-high heat, melt 2 tablespoons **butter** or margarine. Add mushrooms, sprinkle with 1½ tablespoons **lemon juice,** and cook until mushrooms are

soft. Pour out of pan and set aside.

Trim and pound 1½ pounds **boneless veal** according to Basic Veal Scaloppine. Cut veal into strips about 1 inch wide and dust in ¼ cup **all-purpose flour** seasoned with ½ teaspoon **salt** and ¼ teaspoon **pepper;** shake off excess. In same frying pan over high heat, melt 2 tablespoons **butter** or margarine. Add veal and brown on both sides; remove meat when browned and keep warm.

To same pan, add ¾ cup **Marsala** or dry sherry and 1 teaspoon **beef stock base** granules. Cook rapidly, stirring constantly, until all browned particles are scraped free from pan and are incorporated into sauce. Return mushrooms and meat to pan and heat through.

Serve at once, garnished with 1 tablespoon minced fresh **parsley.** Makes 4 servings.

VEAL ROLLS
SALTIMBOCCA

"Jump-in-the-mouth" is the translation of saltimbocca—as in "I didn't eat all six of them, they just jumped in my mouth!" The delectable little morsels are made by rolling veal (cut for scaloppine) around prosciutto and cheese, with sage and basil for flavoring. The Roman version leaves out the cheese; the herbs are more prominent that way.

4	veal round steaks (about 2 lbs. total) each cut ½ inch thick
24	very thin slices prosciutto (about 6 oz. total)
¼	pound fontina or Swiss cheese, cut into 12 pieces (optional)
¼	cup butter or margarine
¼	teaspoon each sage leaves and dry basil, crumbled
½	teaspoon Dijon mustard
⅓	cup dry white wine

Trim and pound veal according to directions for Basic Veal Scaloppine (page 62). Divide meat into 12 pieces of fairly equal size. (You can join scraps into larger pieces, if necessary, by overlapping edges and pounding

between sheets of wax paper; handle gently.) Top each piece of veal with several slices of prosciutto and a piece of cheese. Roll meat to enclose filling completely, turning in edges; secure with small skewers.

Melt butter in a wide frying pan over high heat, and blend in sage, basil, and mustard. Add meat rolls and brown quickly on all sides, turning frequently (4 to 5 minutes). Remove rolls and keep warm. Add wine to pan and bring to a boil, scraping brown particles free from pan. Pour sauce over veal. Makes 6 servings.

BOLOGNESE VEAL CUTLETS
COSTOLETTE ALLA BOLOGNESE

(Pictured on page 66)

The people of Bologna are renowned for hearty appetites—never heartier than when confronted with this somewhat more substantial version of the Roman saltimbocca. It is usually accompanied by mashed potatoes and a cooked leafy green vegetable such as spinach or chard.

A lavish Bolognese gesture is the addition of thinly sliced white truffles just before adding the creamy sauce.

1½	pounds boneless veal round steak, ¼ to ⅓ inch thick, cut into serving-size pieces
	Salt, white pepper, and nutmeg
	All-purpose flour
1	egg beaten with 1 tablespoon water
2	tablespoons each butter and olive oil
¼	pound thinly sliced prosciutto
½	cup freshly shredded Parmesan cheese
¼	cup dry white wine
½	cup whipping cream

Lightly sprinkle veal on both sides with salt, pepper, and nutmeg. Coat each piece of veal lightly with flour and shake off excess. Dip and turn in egg mixture; drain briefly. Heat butter and oil in a wide frying pan over medium heat. Add veal, about half at a time, and cook until golden brown on both sides (turn once). As veal browns, arrange in a single layer in a shallow baking pan or on an ovenproof platter. Cover each piece with a slice of prosciutto and sprinkle with Parmesan cheese.

Bake, uncovered, in a 400° oven for 10 to 12 minutes or until cheese browns lightly. Add wine and cream to drippings in frying pan and cook, stirring, over medium-high heat until mixture is reduced to about ½ cup. Pour sauce over veal. Serve at once. Makes 6 servings.

SPICY VEAL CHOPS
BISTECCA ALLA PIZZAIOLA

Although the Italian name for this Neapolitan recipe suggests that it contains beef, in truth it is usually prepared with veal that is somewhat mature. You can also cook pork chops this way, but extend the simmering time to 40 to 45 minutes.

4 to 6	one-inch-thick veal shoulder or loin chops
	Salt and pepper
¼	cup olive oil
1	medium-size onion, finely chopped
2	cloves garlic, slivered
½	teaspoon marjoram leaves
1	can (1 lb.) tomatoes
¼	cup tomato paste
½	cup dry white wine
	Chopped parsley

Sprinkle veal chops with salt and pepper. Brown in olive oil in a large frying pan over medium-high heat; remove chops when browned and set aside.

Add onion to pan and cook until soft and golden. Mix in garlic, marjoram, tomatoes (break up with a spoon) and their liquid, tomato paste, and wine. Return chops to pan, spooning sauce over them. When sauce comes to a boil, reduce heat; cover and simmer until veal is tender when pierced (20 to 25 minutes). Remove chops to a warm platter and keep warm.

Raise heat to high and bring sauce to boil; cook, stirring, until liquid is reduced by about a fourth. Taste and add salt, if needed. Spoon sauce over chops. Sprinkle with parsley. Makes 3 or 4 servings.

VEAL CHOPS WITH SAGE
NODINI ALLA SALVIA

The penetrating flavor of fresh sage with veal is a favorite Roman combination. It's almost worth planting a pot of sage to enjoy this dish. To enhance the veal, accompany with Roast Potatoes & Artichokes (page 48).

4 to 6	one-inch-thick veal loin chops
	Salt and white pepper
¼	cup butter or margarine
2	tablespoons fresh small whole sage leaves or 1 teaspoon dry sage leaves
¼	cup dry vermouth

Sprinkle chops with salt and pepper. Melt butter in a large frying pan over medium heat. Add chops and cook slowly on one side until well browned (about 10 minutes). Turn chops, sprinkle sage into butter between chops, and cook until chops are well browned (about 10 minutes). Arrange on a platter; keep warm.

Add vermouth to pan. Raise heat to high, bring mixture to boil, and cook, stirring, until reduced by about half. Drizzle over chops. Makes 3 or 4 servings.

STUFFED VEAL BREAST
PETTO DI VITELLO FARCITO

The luscious spinach and ground veal stuffing more than makes up for what breast of veal lacks in meatiness. You can stuff the breast up to eight hours ahead and refrigerate until ready to cook. If there are drippings stuck to the pan, you can make a sauce by stirring in about 1 cup broth, wine, or water. Bring to boiling and stir in enough cornstarch-water paste to thicken the sauce.

1	tablespoon olive oil
¼	pound each ground veal and ground, cooked ham (or all veal or all ham)
3	strips bacon, finely chopped
1	large onion, finely chopped
1	large clove garlic, minced or pressed
1	teaspoon dry basil or tarragon leaves
⅓	cup finely chopped parsley
½	pound mushrooms, finely chopped
2	pounds fresh spinach, cooked, chopped, and well drained, or 2 packages (10 oz. each) frozen chopped spinach, thawed and very well drained
¾	cup (3 oz.) shredded Gruyère, Swiss, or jack cheese
1	cup soft bread crumbs (2 slices bread)
1	egg
½	teaspoon salt
¼	teaspoon pepper
3½ to 4-pound	veal breast, split to form a pocket for stuffing
	Salad oil or butter
	Dry basil, thyme leaves, and 1 bay leaf

Heat olive oil in a wide frying pan over medium-high heat; add ground meats and bacon and cook, stirring, until browned. Add onion, garlic, basil, and parsley to meat mixture and continue cooking, stirring occasionally, until onion is soft (about 10 minutes). Remove from heat and combine with mushrooms, spinach, cheese, bread crumbs, egg, salt, and pepper; mix until thoroughly combined.

Pack stuffing into veal breast; fasten

(Continued on page 67)

opening securely with small skewers, or sew with string to hold stuffing inside. Place meat, bone side down, in a well-oiled shallow roasting pan. Rub meat with oil or butter and sprinkle lightly with crumbled basil and thyme; add bay leaf.

Cover pan and bake in a 350° oven for 2 to 2¼ hours or until meat is tender when pierced. Remove cover and bake for about 15 minutes longer to brown surface. Remove skewers or string and slice between bones to serve. Makes 8 servings.

VEAL SHANKS MILANESE
OSSO BUCO

Literally, osso buco means "hollow bones." But veal shanks aren't exactly hollow, they're filled with succulent marrow which you can scoop out with a special spoon or extract with the tip of a knife. This version comes from Milan and is garnished with a mixture of lemon peel, garlic, and parsley known as gremolata. Saffron-flavored Risotto (page 36) is a superlative accompaniment.

7	to 8 pounds meaty veal shanks with marrow in bone, cut through bone in 2-inch-thick slices (12 to 18 pieces)
	Salt
	All-purpose flour
½	cup butter or margarine
1½	cups dry white wine
1	cup chicken broth
1½	tablespoons grated lemon peel
½	cup chopped fresh parsley
1	clove garlic, minced or pressed

Really a hearty version of Saltimbocca geared to satisfy Bolognese appetites, these Bolognese Veal Cutlets (page 64) are crowned with prosciutto, a simple cream sauce, and Parmesan cheese. They're paired with traditional accompaniments—mashed potatoes sprinkled with parsley, and spinach topped with zest of lemon.

Sprinkle shanks with salt, then roll in flour and shake off excess. In a 6 to 8-quart kettle over medium heat, melt butter. Add veal shanks to butter, a portion at a time, and brown on all sides; remove when browned and set aside. When all shanks have been browned, return meat to pan; add wine and broth. Reduce heat; cover and simmer for 1½ to 2 hours or until meat is very tender when pierced and pulls easily from bone. (At this point you may cool, cover, and refrigerate until next day, if you wish. Reheat slowly when ready to continue.)

Combine lemon peel, parsley, and garlic; set aside. With a slotted spoon, transfer meat to a heated platter and keep hot. Bring sauce to a rolling boil, scraping brown particles free from kettle. Add half of lemon-garlic mixture to sauce and let simmer just until parsley wilts. Pour sauce over meat and garnish with remaining lemon-garlic mixture. Makes 6 to 8 servings.

FRITTER DINNER
FRITTO MISTO

Along the lengthy coastline of Italy, fritto misto is usually a combination of crisply fried seafoods. But in the north and inland, it's more likely to be this whole-meal mélange of veal, other meats, and vegetables.

Regarded as family fare in Italy, fritto misto can be remarkably light and delicate. We think this makes it a delightful dinner for guests as well. Our recipe yields eight to ten servings. You can scale it down to serve six by eliminating some of the ingredients; use only artichokes, zucchini, eggplant, and veal.

Assembling this meal of meat and vegetable fritters is easier than you might think. You need only a small portion of each food, and you have them all prepared and waiting before you begin cooking.

Keep the fritters warm in the oven while you cook the remaining food, then serve them all at once with a green salad and crusty bread.

1¼	to 1½ pounds boneless veal
4	or 5 chicken thighs
1	set (about ¾ lb.) of beef brains (optional)
1	pound veal sweetbreads (optional)
4	or 5 whole chicken livers (about ¼ lb.)
3	medium-size zucchini
3	small crookneck squash
1	small eggplant (about ¾ lb.)
6	small artichokes (each 2½-inch diameter or less), or 10 to 12 frozen artichoke hearts, thawed
	Acid water (1 tablespoon vinegar to each 1 quart water)
16	to 20 small mushrooms
	Salt
6	eggs
	All-purpose flour
	Olive oil or salad oil, or half butter and half oil
4	or 5 lemons

Trim and pound veal according to directions on page 62. Remove and discard skin from chicken thighs; cut out bone, if desired; cut each thigh lengthwise into 2 or 3 portions. With your fingers, gently pull membrane from brains and sweetbreads; rinse meats well and cut into ½-inch-thick slices. Cut each chicken liver in half.

Cut zucchini into ⅜-inch-thick diagonal slices. Cut crookneck squash lengthwise into ¼-inch-thick slices. Cut eggplant crosswise into ¼-inch-thick slices or cut lengthwise into ⅜-inch-thick sticks.

Remove tough outer leaves from artichokes, cut off top third (be sure all thorns are removed), and trim stem end. Cut each artichoke in half (if very small) or in quarters. Immerse in acid water until all are prepared; drain well before frying. Trim ends from mushroom stems, if necessary.

Season meats and vegetables by sprinkling with salt. In a bowl, beat eggs until blended. Coat each piece of food with flour and shake off excess.

In a wide frying pan over medium-high heat, pour oil to a depth of about ½ inch. When oil is hot, dip each piece of vegetable into beaten eggs, then fry until richly browned. Remove pieces when browned and place on baking sheets lined with paper towels; keep warm in a 150° oven.

Add more fat as needed, spooning out small browned particles as they accumulate. Next fry meats, leaving veal for last. Cook veal just until lightly browned.

When all food is cooked, transfer fritters to warm serving plates, grouping each kind of meat and vegetable separately. Accompany with lemon wedges to squeeze over fritters, allowing about half a lemon per person. Makes 8 to 10 servings.

POACHED VEAL WITH TUNA SAUCE
VITELLO TONNATO

Thinly sliced, simmered boneless veal served cold with a mellow Tuna Sauce is a classic summer buffet dish. Offer it as a first course, or serve as a main dish with a well-seasoned rice salad and sliced tomatoes.

Veal leg produces the nicest slices, but you may use less costly veal shoulder if it's available.

Or you may use turkey breast—in which case, the dish should probably be called tacchino tonnato.

4	to 5 pounds veal leg or shoulder, or turkey breast, boned, rolled, and tied
1½	cups dry white wine
1	large carrot, sliced
1	large stalk celery, sliced
1	small onion, chopped
1	bay leaf
6	sprigs parsley
1	clove garlic, minced or pressed
	Water
	Tuna Sauce (recipe follows)
	Lemon slices, anchovy fillets, ripe olives, capers, and parsley

In a 5 to 6-quart kettle or Dutch oven, place veal, wine, carrot, celery, onion, bay leaf, parsley, garlic, and just enough water to barely cover meat. Bring to a boil, then lower heat; cover and simmer until meat is easily pierced with a fork or meat thermometer registers 170° when inserted in thickest part (1½ to 2 hours). Let meat cool in cooking liquid, then cover and refrigerate until cold.

Meanwhile, prepare Tuna Sauce.

Remove meat from liquid (strain and refrigerate or freeze for soup); slice meat thinly. Pour a third of the Tuna Sauce in a large shallow serving dish. Arrange meat slices in dish and cover with remaining sauce. Cover and chill for at least 2 hours or until next day.

Shortly before serving, garnish veal with lemon slices, anchovies, olives, capers, and parsley. Makes about 12 main-dish servings or about 24 first-course servings.

Tuna Sauce. Drain oil from 1 small can (about 3 oz.) **tuna** into a measuring cup. Add more **olive oil** or salad oil to make 1 cup. In a blender or food processor combine tuna, 5 **anchovy fillets**, 3 tablespoons **lemon juice**, 2 **eggs**, and 1½ tablespoons **capers**; whirl until smooth. Gradually add oil in a thin steady stream until thick and well blended. Cover and chill up to 1 week. Makes about 1½ cups.

ROLLED PORK LOIN WITH LIVER
PORCHETTA

The porchetta vendor is a familiar sight in Italian street markets. The aroma of spit-roasted pork draws customers eager to taste some of the warm meat on thick slices of casareccio (home-style bread).

This flavorful rolled pork roast is a modest adaptation of an elegant Roman version of porchetta in which suckling pig is pungently seasoned with sage and fennel, and stuffed with its own liver.

1	teaspoon fennel seeds
2	cloves garlic
½	teaspoon each sugar, salt, and coarse ground pepper
¾	teaspoon rubbed sage
3	-pound boneless pork loin or loin end roast
½	pound pork, lamb, or beef liver
1	cup beef broth
1	tablespoon cornstarch mixed with 2 tablespoons water

With a mortar and pestle (or flat bottom of a glass), crush fennel seeds. Add garlic, sugar, salt, pepper, and sage and crush until mixture forms a rough paste. Open pork roast and lay fat side down; slash meat if necessary to make it lie flat. Rub surface of meat with about half the garlic paste.

Trim off and discard any tough membrane from liver. Cut into ⅓-inch-thick strips. Place strips of liver in a single layer over meat. Tightly roll meat lengthwise with seasoned surface inside; tie with heavy string at 2-inch intervals. Rub remaining seasoning paste over outside surface.

Place meat on a rack in a pan; roast uncovered in a 375° oven for 1½ to 1¾ hours or until meat thermometer inserted into thickest part registers 170°. Transfer roast to a serving platter and keep warm.

Place roasting pan over medium-high heat. Pour broth into drippings in pan and bring to a boil, scraping brown particles free from pan. Stir in cornstarch mixture, a little at a time, until sauce reaches desired thickness. Pour sauce into a serving bowl. Cut strings and carve roast into thin slices. Makes 8 servings.

PORK & OLIVE STEW
SPEZZATINO DI MAIALE

Dried mushrooms and either black or green ripe olives flavor the generous tomato sauce of this savory stew.

¼	cup dried Italian mushrooms
	Hot water
2	tablespoons olive oil or salad oil
2	pounds boneless lean pork butt or shoulder, cut into ¾-inch cubes
1	medium-size onion, finely chopped
1	stalk celery, finely chopped
¼	cup chopped parsley
1	clove garlic, minced or pressed
½	teaspoon each salt and dry rosemary
⅛	teaspoon sage leaves
	Dash of ground red pepper (cayenne)
1	can (1 lb.) tomatoes
1	can (8 oz.) tomato sauce
1	can (about 6 oz.) pitted black or green ripe olives, drained

Place mushrooms in a small bowl and barely cover with hot water; set aside.

Heat oil in a wide frying pan or 5 to 6-quart Dutch oven over medium heat. Add pork, about half at a time, and brown on all sides; remove when browned and set aside.

When all pork is browned, add onion and celery to pan and cook, stirring, occasionally, until soft. Mix in parsley, garlic, salt, rosemary, sage, red pepper, tomatoes (break up with a spoon) and their liquid, tomato sauce, and olives. Pour in all of mushroom soaking liquid but last bit (containing residue). Chop mushrooms and add to mixture along with browned pork. Bring to a boil; cover, reduce heat, and simmer until meat is very tender when pierced (1¼ to 1½ hours). If necessary, skim and discard fat. Makes 6 servings.

SWEET-SOUR RIBS
SPUNTATURE DI MAIALE

In Italy the sauce in which these tender ribs cook is used to enhance game, such as wild boar (cinghiale). This tamer version is well suited as a companion to serve with Polenta (page 33).

2	tablespoons each butter or margarine and olive oil
3½	to 4 pounds country-style spareribs, cut into 2-inch lengths
1	large onion, finely chopped
2	cloves garlic, minced or pressed
1	can (15 oz.) tomato purée
½	cup red wine vinegar
¼	cup dried currants
⅓	cup chopped fresh parsley
¾	teaspoon salt
½	teaspoon thyme leaves
¼	teaspoon each whole allspice, whole cloves, and black peppercorns
¼	cup pine nuts (optional)
2	tablespoons sugar

Heat butter and oil in a 5-quart Dutch oven over medium heat. Add spareribs, a few at a time, and brown. Remove ribs when browned and set aside.

When all ribs are browned, add onion to pan and cook, stirring, until soft. Mix in garlic, tomato purée, ⅓ cup of the vinegar, currants, parsley, salt, thyme, allspice, cloves, and peppercorns.

Add ribs, stirring to coat with sauce. Bring to a boil, then reduce heat; cover and simmer until meat is fork-tender (2½ to 3 hours). Skim and discard fat.

In a small frying pan over medium heat, stir nuts (if used) until lightly browned (6 to 8 minutes). Set aside.

In a small pan, heat sugar over medium heat until it melts and turns a medium-amber color; remove from heat and gradually stir in remaining vinegar (reheat, if necessary, to dissolve sugar). Stir sugar mixture into sauce. Sprinkle with toasted pine nuts, if desired. Makes 6 servings.

ITALIAN SAUSAGES WITH PEPPERS
SALSICCE CON PEPERONI

This informal main dish features green Italian frying peppers or a combination of green and red bell peppers. In either case the peppers are roasted and peeled. If you grow your own peppers, you can roast, peel, and freeze them for cooking.

8	Italian frying peppers, or 4 large green or red bell peppers, or a combination of green and red bell peppers
8	mild or hot Italian sausages (about 2 lbs. total)
	Water
2	tablespoons olive oil or salad oil
1	large onion, finely chopped
2	cloves garlic, minced or pressed
1	can (14½ oz.) Italian-style tomatoes
1	can (15 oz.) tomato purée
1½	teaspoons each sugar and dry basil
½	teaspoon oregano leaves
	Salt and pepper

Arrange peppers in a single layer in a broiler pan and broil about 1 inch from heat, turning frequently, until skins are blistered and charred on all sides. Transfer them to a paper or plastic bag and let them sweat for 15 to 20 minutes. Using a paring knife, pull or strip off skin and remove seeds and stems. (At this point you may cool, wrap, and refrigerate for up to 3 days; freeze for longer storage.) Cut Italian peppers in half lengthwise, or quarter bell peppers; set aside.

Pierce each sausage in several places with a fork. Place in a 5 to 6-quart Dutch oven and add water to barely cover. Bring to a boil, then reduce heat; cover and simmer until sausages are no longer pink inside (about 20 minutes). Remove from pan; set aside. Discard water.

To the same pan add oil, onion, and garlic. Cook, stirring, over medium-high heat until soft. Add tomatoes (break up with a spoon) and their liquid, tomato pureé, sugar, basil, and oregano. Simmer, uncovered, stirring occasionally, until thickened (about 20 minutes).

Cut sausages into 1½ to 2-inch chunks and add to sauce; add peppers. Simmer, uncovered, until sausages are hot (5 to 10 minutes). Add salt and pepper to taste. Makes 8 servings.

GRILLED SAUSAGES WITH SPINACH
SALSICCE ALLA GRIGLIA CON SPINACI

Grilled meats and fresh spinach often go together to make an Italian main dish, as in this combination featuring Italian sausages.

2	bunches spinach (about ¾ lb. each)
8	mild Italian sausages (about 2 lbs. total)
2	tablespoons each olive oil and butter or margarine
1	medium-size onion, slivered
1	clove garlic, minced or pressed
¼	teaspoon dry basil
1	medium-size tomato, peeled and chopped
¼	cup dry white wine
½	teaspoon salt
⅛	teaspoon each ground nutmeg and white pepper
	Lemon wedges

Remove and discard stems from well-rinsed spinach; set spinach aside. Pierce each sausage in several places with a fork. Place on grill about 6 inches above a bed of glowing coals, turning as needed to brown well. Grill for 25 to 30 minutes or until sausages are cooked in center (cut a gash to test).

Meanwhile, in a large frying pan, over medium heat, place oil and butter. When butter is melted, add onion and cook, stirring, until soft and golden. Mix in garlic, basil, tomato, wine, salt, nutmeg, and pepper. Cook, stirring, until mixture is thick (8 to 10 minutes). Add spinach

and continue cooking and stirring until spinach is just wilted and thoroughly combined with tomato mixture.

Place spinach on a warm platter. Top with sausages and garnish with lemon. Makes 4 servings.

BIROLDO & BEAN SAUTÉ
BIROLDO E FAGIOLINI

Pine nuts and raisins distinguish the sweetly spiced, Italian-style blood sausage known as biroldo. You'll especially enjoy its subtle flavors if you serve it hot with sautéed onions and Italian green beans.

6	tablespoons butter or olive oil
3	medium-size onions, thinly sliced
½	teaspoon dry basil
1½	to 1¾ pounds biroldo ring sausage (or a length of biroldo the same weight)
2	packages (9 oz. each) frozen Italian green beans, thawed
2	tablespoons water
	Salt

In a wide frying pan over medium heat, melt butter. Add onions and basil and cook, stirring frequently, until onions are golden with faint signs of browning (about 15 minutes).

Push onions to sides of pan and lay sausage in center of pan. Reduce heat to medium-low, cover and cook gently for 5 to 6 minutes, then turn and cook until heated through (5 to 6 minutes more).

(If you prefer sausage slightly crisp, use this alternate cooking method: Cut uncooked sausage in 2-inch lengths. Place slices, cut sides down, in pan with onions; cook, uncovered, for 10 to 12 minutes, turning once.)

Transfer biroldo to a serving dish and keep warm.

Add beans and water to pan. Leave uncovered, raise heat to high, and cook, stirring, until beans are hot and lightly cooked (about 3 minutes). Salt to taste. Spoon beans and onions in and around sausage on serving dish. Makes 6 servings.

COTEGHINO WITH LENTILS
COTEGHINO CON LENTICCHIE

If fresh coteghino sausage (sometimes spelled cotechino) isn't available at Italian delicatessens, use more finely textured, garlic-flavored Italian sausage. Either one acts like a flavor-packet when cooked in this family-style lentil dish, traditional on New Year's Day. The lentils symbolize coins or hoped-for wealth.

3	strips bacon, diced
1	large onion, coarsely chopped
2	medium-size carrots, cut in ¼-inch-thick slices
2½	cups water
1	bay leaf
1	to 1½ pounds coteghino sausage or mild Italian sausages
1	cup (about 6 oz.) lentils
2	cups packed, finely chopped Swiss chard or 1 package (12 oz.) frozen Swiss chard, thawed
	Salt
2	tablespoons minced parsley

In a 4 to 6-quart kettle over medium-high heat, cook bacon, onion, and carrots, stirring frequently, until onion is soft (about 10 minutes). Add water, bay leaf, and coteghino; bring to a boil. Reduce heat, cover, and simmer for 45 minutes (10 minutes for Italian sausages).

Sort lentils, discarding any foreign matter; rinse well. Add to pan, cover, and simmer for 30 minutes. Remove sausage and keep warm.

Gently stir chard into lentils and cook, uncovered, until chard and lentils are tender (about 10 minutes).

(Continued on page 72)

Luscious layers of eggplant, mozzarella, meat sauce, and Parmesan cheese amount to an extraordinary Eggplant Parmesan (page 74). The rich meat sauce combines mild Italian sausages with beef, onions, green pepper, and mushrooms for a substantial entrée.

Salt to taste. Pour lentils into serving dish. Remove casing from coteghino, then slice ¼ inch thick. (If using Italian sausages, cut into chunks.) Arrange sausage on top of lentils; sprinkle with parsley. Makes 4 to 6 servings.

BULK ITALIAN SAUSAGE
SALSICCIA

Making your own sausage has many advantages: you can control the amount of fat and salt, eliminate preservatives, and adjust the spices to suit your taste. (For hot-spiced sausage, add 1 teaspoon chili powder, or ¼ teaspoon cayenne with other seasonings.) Pork butt or shoulder has enough marbled fat to make sausage that is moist and juicy when cooked. Leaner cuts yield drier-tasting sausage.

Serve this sausage by itself, if you wish, or add it to pizza, lasagne, frittatas, or spaghetti sauce.

2½	pounds boneless pork butt or shoulder, cut into 1-inch cubes
1½	teaspoons *each* coriander seeds and dried parsley flakes
1	tablespoon fennel seeds
1	large clove garlic, minced or pressed
¾	teaspoon salt
¾	teaspoon coarse ground black pepper
	Butter, salad oil, or olive oil

Using a coarse blade, put pork cubes through a food chopper twice; or coarsely chop in a food processor. (If you use a processor, first place meat cubes in a single layer on a baking sheet and chill in the freezer for about 20 minutes or until meat is firm but not hard. This makes cleaner cuts when chopping.)

With a mortar and pestle, or blender, grind coriander, parsley, and fennel into small particles. Add to chopped meat. Add garlic, salt, and pepper. Mix well with your hands to distribute seasonings. Cover and refrigerate for at least 8 hours to blend flavors. Makes 2½ pounds.

To use in recipes, crumble sausage into a frying pan, and use as directed.

To make patties, divide sausage equally into 10 patties and stack with 2 sheets of wax paper between each patty. Wrap airtight and refrigerate for up to 2 days or freeze for as long as 3 months. To cook patties, place them (thawed, if frozen) in a frying pan lightly coated with butter or oil. Cook over medium heat until browned on both sides (turn once) and no longer pink in center.

To make Italian sausage links, force seasoned meat through a sausage press into casings (order from a meat market). Fill casings to make sausages ¾ to 1 inch in diameter. Tie with string in 4 to 6-inch lengths. Store as directed for bulk sausage. Use as you would purchased Italian sausage.

GRILLED STEAK FLORENTINE
BISTECCA ALLA FIORENTINA

Steak is never grilled more meticulously than in Florence, known for its exceptional beef. The preferred cut is a thick porterhouse or T-bone. When possible it's cooked over a wood fire, and unless you specify otherwise, it will be rare.

With a similar cooking technique and presentation, you can approximate this sumptuous dish at home, grilling the steak on the barbecue or an indoor grill; it can also be broiled or pan-broiled.

2	porterhouse, T-bone, club, or rib steaks, each 1 inch thick
¼	cup olive oil
	Freshly ground black pepper
	Salt
	Lemon wedges

Brush steaks with oil and sprinkle generously with pepper; let stand for about 15 minutes. Slash edge fat at 3-inch intervals to prevent curling. Lightly brush barbecue grill with olive oil. Place steaks on grill 4 to 6 inches above a solid bed of glowing coals. Cook, turning only once, for 4 to 6 minutes on each side for rare (or until done to your liking when slashed). Transfer steaks to a serving platter; season with salt. Serve with lemon wedges to squeeze over each serving. Makes 4 to 6 servings.

Note: Steaks can also be broiled about 4 inches from heat or pan-broiled in an oiled frying pan over medium-high heat.

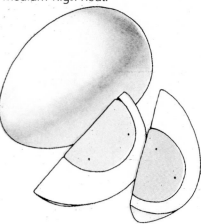

ROLLED FLANK STEAK
BRACIOLA

Filled with cheese, salami, bacon, and hard-cooked eggs, these flank-steak rolls simmer in a robust Neapolitan tomato sauce. When sliced they have an appealing pinwheel design. Serve hot with spaghetti and Parmesan cheese, or serve cold.

You can even serve one steak hot with the sauce and refrigerate the other to slice later for a cold meat tray. Any leftover sauce can be refrigerated for up to a week, or frozen for longer storage; you could use it as a sauce for pasta.

	Neapolitan Gravy (recipe follows)
2	large flank steaks (1½ to 2 lbs. each)
¼	cup freshly grated Parmesan cheese
10	strips bacon
8	slices (about 10 oz.) provolone cheese
12	thin slices salami
6	hard-cooked eggs
2	tablespoons olive oil or salad oil

Prepare Neapolitan Gravy.

Trim excess fat from flank steaks. Butterfly each steak by splitting it horizontally through center, leaving one edge attached. Open and place between pieces of plastic wrap; pound each with flat side of mallet until evenly flattened, especially at center ridge. Discard top piece of plastic wrap. Evenly sprinkle meat with Parmesan cheese.

In a wide frying pan over medium heat, partially cook bacon to render excess fat; bacon should still be limp. Arrange 5 bacon strips on each steak, crossing center ridge. Cover each with 4 slices provolone and 6 slices salami; arrange 3 hard-cooked eggs on salami, crossing ridge.

Using the plastic wrap to help you lift, roll up meat as tightly as possible to enclose filling. With cord, tie each roll lengthwise, tucking in ends, then tie around each roll in 6 to 8 places.

Heat oil in a 6 to 8-quart kettle over medium heat; add meat rolls, one at a time, and brown well on all sides. Return both rolls to pan. Pour in Neapolitan Gravy, bring to a boil, then cover and reduce heat. Simmer for 3 hours or until meat is very tender when pierced. Lift out meat; skim and discard fat from cooking liquid.

To serve hot, cut in ½-inch-thick slices and pass sauce to spoon over individual servings. Or let rolls cool, then cover and refrigerate; cut in thin slices to use as a cold cut or in sandwiches. Makes 10 to 12 servings.

Neapolitan Gravy. In a large bowl, combine 2 large cans (1 lb. 13 oz. each) tomato purée, 2 cloves **garlic** (minced or pressed), ½ cup chopped **parsley**, ½ pound **mushrooms** (sliced), ¾ cup **dry red wine**, 2 tablespoons **dry basil**, 1 tablespoon **oregano leaves**, 1 teaspoon **salt**, 1 teaspoon **sugar**, ½ teaspoon **pepper**, and 1½ cups **water**.

BOILED DINNER
BOLLITO MISTO CON COTEGHINO
(Pictured on page 75)

Chubby coteghino, a fresh sausage sold in some Italian delicatessens, has a coarser texture than garlic-flavored Italian sausage—though they're similar in taste. Here it flavors beef brisket, vegetables, and sauce in a boiled dinner such as you might

have in Rapallo on the Italian Riviera, just south of Genoa.

Be sure you select fresh, not corned, brisket. You can choose one or both of the sauces that follow.

5	-pound piece fresh beef brisket
2 to 3	quarts water or Brown Stock (page 38)
1	each **medium-size carrot, onion, and celery stalk, cut into chunks**
3 or 4	parsley sprigs
1	bay leaf
8 to 10	black peppercorns
4 to 6	whole allspice
	Salt (optional)
1 to 1½	pounds coteghino sausage
3 to 5	large carrots, cut in half lengthwise
8 to 10	small thin-skinned potatoes
8 to 10	small boiling onions
4	large stalks celery, cut in half
	Chive Sauce (recipe follows)
	Green Sauce (recipe follows)

Place brisket in a shallow roasting pan. Bake in a 500° oven for 35 minutes, turning meat over after 25 minutes. If drippings begin to char, add 3 to 4 tablespoons water to pan. Transfer brisket to a 6 to 8-quart kettle; skim and discard fat from roasting pan.

Add some of the water or stock to pan, scraping browned particles free. Pour this liquid and remaining water or stock over meat in kettle.

Add chunks of carrot, onion, and celery to pan along with parsley, bay leaf, peppercorns, allspice, and 1 teaspoon salt (omit if cooking liquid is salted). Bring to a boil then reduce heat; cover and simmer until meat is slightly tender when pierced (about 2 hours). Add the sausage and cook for 2 more hours until both meats are very tender when pierced.

Remove brisket and sausage from broth and keep warm in a 150° oven while you make sauce and cook remaining vegetables. Pour broth through a wire strainer; discard residue. Measure out and set aside 2

cups of the broth if making Chive Sauce.

Bring remaining broth to a boil. Add carrot halves, potatoes, and boiling onions; cook, uncovered, until potatoes are tender when pierced (about 20 minutes). Add celery; cook for another 5 minutes. With a slotted spoon, transfer vegetables from broth to a warm platter. (Refrigerate or freeze broth for other uses.) Arrange brisket and coteghino on platter with vegetables. Slice meats and serve with Chive Sauce or Green Sauce, or both, to pour over meat. Makes 8 to 10 servings.

Chive Sauce. In a pan over medium heat, melt 1 tablespoon **butter** or margarine. Add 1 tablespoon minced **shallots** or green onions and cook until soft and golden. Blend in 2 tablespoons **all-purpose flour**; gradually add the 2 cups reserved **broth**.

Reduce heat and simmer gently, uncovered, for about 10 minutes, stirring occasionally. Blend in 4 to 6 tablespoons minced **chives** (fresh, frozen, or freeze-dried) and 2 to 4 tablespoons **half-and-half** (light cream). Makes about 2 cups.

Green Sauce. Combine the following ingredients in a blender or food processor and whirl or process until well blended: ½ cup **olive oil**, ¼ cup **white wine vinegar**, ½ small **onion** (cut into chunks), 1 cup lightly packed fresh **parsley leaves**, 2 tablespoons **capers**, 1 small clove **garlic**, 3 canned **anchovy fillets**, a dash of **pepper**, and ½ teaspoon **each oregano** leaves, **basil**, and **salt** to taste. Serve at room temperature. Makes about 1½ cups.

BRAISED CHUCK ROAST
STRACOTTO

Choose a thick, flat chuck roast (blade-cut or 7-bone) or—for a more handsome presentation—a boneless rolled chuck roast.

The sauce in which the roast cooks is rich, red, and plentiful; serve it over a pasta such as rigatoni as a side dish for the meat. Freeze any extra sauce to serve with pasta at another meal.

(Continued on next page)

3	to 4-pound **beef chuck roast,** bone in (or boned, rolled, and tied)
1	large **onion,** chopped
2	tablespoons **olive oil** (optional)
3	cans (8 oz. each) **tomato sauce**
1	can (6 oz.) **tomato paste**
½	cup each **water** and **dry red wine**
½	teaspoon each ground **allspice, poultry seasoning,** and **thyme leaves**
6	cloves **garlic,** minced or pressed
¼	cup chopped **parsley**
½	pound **mushrooms,** sliced
	Salt and **pepper**

Trim any fat from meat and place in a Dutch oven or deep, wide frying pan over medium heat. Slowly brown meat and onion in fat, adding olive oil if needed. Then add tomato sauce, tomato paste, water, wine, allspice, poultry seasoning, thyme, garlic, and parsley. Cover and simmer slowly for 2 to 2½ hours for bone-in roast (2½ to 3 hours for a boneless, rolled roast) until meat is very tender when pierced. About 15 minutes before serving, add mushrooms and salt and pepper to taste; simmer. Skim and discard fat. Makes 6 to 10 servings.

EGGPLANT PARMESAN
MELANZANE ALLA PARMIGIANA
(Pictured on page 71)

This hearty casserole makes eight to ten generous servings and is perfect for a buffet. You can layer the eggplant, meat sauce, and cheese well ahead of time, then bake it just before serving.

	Meat Sauce (recipe follows)
2	medium-size **eggplants** (about 1 pound each)
	All-purpose flour
	Olive oil or **salad oil**
3	**eggs** beaten with ⅓ cup water
1	pound **mozzarella cheese,** sliced
½	cup freshly grated **Parmesan cheese**

Prepare Meat Sauce.

Cut eggplants lengthwise into slices about ¼ inch thick. Coat each slice with flour and shake off excess. Heat about ¼ inch oil in a wide frying pan over medium-high heat. Dip eggplant slices in egg mixture, drain briefly, and cook, without crowding, adding oil as needed, until well browned and tender when pierced. Drain, when browned, on paper towels.

Arrange about half the eggplant in a shallow 3 to 4-quart casserole. Spoon half the Meat Sauce over it, then cover sauce with about half the mozzarella. Repeat with layers of eggplant, Meat Sauce, and mozzarella. Top with Parmesan cheese. (At this point you may cover and refrigerate, if made ahead.)

Bake, uncovered, in a 375° oven for 40 minutes (50 minutes, if refrigerated) or until bubbly. Makes 8 to 10 servings.

Meat Sauce. In a 5 or 6-quart kettle, crumble 1½ pounds **lean ground beef** and add 1¼ to 1½ pounds thinly sliced **mild Italian pork sausages** (casings removed), 1 seeded **green pepper** (finely chopped), 2 medium-size **onions** (chopped), and ½ pound **mushrooms** (chopped).

Cook over medium-high heat, stirring frequently, until meat is no longer pink. Add 1 large can (1 lb. 12 oz.) **tomatoes** or Italian-style tomatoes (break up with a spoon) and their liquid, and 1 can (6 oz.) **tomato paste.** Cook rapidly, uncovered, until sauce is very thick (about 45 minutes), stirring often. Remove from heat and let stand undisturbed for 5 to 10 minutes, then skim and discard fat. Use sauce hot or cold. (If made ahead, you may cover and refrigerate sauce for up to 4 days; freeze for longer storage.)

BEEF-STUFFED ZUCCHINI
ZUCCHINE RIPIENI

Filled with a meaty stuffing and baked, zucchini makes a fine main dish, particularly in the late summer or fall when home gardens abound with this prolific vegetable.

8	medium-size **zucchini** (2½ to 3 lbs. total)
	Salt
2	tablespoons **olive oil** or **salad oil**
1	large **onion,** finely chopped
1	pound lean **ground beef**
½	cup canned **tomato sauce**
½	teaspoon **thyme leaves**
3	cups diced **French bread** (about 3 slices)
2	cups packed chopped **Swiss chard** or 1 package (12 oz.) frozen **Swiss chard,** thawed
½	cup lightly packed **parsley leaves**
¼	cup freshly grated **Parmesan cheese**
3	**eggs**
	Additional freshly grated **Parmesan cheese**

Trim and discard stem and blossom ends from zucchini; then cut zucchini in halves lengthwise. Cook, covered, in boiling water to cover for 5 minutes; drain. Let stand until cool enough to handle, then scoop out and discard seeds. Sprinkle shells lightly with salt; set aside.

To make meat filling, heat 1 tablespoon of the oil in a wide frying pan over medium heat. Add onion and cook until soft. Crumble ground beef into pan with onions, raise heat to medium-high, and cook, stirring, until meat is no longer pink. Mix in tomato sauce, thyme, and ¾ teaspoon salt; cook on high heat, stirring often, for about 5 minutes; remove from heat.

Meanwhile, place bread in a bowl and add water to cover. Let stand for

(Continued on page 76)

Glossy vegetables and coteghino sausage surround a savory beef brisket for an Italian version of a boiled dinner, Bollito Misto con Coteghino (page 73). The sausage simmers along with the meat and vegetables, flavoring the entire dish. But the Italians aren't content to serve this dish without the additional flavor of a light Chive Sauce or a more vigorous Green Sauce—or both.

a few minutes, then drain. Squeeze moisture from bread; set bread aside.

In a small pan over high heat, bring a small amount of water to boiling. Add chard and parsley and cook just until chard is limp and bright green. (If using frozen chard, combine with parsley and water; heat through.) Drain well; when cool enough to touch, squeeze to remove excess moisture then finely chop.

Combine meat mixture, bread, chard mixture, the ¼ cup Parmesan cheese, and eggs. Beat to blend. Brush edges of zucchini with remaining 1 tablespoon oil. Mound meat filling into zucchini, using about ⅓ cup for each. Place zucchini in a shallow baking dish. Bake, uncovered, in a 350° oven for 25 to 30 minutes or until filling is hot. Serve with additional Parmesan cheese. Makes 6 to 8 servings.

VENETIAN LIVER
FEGATO ALLA VENEZIANA

A touch of grated lemon peel stirred into golden sautéed onions is the Venetian touch that distinguishes this liver and onion dish.

½	cup olive oil
4	large onions, quartered and separated into layers
½	teaspoon grated lemon peel
2	pounds calf or baby beef liver, cut into ½-inch-thick slices and trimmed of any tough membrane
	All-purpose flour
	Salt and pepper
	Lemon wedges
	Chopped parsley

Heat oil in a wide frying pan over medium-high heat. Add onions and cook, stirring, until soft and slightly golden (about 10 minutes). Stir in lemon peel. With a slotted spoon, remove onion mixture to a bowl and set aside. Reserve oil in pan.

Coat liver with flour, shake off excess and lay pieces side by side on wax paper. Sprinkle with salt and pepper.

In same frying pan over medium heat, add liver slices without crowding, and cook until browned well on both sides but still slightly pink in center (about 5 minutes); cut a gash to test. Transfer liver when cooked to a warm platter and keep warm. Return onions to pan when liver is cooked and stir to heat through. Spoon onions over liver and garnish with lemon wedges and parsley. Makes 6 servings.

TUSCAN BEEF TONGUE
LINGUA DOLCE-FORTE

Dolce-forte means "sweet-strong," and that's an accurate description of the seasoning in this recipe. In and around Florence, the practice of balancing sweet and sharp flavors is popular.

3½	to 4-pound fresh beef tongue
6	cups water
3	large onions
4	large carrots
6	to 8 parsley sprigs
½	cup olive oil
2	large stalks celery, finely chopped
1	cup chopped fresh parsley
2	tablespoons tomato paste
2	tablespoons minced candied citron or candied orange peel
½	cup raisins
2	tablespoons *each* sugar and all-purpose flour
½	ounce unsweetened chocolate, finely chopped
6	tablespoons wine vinegar
⅓	cup pine nuts (pignoli), optional

Rinse tongue and place in a 5 to 6-quart Dutch oven. Add water, 1 of the onions (quartered), 2 of the carrots (cut into chunks), and parsley sprigs. Bring to a boil; cover, reduce heat, and simmer until tongue is easily pierced with a fork (2½ to 3 hours). Remove from heat and let stand in broth until cool enough to touch.

Remove tongue from broth. Strain and reserve broth; discard vegetables. Peel skin from tongue, trim off fat, and remove and discard any bones. Cut tongue crosswise into ¼-inch-thick slices; set aside.

Finely chop remaining onions and carrots. Heat oil in a wide frying pan over medium heat. Add onions, carrots, celery, and chopped parsley. Cook, stirring, until vegetables are soft (about 15 minutes); do not brown. Stir in tomato paste, citron, raisins, sugar, flour, and chocolate. Then stir in vinegar and 1 cup of the reserved broth (refrigerate or freeze balance for other uses). Bring to a boil, stirring; remove from heat and season to taste with salt.

Layer tongue and sauce in a 2-quart shallow casserole, finishing with a layer of sauce. Sprinkle with nuts. (At this point you may cover and refrigerate until next day.) Bake, covered, in a 325° oven for 45 minutes (1 hour, if refrigerated). Makes 6 to 8 servings.

FLORENTINE TRIPE
TRIPPA ALLA FIORENTINA

Florentine-style cooking presents a wonderful opportunity to use a food processor, since it typically begins with finely chopped onion, carrots, and celery. Here, the vegetable mixture is the beginning of a richly flavored tomato sauce that coats slivers of tripe.

1½	pounds plain or honeycomb tripe
3	quarts water
6	tablespoons olive oil
2	large onions, finely chopped
2	cloves garlic, minced or pressed
1	large stalk celery, finely chopped
3	large carrots, finely chopped
1	cup lightly packed chopped parsley
1	large can (1 lb. 12 oz.) tomatoes
1	can (6 oz.) tomato paste
½	teaspoon dry rosemary
1	can (14½ oz.) regular-strength beef broth
	Salt

Rinse tripe and place in a 5 to 6-quart kettle with water. Cover and bring to a boil; reduce heat and simmer for 2 hours or until tripe is very easy to pierce.

Meanwhile, heat olive oil in a wide frying pan over medium heat. Add onions, garlic, celery, and carrots. Cook, stirring frequently, until vegetables are soft but not browned (about 15 minutes). Stir in parsley, tomatoes (break up with a spoon) and their liquid, tomato paste, rosemary, and beef broth. Boil, uncovered, stirring occasionally, until quite thick; then stir more frequently to prevent scorching until sauce is reduced to about 3½ cups. Set aside.

Drain cooked tripe; when cool enough to handle, cut in slivers ⅛ to ¼-inch wide. Mix tripe into sauce and add salt to taste. Spoon into a shallow 2-quart casserole. (At this point you may cover and refrigerate until next day.)

Bake, uncovered, in a 425° oven for 45 minutes (50 minutes, if refrigerated) or until top is slightly crusty and browned. Makes 5 or 6 servings.

ROMAN LAMB CHOPS
ABBACCHIO ALLA SCOTTADITO

One typical meat dish of Rome is quickly grilled chops from a young lamb—cooked so fast and on such a hot grill that they "burn the fingers" (**scottadito**) as the cook turns them.

6	to 8 rib or shoulder lamb chops, about ¾ inch thick
	Freshly ground black pepper
3	tablespoons olive oil
1	teaspoon dry rosemary
2	cloves garlic, slivered
	Salt

Slash any fat around edges of chops about every 2 inches to prevent curling during cooking. Sprinkle chops with pepper. Pour oil into a wide frying pan over medium-high heat. Add rosemary and garlic and swirl until oil is hot; remove garlic and rosemary with a slotted spoon. Cook chops, turning once, until well browned on both sides (2½ to 3 minutes on each side). Sprinkle with salt and serve at once. Makes 3 or 4 servings.

HERBED LAMB STEW
AGNELLO ALLA CACCIATORA

Reasonably priced and fat-trimmed lamb shoulder is an excellent choice for this succulent Sienese stew. You can also use chunks of bone-in lamb neck, but you'll need about five pounds of it instead of three.

3	pounds cubed lean lamb shoulder or other lamb stew meat
	Salt and pepper
2	tablespoons each butter or margarine and olive oil
1	large onion, finely chopped
1	medium-size carrot, shredded
1	large stalk celery, finely chopped
3	cloves garlic
1	teaspoon dry rosemary
½	teaspoon sage leaves
1	large can (1 lb. 12 oz.) tomatoes
1	can (6 oz.) tomato paste
½	cup dry red wine
2	tablespoons wine vinegar
	Chopped parsley

Sprinkle lamb lightly with salt and pepper. Place butter and oil in a 5 to 6-quart Dutch oven over medium heat. When mixture is hot, brown lamb, without crowding. Remove pieces when browned and set aside.

When all lamb is browned, pour off all but 2 tablespoons of the drippings. Add onion, carrot, celery, and garlic; cook, stirring occasionally, until vegetables are soft. Return meat to pan; add rosemary, sage, tomatoes (break up with a spoon) and their liquid, tomato paste, and wine. Bring to a boil, then reduce heat; cover and simmer until lamb is tender when pierced (1 to 1½ hours).

Skim and discard fat, then continue cooking, uncovered, until sauce is thick (about 20 minutes). Stir in vinegar. Sprinkle with parsley and serve. Makes 6 to 8 servings.

ROAST CHICKEN
POLLO ARROSTO

Garlic, lemon, and marjoram flavor the chicken as it roasts, then you add a touch of Madeira to the pan juices to finish the sauce.

3½	to 4-pound broiler-fryer chicken or 5 to 6-pound roasting chicken
	Salt
1	clove garlic, minced or pressed
⅛	teaspoon pepper
1	teaspoon marjoram leaves
2	tablespoons lemon juice
3	tablespoons Madeira

Remove giblets from chicken; set aside for other uses. Pull off and discard lumps of fat from chicken.

Lightly sprinkle chicken inside and out with salt. Place chicken, breast up and wings tucked under back (do not truss), on a rack in a roasting pan. In a small bowl, mix together garlic, pepper, marjoram, and lemon juice; brush over chicken.

Roast, uncovered, in a 375° oven for 1¼ to 1½ hours (about 2 hours for a heavier roasting chicken) or until chicken is well browned and meat near thigh bone is no longer pink when slashed.

Drain juices from cavity of cooked chicken into roasting pan. Transfer chicken to a serving dish; cover loosely and keep warm. Skim and discard fat from pan juices. Add Madeira to pan and bring mixture to a boil, scraping brown particles free from

(Continued on page 79)

pan. Serve in a small bowl; spoon over portions of carved chicken. Makes 4 or 5 servings (a roasting chicken yields 6 servings).

GRILLED CHICKEN HALVES
POLLO ALLA DIAVOLA

To prepare this specialty from Rome, you cut a small, whole chicken down its backbone, open it flat, and cook it in a red-hot pan. Using a more gentle cooking temperature tends to rob the dish of the inspiration for its fiery Italian name, but we find that it results in juicier chicken.

2	to 2½-pound broiler-fryer chicken
¼	cup olive oil
½	teaspoon salt
¼	teaspoon coarse ground pepper
	Lemon wedges

Remove chicken giblets and reserve for other uses. Using a sharp knife, kitchen scissors, or poultry shears, cut out chicken backbone (vertebrae that run from tail to neck). Pull free and discard any excess fat from inside. Open chicken out so it lies flat, pressing down on breast bone to snap cartilage open.

In a small bowl, mix together oil, salt, and pepper; brush chicken generously on both sides with some of the mixture. Brush a wide frying pan large enough to hold opened-out chicken with some of the remaining oil mixture. Place over medium heat.

Place chicken, breast down, in

Al fresco—in the fresh air. What a delightful way to enjoy an Italian repast. Golden Chicken Cutlets (page 81), sliced cheese, and a salad of red peppers, olives, watercress, and capers form the main course. Picnickers also enjoy a ring of Italian bread, white wine, and a thermosful of hot espresso. The dessert selection includes oranges, chocolate truffles, and almond macaroons.

---

pan; weight with a heavy dinner plate to flatten chicken as it cooks. Turn occasionally, each time removing plate, brushing with oil mixture, and replacing plate. Continue to cook chicken until well browned on both sides and meat near thigh bone is no longer pink when slashed (a total of 15 to 20 minutes on each side). Cut in half along breast bone (then into quarters, if you wish). Serve with lemon. Makes 2 to 4 servings.

HUNTER-STYLE CHICKEN
POLLO ALLA CACCIATORA

One whiff of this chicken simmering in its robust sauce of tomatoes, herbs, and red wine and you'll know it's Italy's famous chicken cacciatora. The same savory method of preparation can be used for rabbit.

3	-pound broiler-fryer chicken, cut into pieces
	Salt and pepper
2	tablespoons each butter and olive oil
1	medium-size onion, chopped
1	clove garlic, minced or pressed
1	large stalk celery, finely chopped
1	medium-size carrot, shredded
¼	pound medium-size mushrooms, quartered
1	can (about 1 lb.) tomato wedges, or tomatoes, coarsely chopped
⅓	cup each dry red wine and chopped fresh parsley
½	teaspoon dry rosemary
¼	teaspoon each dry basil and oregano leaves

Sprinkle chicken with salt and pepper. In a wide frying pan over medium-high heat, place butter and oil. When butter is melted, add chicken pieces and cook, turning, until browned on all sides. Remove when browned and set aside. Pour off and discard all but 3 tablespoons pan drippings.

To the pan, add onion, garlic, celery, carrot, and mushrooms. Cook, stirring occasionally, until onions are soft and lightly browned (about 10 min-

utes). Return chicken to pan and add tomatoes and their liquid, wine, ¼ cup of the parsley, rosemary, basil, and oregano; stir well. Cover and simmer gently for about 45 minutes or until meat is no longer pink in thickest part when slashed. With a slotted spoon, transfer chicken and mushrooms to a serving dish; keep warm.

Over high heat cook sauce, stirring, until slightly thickened. Add salt to taste. Spoon sauce over chicken and sprinkle with the remaining chopped parsley. Makes 4 or 5 servings.

Hunter-style Rabbit. Follow preceding directions for chicken, but dust 2½ to 3-pound **rabbit**, cut in pieces, with **all-purpose flour**, then shake off excess before browning. Increase simmering time to 50 minutes to 1 hour or until rabbit is very tender when pierced.

CHICKEN SAN MARINO
POLLO ALLA SAN MARINO

Named for a small republic in eastern Italy, this dish features chicken breasts stuffed with ham and melted cheese. Most of the preparation can be done ahead. The chicken is baked and served with a brandy cream sauce.

4	whole chicken breasts (about 4 lbs. total), cut in half, boned, and skinned
8	slices fontina or Gruyère cheese, each ¼ inch thick and cut into 1 by 2½-inch rectangles
8	very thin slices prosciutto or Westphalian ham
	Salt
	All-purpose flour
1	or 2 eggs, well beaten
	Fine dry bread crumbs
3	to 4 tablespoons butter
3	tablespoons brandy
½	cup whipping cream

Place chicken pieces, one at a time, between pieces of wax paper or plastic wrap and pound with flat side of a mallet until about ¼ inch thick. On each flattened piece, lay a rectangle of cheese wrapped in a slice of ham. Wrap the chicken around the ham, enclosing completely. Sprinkle with salt, then coat with flour and shake off excess. Dip each roll in beaten egg, then roll in bread crumbs. (At this point you may cover, and refrigerate, if made ahead.)

In a wide frying pan large enough to hold all the rolls, melt 3 tablespoons butter over medium heat. Cook rolls, browning evenly and well on all sides, for about 15 minutes, adding more butter if needed to keep rolls moist. Transfer to an oven proof serving dish, arranging rolls side by side in a single layer. Bake, uncovered, in a 350° oven for 15 minutes.

To the pan in which you browned the chicken, add brandy; set aflame (**not** beneath an exhaust fan or flammable items), tipping and tilting pan until flame dies. Add cream and boil until large shiny bubbles form and sauce has thickened slightly. Pour sauce over chicken to serve. Makes 6 to 8 servings.

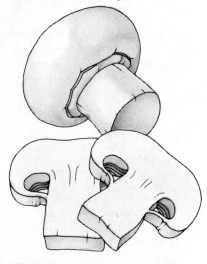

TUSCAN CHICKEN & STUFFED MUSHROOMS
POLLO ALLA TOSCANA
(Pictured on page 63)

For a special Italian dinner, this is a very handsome dish. It's complicated, but you can do the major part of the preparation in advance. The only accompaniments needed are a fresh green vegetable, such as asparagus, and perhaps a loaf of crusty bread.

3	-pound broiler-fryer chicken, cut in pieces (giblets optional)
1	whole chicken breast (about 1 lb.)
	Salt
2	tablespoons *each* olive oil and butter
	Stuffed mushrooms (recipe follows)
¼	cup chopped onion
1	large tomato, peeled, seeded, and diced
½	teaspoon dry basil
⅛	teaspoon dry rosemary
½	cup *each* dry white wine and water
¼	cup minced prosciutto or cooked ham
8	ounces vermicelli or other thin noodles, hot, cooked, and drained
	Minced parsley

Bone chicken breasts and thighs; cut meat into large pieces. (Reserve bones, neck, and back of chicken for stock.) Salt meat lightly. In a wide frying pan over medium heat, place oil and butter. When butter is melted, add wings, drumsticks, thighs, gizzard, and heart. Brown on all sides, then push to corner of pan to continue cooking. Without crowding, lightly brown pieces of breast and liver (they should remain pink inside); then remove all chicken from pan and set aside.

In same pan, brown stuffed mushrooms on flat side only; carefully set aside.

To pan drippings, add onion, tomato, basil, and rosemary, and cook until onion is soft. Add wine and water and boil rapidly until reduced by about half. Return chicken and any juices to pan, add prosciutto, and simmer for 10 minutes.

Put chicken into a shallow 2 to 3-quart casserole; top with mushrooms and sauce. (At this point you may cover and refrigerate, if you wish.)

Bake, covered, in a 375° oven for 30 minutes (40 minutes, if refrigerated) or until chicken is tender when pierced. To serve, set mushrooms around edge of platter, swirl noodles in center, top with chicken, and spoon sauce over all. Sprinkle with parsley. Makes 4 or 5 servings.

Stuffed mushrooms. Select 8 mushrooms, each about 2 inches in diameter; remove stems and scoop out centers. Mince stems and centers; cook in a small pan in 1 tablespoon melted **butter** with ¼ cup minced **onion** until vegetables are soft; set aside.

Cook ½ pound **sweetbreads** for 10 minutes in boiling salted water to cover. Drain; pull off membrane. Put sweetbreads through fine blade of a food chopper (or mince in a food processor), then blend with cooked mixture, ⅓ cup freshly shredded **Parmesan cheese**, ¼ cup chopped **prosciutto** or cooked ham, and **salt** to taste. Stuff all the filling into mushroom caps.

BONELESS CHICKEN BUNDLES
INVOLTINI DI POLLO AL ROSMARINO

Crispy on the outside, moist and juicy inside, these succulent chicken bundles are actually two whole chicken legs that you bone, then tie together. You can cook them on the barbecue or bake them.

8	whole chicken legs, drumsticks and thighs attached
3	tablespoons olive oil or salad oil
	Salt and pepper
2	cloves garlic, minced or pressed
4	sprigs fresh rosemary or ½ teaspoon dry rosemary

On the inside of each leg, cut meat to bone along entire length. With knife blade, cut and scrape meat free from bone; do not remove skin. (Save bones to make broth.) Brush meaty sides of boned chicken legs with some of the oil; sprinkle with salt, pepper, and garlic. Place a sprig of rosemary or about ⅛ teaspoon of dry rosemary on 4 of the pieces of chicken. Place meaty sides of 2 legs together to make 4 bundles, positioning thigh section of one against drumstick section of the other. For each bundle, pull loose skin from edges of one leg over other leg, tucking in meat to make a neat bundle. Tie each bundle with string at 2-inch intervals. Brush bundles with remaining olive oil.

Grill 4 to 6 inches above glowing coals, turning as needed, or bake in a shallow pan in a 400° oven for about 40 minutes or until well browned on all sides and meat in thickest portion is no longer pink when slashed. Makes 4 large or 8 small servings.

CHICKEN & OLIVE SAUTÉ
POLLO CON LE OLIVE

Only the dark pieces of chicken are used in this dish. Swiss chard is served with it to complement the sauce.

¼	cup olive oil
1	medium-size onion, chopped
2	cloves garlic
6	each chicken drumsticks and thighs, separated
	Salt
½	cup canned tomato sauce
¼	cup water
1	can (7½ oz.) pitted green ripe or black olives, drained
1	jar (2¼ oz.) pimento-stuffed Spanish-style olives, drained
4	cups packed chopped Swiss chard or 2 packages (12 oz. each) frozen Swiss chard, thawed

Heat oil in wide frying pan over medium heat. Add onion and garlic and cook, stirring, until onion is soft; remove from pan with a slotted spoon and set aside. Sprinkle chicken with salt. Raise heat to medium high and brown chicken lightly on all sides. Return onion and garlic to pan, then add tomato sauce, water, and both kinds of olives. Reduce heat to low, cover pan, and simmer gently until chicken is quite tender when pierced (40 minutes).

About 10 minutes before chicken is done, stir in fresh chard, cover and continue to cook. (If using frozen chard, add 5 minutes before chicken is done.)

Transfer chicken pieces to a wide serving dish. With a slotted spoon, lift out chard and spoon alongside chicken. Remove garlic from sauce, if desired. Over high heat, boil sauce rapidly to reduce slightly, then pour over chicken and chard. Makes 6 servings.

CHICKEN SCALOPPINE WITH LEMON
SCALOPPINE DI POLLO AL LIMONE

Though most people associate scaloppine with veal, the term also applies to equally delicious and less costly dishes made with small thin slices (scaloppine) of other meats. In this elegant main dish for two, chicken thighs are prepared by pounding, coating with flour, and sautéeing. Serve them with a lemon-thyme wine and cream sauce.

4	chicken thighs (1 to 1¼ lbs.)
	All-purpose flour
	About 1 tablespoon each butter or margarine and olive oil or salad oil
⅓	cup dry white wine or chicken broth
¼	cup whipping cream
1	teaspoon lemon juice
¼	teaspoon thyme leaves
	Salt and pepper
	Parsley and lemon wedges

Remove skin from chicken. On the inside of each thigh, cut meat to bone along the entire length. With a knife blade, scrape meat free from bone. Place meat between pieces of wax paper or plastic wrap and pound with flat side of a mallet until about ¼ inch thick. Coat chicken with flour and shake off excess.

In a wide frying pan over medium-high heat, place butter and oil. When butter melts, add as many chicken pieces as will fit without crowding and cook quickly just until meat is no longer pink when slashed (about 1½ minutes on each side). Place on a hot platter and keep warm. Cook remaining pieces, adding more butter and oil if needed; add to platter and keep warm.

To pan drippings, add wine and bring to a boil, scraping particles free from pan. Turn heat to high and boil until reduced by about half. Add cream, lemon juice, and thyme; boil until sauce thickens slightly. Salt and pepper to taste. Pour over chicken and garnish with parsley and lemon. Makes 2 servings.

GOLDEN CHICKEN CUTLETS
PETTI DI POLLO DORATI
(Pictured on page 78)

Pounded chicken breasts, lightly breaded and quickly sautéed, can be served crusty and hot—or cold for a picnic or summer buffet.

3	whole chicken breasts (about 3 lbs. total), cut in half, boned, and skinned
⅓	cup all-purpose flour
½	teaspoon salt
⅛	teaspoon each white pepper, ground nutmeg, and marjoram leaves
1	egg beaten with 1 tablespoon water
⅓	cup fine dry bread crumbs
¼	cup freshly grated Parmesan cheese
¼	cup butter or margarine
2	tablespoons olive oil
½	cup dry white wine (optional)
	Lemon wedges

Place chicken breasts, one at a time, between pieces of wax paper or plastic wrap and pound with flat side of a mallet until about ¼ inch thick. Mix flour, salt, pepper, nutmeg, and marjoram in a shallow dish. Have egg mixture ready in a second shallow dish. Mix crumbs and cheese in a third. Coat chicken breasts lightly with flour mixture, then with egg, and finally with crumb mixture.

In a wide frying pan over medium-high heat, place butter and oil. When butter is melted, add chicken breasts, without crowding, and cook, turning once, until golden brown on each side (2 to 3 minutes per side).

To serve hot, transfer cooked

chicken breasts to a warm platter and keep warm. Add wine to cooking pan and bring to a boil on high heat, scraping brown particles free from pan. Cook until well blended and slightly reduced; pour sauce over chicken. Accompany with lemon. To serve cold, omit sauce. Makes 6 servings.

TURKEY LA SCALA
TACCHINO A LA SCALA

Here turkey breast is presented in another version of scaloppine. Thin pounded scallops of turkey are dipped in egg before sautéing, then the turkey scaloppine bakes briefly with peas, prosciutto, and cheese.

Sometimes you can buy fresh turkey breast, whole or sliced. If your only choice is to purchase a whole frozen breast, ask your meat cutter to saw it into smaller sections, about 1½ pounds each. Wrap remaining sections individually and store in the freezer.

	About 1½ pounds boneless turkey breast
¼	cup all-purpose flour
2	tablespoons *each* olive oil and butter or margarine
1	egg beaten with 2 tablespoons water
1	package (10 oz.) frozen tiny peas, thawed
2	ounces very thinly sliced prosciutto
¾	pound (12 oz.) teleme or jack cheese, thinly sliced
⅛	teaspoon *each* ground nutmeg and pepper

Slice turkey across the grain into ½-inch-thick slices. Place slices between pieces of wax paper and pound with flat side of a mallet until about ¼ inch thick. Coat slices with flour and shake off excess.

In a wide frying pan over medium heat, place oil and butter. When butter is melted, dip turkey slices, one at a time, in egg-water mixture to coat thoroughly; drain briefly and then slip each piece into frying pan without crowding. Cook, turning once, until lightly browned on both sides (about 3 minutes **total**).

Remove turkey when cooked and drain briefly.

Arrange cooked turkey, overlapping as needed in a shallow baking dish about 8 by 12 inches. Spoon peas around turkey. Arrange prosciutto evenly over turkey; top with an even layer of teleme cheese over all. (At this point you may cover and refrigerate until next day.)

Bake, covered, in a 400° oven for 20 minutes (35 minutes, if refrigerated) or until cheese melts. Sprinkle with nutmeg and pepper and serve. Makes 6 servings.

RABBIT IN PICKLED ONION SAUCE
CONIGLIO ALLA ROMAGNOLA

A creamy tomato sauce envelops moistly cooked rabbit to make a satisfying stew in the style of Bologna.

2½	to 3-pound frying rabbit, cut into pieces
	Salt, pepper, and nutmeg
¼	cup butter or margarine
1	medium-size onion, finely chopped
1	clove garlic, minced or pressed
1	can (8 oz.) tomato sauce
⅓	cup sweet vermouth
1	bay leaf
¼	teaspoon *each* whole allspice and black peppercorns
¼	cup drained small white pickled onions
½	cup whipping cream

Sprinkle rabbit pieces with salt, pepper, and nutmeg. Melt butter in a wide deep frying pan or 4 to 5-quart Dutch oven over medium heat. Add rabbit, about half at a time, and brown well; remove when browned.

To same pan add chopped onion and cook, stirring, until soft. Mix in garlic, tomato sauce, vermouth, bay leaf, allspice, and peppercorns; then add rabbit pieces and pickled onions. Bring to a boil; cover, reduce heat, and simmer until rabbit is very tender (50 to 60 minutes). Remove to warm serving dish; keep warm.

Skim fat from cooking liquid, if necessary. Add cream and bring to a boil over high heat; continue to cook, stirring, until sauce is slightly reduced and thickened. Taste and add salt, if needed. Pour sauce over rabbit. Makes 4 to 6 servings.

SCAMPI-STYLE SHRIMP
SCAMPI ALL' AGLIO
(Pictured on page 83)

By giving shrimp a quick sauté in lemon-garlic butter you can recreate a favorite Italian preparation for scampi, that crustacean found only in waters of the Adriatic Sea.

6	tablespoons butter or margarine
1	tablespoon minced green onion
1	tablespoon olive oil or salad oil
4	to 5 cloves garlic, minced or pressed
2	teaspoons lemon juice
¼	teaspoon salt
	About ¾ pound medium-size (30 to 40 per lb.) raw shrimp, shelled and deveined
2	tablespoons minced fresh parsley
¼	teaspoon grated lemon peel
	Dash of liquid hot pepper seasoning
	Lemon wedges

In a wide frying pan over medium heat, melt butter. Stir in onion, oil, garlic, lemon juice, and salt; cook until bubbly. Add shrimp to pan and cook, stirring occasionally, until shrimp turn pink (about 5 minutes). Stir in parsley, lemon peel, and hot pepper seasoning. Spoon into serving dish; garnish with lemon wedges. Makes 2 servings.

Cuddle up for a romantic supper for two. Scampi-style Shrimp (page 82) sautéed with garlic and lemon, a vegetable dish of steamed zucchini and sautéed red bell peppers, Whole Wheat Italian Bread (page 88), a crisp white wine, candlelight, and firelight all add up to a most tempting evening.

SEAFOOD STEW
CIOPPINO

Probably invented by an Italian in San Francisco, Cioppino starts with Dungeness crabs. For the authentic version, both crab and shrimp are cooked in the shell. This makes for messy eating, so have plenty of napkins available. Green salad and plenty of sourdough or Italian bread complete the meal.

½	cup (¼ lb.) butter or margarine, or olive oil
2	medium-size onions, chopped
2 or 3	cloves garlic
1	cup lightly packed chopped fresh parsley
2	large cans (1 lb. 12 oz. each) tomatoes
2	cans (14½ oz. each) regular-strength chicken broth
1	bay leaf
1	tablespoon dry basil
½	teaspoon each thyme leaves and oregano leaves
1	cup water
1½	cups dry white wine
1½	pounds large raw shrimp in shells (or boneless, skinless, chunks of rock fish or ling cod)
2	large Dungeness crabs (about 4 lbs. total), live, cleaned, and cracked (have this done at your market)
1½	pounds scallops

In a 6 to 8-quart kettle over medium heat, melt butter. Add onions, garlic, and parsley; cook, stirring, until onions are soft. Add tomatoes (break up with a spoon) and their liquid, along with broth, bay leaf, basil, thyme, oregano, water, and wine. Bring to a boil, then reduce heat; cover and simmer for about 30 minutes.

Devein shrimp in this manner: insert a small metal or wooden skewer along the back of each shrimp (in shell), beneath the vein. Gently pull skewer to surface, drawing out vein; repeat as often as necessary to remove entire vein. Set shrimp aside.

Add crab to simmering sauce and cook, covered, for 10 minutes. Add shrimp and scallops and return stew

to simmering, then cover and simmer until scallops are opaque throughout (5 to 7 minutes more).

Serve stew from the kettle or from a tureen into large soup bowls; also have available a large bowl to hold shells as they're emptied. Makes 8 to 10 servings.

Cooked Crab Cioppino. Prepare recipe as directed above, but use whole, cooked, cleaned, and cracked crab (thaw, if frozen) instead of live crab; add to sauce along with the shrimp.

OVEN SEAFOOD BAKE
PESCE AL CARTOCCIO

Here is a seafood main dish that steams as it bakes, enclosed in a bag, parchment, or foil. When the clams pop open, it is ready to serve with a creamy sauce.

¼	cup butter or margarine, softened
1	clove garlic, minced or pressed
½	teaspoon grated lemon peel
1	teaspoon lemon juice
2	halibut steaks, about 1 lb. each and ¾ inch thick, or other mild-flavored lean fish steaks or fillets of same weight and thickness
	Salt and pepper
½	pound medium-size (30 to 40 per lb.) shrimp, shelled and deveined
12	small hard-shell clams in shells, well scrubbed
¼	cup whipping cream
	Chopped parsley

Beat together butter, garlic, lemon peel, and lemon juice. Lightly season fish steaks with salt and pepper. Spread about half the butter mixture evenly over one side of each steak. Place a large clear roasting bag (about 12 by 18 inches) or a piece of baking parchment paper or heavy foil (about 24 inches long) in a 10 by 15-inch baking pan about 2 inches deep. Place fish steaks side by side, buttered side down, in bag or on parchment or foil. Arrange shrimp on fish, then top with clams and dot evenly with remaining butter. Seal

bag according to manufacturer's directions and pierce 4 to 6 holes in top; fold top and ends of parchment to enclose loosely, fastening with paper clips; or fold and crimp foil to seal.

Bake in a 350° oven for 30 to 40 minutes or until clams have opened. Slash top of bag just enough to remove food without losing juices, or open and fold back parchment or foil. With a slotted spoon, lift out clams; set aside. Using a slotted spatula, transfer fish (with shrimp on top) to a warm serving platter; surround with clams and keep warm.

Pour cooking liquid into a wide pan, add cream, and cook over high heat until liquid is reduced to about ¾ cup. Garnish fish with parsley; pass sauce to pour over each serving. Makes about 6 servings.

CLAMS WITH RICE
VONGOLE IN UMIDO

The wine-flavored broth used to steam the clams makes a fragrant, sturdy soup. Present it in wide rimmed bowls with hot cooked rice.

¼	cup butter or margarine
¼	cup finely chopped fresh parsley
1 or 2	cloves garlic, minced or pressed
2	cups chicken broth or 1 can (14½ oz.) regular-strength chicken broth
1	cup dry white wine (or ¼ cup lemon juice with ¾ cup chicken broth)
3	dozen small hard-shell clams in shells, well scrubbed
1 to 2	cups hot, cooked rice

In a 5 to 6-quart kettle over medium heat, melt butter. Add parsley and garlic and cook, stirring, for 1 to 2 minutes. Pour in broth and wine, raise heat to high, and bring to a boil. Add clams and reduce heat; cover and simmer gently until clams pop open (5 to 10 minutes).

To serve, spoon equal amounts of hot rice into large soup bowls or soup plates; top with clams, then pour in broth and serve. Makes 4 servings.

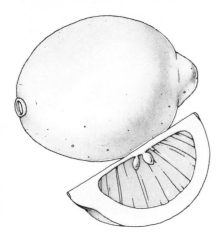

SOLE WITH GARLIC SAUCE
SOGLIOLE ALL' AGLIO

Bits of garlic fried golden in butter make a bold sauce to serve with sole.

	About ¼ cup butter or margarine
¼	cup minced garlic (about 12 large cloves)
1	pound sole fillets
	Salt and pepper
1	tablespoon olive oil or salad oil
1	egg, lightly beaten with 1 tablespoon water
	Lemon wedges

Melt 3 tablespoons of the butter in a small pan over medium-low heat. Add garlic and cook, stirring occasionally, until garlic just begins to turn golden (15 to 20 minutes); take care not to scorch garlic or it will be bitter. Remove from heat and keep warm.

Lightly sprinkle fillets with salt and pepper. In a wide frying pan over medium heat, melt another 1 tablespoon butter with oil until frothy. Dip each fillet in egg mixture, drain briefly, and place in frying pan without crowding.

Cook until lightly browned (about 2 minutes). Turn carefully with a wide spatula (adding more butter if needed) and cook until lightly browned on second side and fish flakes readily when prodded in thickest portion with a fork (about 2 minutes more). As each piece is finished, place on serving platter and keep warm. Repeat until all fillets are cooked.

Pour garlic sauce over fish and serve with lemon wedges. Makes 3 or 4 servings.

ROMAN SOLE
SOGLIOLE ALLA ROMANA

The Roman way with sole calls for oven-frying—a one-step technique that eliminates turning the fragile fish as it cooks.

You can choose English, Dover, rex, sand dab, or petrale sole.

1½	pounds sole fillets
	Salt and pepper
	All-purpose flour
4	tablespoons butter (or 2 tablespoons each butter and olive oil)

In a 500° oven place a shallow baking pan in which fish will just fit without overlapping. Sprinkle fish with salt and pepper; coat with flour and shake off excess.

Remove pan from oven and add butter, swirling until butter is melted. Turn fish in butter to coat both sides. Bake in the 500° oven for 4 to 6 minutes or until fish is browned and flakes easily when prodded in thickest portion with a fork. Makes 4 servings.

BRAISED SALT COD
BACCALÁ CON MORSELATA

Dried salt cod, an Old World staple, is treated with respect and imagination in many cuisines, especially around the Mediterranean. We especially enjoy this hearty, peasant version that simmers the salt cod in a robust tomato sauce with onions, cabbage, and Swiss chard. Serve in wide bowls over hot Polenta.

You can find salt cod in stores specializing in foods from Italy, Portugal, Greece, Spain, or Mexico. You must soak the fish in water for 1 to 2 days before cooking.

	About 2 pounds (1 average-size) salt cod
2	bunches (or about 2 lbs.) Swiss chard
¾	cup olive oil
2	large onions, chopped
8	leeks (including tender green parts), thinly sliced
½	small head cabbage, coarsely chopped
1½	cups dry white wine
1	can (about 1 lb.) Italian-style tomatoes
3	cans (8 oz. each) tomato sauce
1	can (14½ oz.) regular-strength chicken broth
	Hot cooked Polenta (page 33)

Wash cod under cold running water, then immerse in a container of cold water (cut cod into pieces, if necessary, to fit into container). Cover and refrigerate, changing water 2 or 3 times, for 24 to 48 hours.

Place cod in a 3 to 4-quart pan and add boiling water to cover. Simmer, uncovered, for 15 minutes; drain, then cover with cold water.

When cool enough to touch, remove and discard all bones, skin, and cartilage. Cover and refrigerate cod until ready to use.

Chop chard; reserve 2 cups of the green tops. In a 5 to 6-quart kettle, heat oil. When oil is hot, add remaining chard, along with onions, leeks, and cabbage. Cook, stirring, over high heat until vegetables are soft.

Blend in wine, tomatoes (break up with a spoon) and their liquid, tomato sauce, and chicken broth. Bring to a boil, then reduce heat; cover and simmer, stirring occasionally, for 1½ to 2 hours. (At this point you may cover and refrigerate sauce, if made ahead; reheat to use.) Add cooked cod to sauce. Cover and simmer gently, stirring occasionally, for 1 more hour.

Immerse reserved chard greens in boiling water and cook over high heat, uncovered, for 5 minutes. Drain well and stir into cod mixture.

Ladle into wide bowls over spoonfuls or slices of hot Polenta. Makes 8 to 10 servings.

7

RUSTIC ROUND LOAVES SEASONED WITH OLIVE OIL, SPARKLING

BREADS &

HOLIDAY BREADS, CRUNCHY BREAD STICKS, SWEET BREADS

PIZZA

PLUMP WITH FRUIT AND NUTS...AND DON'T FORGET PIZZA!

No Italian meal is complete without bread in some form: big, country-style crusty loaves; bread sticks, thin or fat, short or long; rolls, imaginatively coiled, twisted, or slashed. From the baker's oven, too, come such treats as pizza and some of its relatives: Focaccia and Calzone (both on page 93).

For a brunch, afternoon, or late-evening refreshment, the perfect offering is a slice of a special sweet bread such as Pandolce Genovese (page 96), Schiacciata (page 97), or Pandoro di Verona (page 95) with a cup of espresso or a glass of sweet, dry, or sparkling wine.

This chapter explores all these breads in their tantalizing variety.

Sparkling with holiday joy, this quartet of sweet breads presents a splendid choice to bake for an Easter brunch or any special occasion. Starting clockwise from center left, you see Tuscan Almond-crusted Flat Bread, Golden Christmas Bread, Venetian Sugar Buns, and Sicilian Easter Ring—an Easter basket and Paschal bread all in one. The recipes are on pages 95 and 97.

PHILADELPHIA PEPERONI BREAD

A tangy center of sliced peperoni sausage is hidden in each of two puffy loaves. The recipe for this bread is based on a specialty of Sarcone's bakery in Philadelphia's Italian section. It is a wonderful accompaniment to vegetable soup or a meatless pasta.

1	package active dry yeast
1/4	cup warm water (about 110°)
1	cup warm milk (about 110°)
1	tablespoon sugar
1	teaspoon salt
2	tablespoons olive oil
3	to 3½ cups all-purpose flour
1	cup thinly sliced peperoni

In a large bowl, sprinkle yeast over warm water and let stand for 5 minutes to soften. Stir in milk, sugar, salt, and oil. Add 1 cup of the flour and mix to blend; stir in 1½ cups more flour. With a heavy-duty mixer or wooden spoon, beat until dough is smooth and elastic (about 5 minutes). Stir in ½ cup more flour to make a soft dough.

Turn out onto a board or pastry cloth floured with some of the remaining ½ cup flour; knead until dough is smooth and springy and develops small bubbles just under surface (about 15 minutes). Place in a greased bowl; turn dough to grease top. Cover and let rise in a warm place until doubled (about 1 hour).

Punch dough down, turn out onto a floured surface, and divide in half. Roll each half out to a long strip about 12 by 6 inches; arrange ½ cup peperoni slices evenly down center of each. Roll each up tightly to make a long slender loaf, pinching long edge to seal. Place on a greased baking sheet, cover lightly, and let rise until nearly doubled (30 to 40 minutes).

Bake in a 375° oven for 20 to 25 minutes or until loaves are a rich golden brown and sound hollow when tapped. Slide out onto wire racks to cool before slicing. Serve warm or at room temperature. Makes 2 loaves.

ROSEMARY RAISIN BREAD

PANE DI RAMERINO

In the Florentine tradition, this plump round raisin loaf is seasoned with rosemary and olive oil. You can enjoy it warm and buttered for brunch, or with salad or soup for lunch. It also makes excellent toast, lifting breakfast above the ordinary.

1	package active dry yeast
¼	cup warm water (about 110°)
½	cup milk
3	tablespoons sugar
1	teaspoon each salt and dry rosemary
2	eggs
¼	cup olive oil
3 to 3½	cups all-purpose flour
½	cup raisins
	Olive oil
1	tablespoon cold water

In a large bowl, sprinkle yeast over warm water and let stand for 5 minutes to soften. Meanwhile, in a pan, combine milk, sugar, salt, and rosemary; heat until warm (about 110°). Beat in 1 whole egg, 1 egg white (reserve yolk of second egg for glaze), and the ¼ cup olive oil; add to yeast mixture. Gradually beat in about 2½ cups of the flour to make a stiff dough.

Turn out onto a well-floured board and knead until smooth and satiny (10 to 20 minutes), adding flour as needed to prevent sticking. Flatten dough, top with raisins, and knead lightly to work them into dough (some pop out, but just push them back in). Place in a bowl oiled with olive oil; turn dough to grease top. Cover and let rise in a warm place until doubled (1 to 1½ hours).

Punch dough down; knead briefly on a lightly floured board just to release air; shape into a smooth ball. Place on an olive-oil-coated baking sheet and pat into a flat round, about 8½ inches in diameter. Brush generously with olive oil; cover lightly and let rise in a warm place until puffy (about 30 minutes).

Using a floured razor blade or sharp knife, slash a cross in top of loaf. Beat reserved egg yolk with the 1 tablespoon cold water and brush over loaf. Bake in a 350° oven for about 35 minutes or until loaf is browned and sounds hollow when tapped. Turn out onto a wire rack to cool. Makes 1 loaf.

WHOLE WHEAT ITALIAN BREAD
PANE INTEGRALE
(Pictured on page 83)

Slender wheat loaves are a good accompaniment to any Italian meal—or to take on a picnic with cheese and cold meats.

1	package active dry yeast
1⅓	cups warm water (about 110°)
1	tablespoon each sugar and salad oil
1	teaspoon salt
1	cup whole wheat flour
2½ to 3	cups unbleached all-purpose flour
½	cup wheat germ
1	teaspoon cornstarch dissolved in ⅓ cup water

In a large bowl, sprinkle yeast over warm water and let stand for 5 minutes to soften. Stir in sugar, oil, and salt. Add whole wheat flour and 1½ cups of the unbleached flour; mix to blend. With a heavy-duty mixer or wooden spoon, beat until dough is elastic (about 5 minutes). Stir in wheat germ and about 1 cup more unbleached flour to make a stiff dough.

Turn out onto a board or pastry cloth floured with some of the remaining ½ cup unbleached flour; knead until dough is smooth and springy and develops small bubbles just under surface (20 to 25 minutes). Place in a greased bowl; turn dough to grease top. Cover and let rise in a warm place until doubled (about 1 hour).

Punch dough down, turn out onto a floured surface, and divide in half. Shape each half into a slender oval loaf about 14 inches long. Place on greased baking sheets; cover lightly and let rise until nearly doubled (30 to 40 minutes).

Bring cornstarch mixture to a boil, stirring until thick and clear. Brush loaves with warm cornstarch mixture. Using a floured razor blade or sharp knife, make a ½-inch-deep slash down center of each loaf.

Bake in a 375° oven for 25 to 30 minutes or until loaves are browned and sound hollow when tapped. Cool on wire racks. Makes 2 loaves.

WHOLE WHEAT OLIVE RING
PANE ALLE OLIVE

This olive-flecked bread ring is Venetian in origin. You can break it apart for easy serving.

1	package active dry yeast
1	cup warm water (about 110°)
2	tablespoons sugar
¾	teaspoon salt
¼	cup butter or margarine, melted and cooled
1½	cups whole wheat flour
2 to 2½	cups unbleached all-purpose flour
1	egg
½	cup chopped ripe olives
	Olive oil or salad oil

In a large bowl, sprinkle yeast over hot water and let stand for 5 minutes to soften. Stir in sugar, salt, and butter. Add whole wheat flour and 1 cup of the unbleached flour; mix to blend. With a heavy-duty mixer or wooden spoon, beat for 5 minutes at medium speed. Beat in egg, then stir in 1 cup more unbleached flour to make a soft dough.

Turn dough out onto a board or pastry cloth floured with some of the remaining ½ cup unbleached flour; knead until smooth and springy (10 to 15 minutes). Place in a greased bowl; turn dough to grease top. Cover and let rise in a warm place until doubled (about 1 hour).

Punch dough down, turn out on a floured surface, and knead in olives. Divide dough into 8 equal portions; knead each into a ball. Place at regular intervals next to inside edge of a 9-inch round cake pan generously brushed with oil. Brush tops of balls lightly with olive oil. Cover lightly and let rise until nearly doubled (35 to 40 minutes).

Bake in a 400° oven for 25 to 30 minutes or until well browned. Remove loaf from pan and pull apart to serve hot, or let cool on wire rack. Makes 1 ring.

PROSCIUTTO & CHEESE SWIRLS
LUMACHELLE

A pizza baker in the spectacularly situated hilltop town of Orvieto makes these savory, coiled yeast rolls.

They're a delicious snack and a perfect accompaniment to a salad supper.

1	package active dry yeast
1½	cups warm water (about 110°)
1	tablespoon sugar
2	tablespoons olive oil
1	teaspoon salt
⅛	teaspoon coarse ground pepper
3½	to 4 cups unbleached all-purpose flour
½	cup finely chopped prosciutto or baked ham
⅓	cup grated Parmesan cheese

In a large bowl, sprinkle yeast over warm water and let stand for 5 minutes to soften. Stir in sugar, oil, salt, and pepper. Add 2½ cups of the flour; mix to blend. With a heavy-duty mixer or wooden spoon, beat until dough is elastic (about 5 minutes). Stir in prosciutto, cheese, and about 1 cup more flour to make a soft dough.

Turn out onto a board or pastry cloth floured with some of the remaining ½ cup flour; knead until dough is smooth and springy and develops small bubbles just under surface (20 to 25 minutes). Place in a greased bowl; turn dough to grease top. Cover and let rise in a warm place until doubled (about 1 hour).

Punch dough down, turn out onto a floured surface, and divide into 12 equal pieces. Roll each under your palms to form an 18-inch-long strip. On greased baking sheets, coil each strip loosely to make a 3½-inch-diameter circle; tuck end under. Place circles about 3 inches apart. Cover lightly and let rise until nearly doubled (20 to 25 minutes).

Bake in a 375° oven for 18 to 20 minutes or until well browned. Serve warm, or cool on wire racks. Makes 12 rolls.

VENETIAN TOMATO ROLLS
POMPOMODORI

The tomato filling of these crusty yeast rolls rises and spills over a bit, giving them the appearance of small, savory volcanoes.

1	package active dry yeast
1⅓	cups warm water (about 110°)
1	tablespoon sugar
2	tablespoons olive oil
1	teaspoon salt
3½	to 4 cups unbleached all-purpose flour
	Tomato Filling (recipe follows)
¼	cup grated Parmesan cheese

In a large bowl, sprinkle yeast over warm water and let stand for 5 minutes to soften. Stir in sugar, oil, and salt. Add 2½ cups of the flour; mix to blend. With a heavy-duty mixer or wooden spoon, beat until dough is elastic (about 5 minutes). Stir in about 1 cup more flour to make a stiff dough.

Turn out onto a board or pastry cloth floured with some of the remaining ½ cup unbleached flour; knead until dough is smooth and springy and develops small bubbles just under surface (20 to 25 minutes). Place in a greased bowl; turn dough to grease top. Cover and let rise in a warm place until doubled (1 to 1¼ hours).

Punch dough down, turn out onto a floured surface, and divide into 12 equal pieces. Roll each between your hands to form a ball. Place balls 2 to 3 inches apart on greased baking sheets. With floured fingers, make a deep indentation in center of each and fill it with a generous tablespoon of the filling; sprinkle with about 1 teaspoon cheese. Cover lightly and let rise until nearly doubled (20 to 25 minutes).

Bake in a 375° oven for 25 to 30 minutes until rolls are well browned and sound hollow when tapped. Serve warm, or let cool on wire racks. Makes 12 rolls.

Tomato Filling. In a medium-size frying pan over medium heat, cook 1 small **onion** (finely chopped) in 1 tablespoon **olive oil** until onion is soft. Mix in 1 medium-size **tomato** (peeled and chopped), 1 clove **garlic** (minced or pressed), 1 can (8 oz.) **tomato sauce**, 1 teaspoon **dry basil**, ¼ teaspoon **salt**, and a dash of **pepper**. Bring to a boil and cook over medium heat, stirring often, until mixture is reduced to about 1 cup.

PINE NUT STICKS
GRISSINI AI PIGNOLI
(Pictured on page 47)

The faintly sweet, distinctive flavor of pine nuts becomes more apparent with each bite of these bread sticks.

1	package active dry yeast
⅔	cup warm water (about 110°)
½	teaspoon anise seeds, crushed
2	tablespoons each salad oil and olive oil
¼	teaspoon grated lemon peel
½	teaspoon salt
1	tablespoon sugar
	About 2¼ cups all-purpose flour
⅔	cup pine nuts (pignoli)
1	egg, lightly beaten
2	tablespoons coarse salt

In a large bowl, sprinkle yeast over warm water and let stand for about 5 minutes to soften. Stir in anise seeds, salad oil, olive oil, lemon peel, salt, sugar, and 1 cup of the flour. Beat until smooth. Add pine nuts and enough of the remaining flour to make a stiff dough. Turn out onto a floured board and knead until smooth and elastic (about 5 minutes), using additional flour as needed. Place dough in a greased bowl; turn dough to grease top. Cover with plastic wrap and let rise in warm place until doubled (about 1 hour).

Punch dough down and divide in half. Cut each half into 20 equal-size pieces. Using palms of hands, roll each piece into a 7-inch length. Place parallel and about ½ inch apart on greased baking sheets. Cover and let rise until puffy (about 30 minutes). Brush with egg, and sprinkle lightly with salt. Bake in a 325° oven for 35 to 40 minutes or until lightly browned. Serve hot or cool on wire racks. Store airtight at room temperature for 3 to 4 days; freeze for longer storage. Makes 40 bread sticks.

FENNEL BREAD STICKS
GRISSINI AL FINOCCHIO
(Pictured on page 10)

The same seed that flavors mild Italian pork sausage makes these crisp bread sticks appealingly aromatic.

1	package active dry yeast
¾	cup each warm water, (about 110°), salad oil, and beer
1	teaspoon salt
1	tablespoon fennel seeds
4½	cups all-purpose flour
1	egg beaten with 1 tablespoon water

In a large bowl, sprinkle yeast over warm water and let stand 5 minutes to soften. Stir in salad oil, beer, salt, and fennel seeds. With a heavy-duty mixer or wooden spoon, beat in 3½ cups of the flour until dough is elastic (about 5 minutes). On a board or pastry cloth, spread remaining 1 cup flour and turn out dough. Knead, using this technique: lift edge of dough, coated well with flour, and fold toward center, avoiding contact with sticky part of dough. Continue folding toward center and kneading, turning dough as you work, until it is smooth and elastic. Place dough in a greased bowl; turn dough to grease top. Cover and let rise in a warm place until doubled (1 to 1¼ hours).

On a floured surface, knead just to expel air. Pinch off lumps (1½ inches in diameter) and roll each into a strip that is 18 inches long. Cut each strip in half. Set wire racks on baking sheets and arrange strips across racks ½ inch apart. Brush strips with egg-water mixture. Bake in a 325° oven for about 35 minutes or until evenly browned. Serve hot, or cool on wire racks. Makes about 5 dozen.

GARLIC TOAST
LA BRUSCHETTA

Make garlic toast the way they do in Rome or the hills of Umbria and you will have some ready to eat in about the time it takes to toast the bread. The more flavorsome the olive oil (see page 44), the better the bread.

6	slices sweet or sourdough French or Italian bread
3	cloves garlic
6	tablespoons olive oil
	Salt

Lightly toast both sides of bread. On one side of each slice, rub a cut clove of garlic, then brush with oil. Sprinkle lightly with salt. Serve warm. Makes 6 slices.

SAUSAGE PIZZA
PIZZA ALLE SALSICCE

Pizza, Naples' gift to the world, is considered either a preliminary course or a main dish. Crumbled Italian sausage flavors this version.

	Pizza Dough (recipe follows)
3	cans (about 14½ oz. each) Italian-style tomatoes
1	can (6 oz.) tomato paste
1	teaspoon dry basil
½	teaspoon each dry rosemary and oregano leaves
1	pound mild Italian sausages
	Olive oil
3	cups (12 oz.) shredded mozzarella cheese

Prepare pizza dough; while it is rising, prepare sauce and toppings.

In a large pan over medium heat, combine tomatoes (break up with a spoon) and their liquid, tomato paste, basil, rosemary, and oregano; bring to a boil. Continue to boil, stirring occasionally, until thick and reduced to about 2 cups; set aside. Remove casings from sausages; crumble meat into a large frying pan, and cook, stirring, over medium heat until lightly browned. With a slotted spoon, remove meat from pan; drain on paper towels.

When dough has risen, punch dough down, knead on a lightly floured surface, and shape into a smooth ball. Divide dough in half and roll out each half to about ¾-inch thickness. Gently pull each portion into an oval 12 to 14 inches long and 8 to 10 inches wide. Place each oval of dough on a greased baking sheet and brush generously with olive oil. For each pizza, spread half of the tomato sauce to within ¾ inch of the rim; top with half of the cooked sausage and sprinkle evenly with half of the cheese.

Place one baking sheet at a time on the lowest rack of a 500° oven. Bake for 12 to 15 minutes or until crust is browned. To serve, cut hot pizzas into wedges. Makes 2 pizzas, 2 servings each.

Pizza Dough. In a large bowl, sprinkle 1 package active dry yeast over 1 cup warm water (about 110°) and let stand for 5 minutes to soften. Stir in ½ teaspoon salt and 2 teaspoons olive oil. Add 2 cups all-purpose flour; mix to blend. With a heavy-duty mixer or wooden spoon, beat until dough is elastic (about 5 minutes). Stir in ¾ cup more flour to make a soft dough.

Turn dough out onto a board or pastry cloth floured with about ½

(Continued on page 92)

A dome-shaped loaf of Panettone (page 97) stars at this brunch. Filled with pine nuts, raisins, and candied fruit, the sweet, cakelike bread is delicious with fruit, fontina cheese, and plump Italian sausage. Combine equal portions of hot strong coffee and hot milk for caffè e latte— the perfect beverage.

cup more flour and knead until smooth and springy (5 to 10 minutes). Place in a greased bowl; turn dough to grease top. Cover and let rise in a warm place until doubled (about 1 hour).

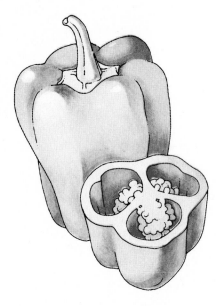

DEEP-DISH PEPERONI PIZZA
PIZZA ALLA SICILIANA

Unlike thin, Neapolitan-style pizza this deep-dish pizza has a softer, thicker, breadlike crust and lots of filling. The crust is partly baked before the filling is added—to be sure it bakes all the way through the second time in the oven.

	Pizza Dough (recipe follows)
2	tablespoons olive oil or salad oil
1	small onion, finely chopped
1	small red bell pepper, seeded and cut into strips
1	clove garlic, minced or pressed
1	can (8 oz.) tomato sauce
½	teaspoon dry basil
⅛	teaspoon oregano leaves
1	tablespoon grated Parmesan cheese
¼	cup sliced ripe olives
1	cup (¼ lb.) thinly sliced peperoni
1½	cups (6 oz.) shredded mozzarella cheese

Prepare pizza dough. While it is rising, prepare sauce and toppings.

Heat oil in a medium-size frying pan over medium heat. Add onion and red pepper and cook, stirring often, until soft but not browned. Add garlic, tomato sauce, basil, and oregano; cook, stirring occasionally, until thick (about 5 minutes). Remove from heat, mix in Parmesan cheese, and set aside.

Punch dough down; knead briefly on a lightly floured board just to release air. Pat and stretch dough to cover bottom and about 1½ inches up sides of a greased, heavy, 10-inch cast-iron frying pan or deep-dish pizza pan. Dough shrinks back at first, but as you continue to stretch and press it in pan, it stays in place. Bake in a 375° oven for 18 to 20 minutes or until lightly browned.

Remove pan from oven and spread tomato sauce over crust. Distribute olives and peperoni over sauce. Sprinkle with mozzarella cheese. Bake for 20 to 25 minutes longer, or until crust is browned. Use a serrated knife to cut into wedges directly in pan, or loosen with a wide spatula and lift entire pizza onto a board to serve. Makes 3 or 4 servings.

Pizza Dough. In a large bowl, dissolve 1 package **active dry yeast** in ⅔ cup **warm water** (about 110°). Let stand for 5 minutes to soften. Stir in 2 teaspoons **sugar**, ½ teaspoon **salt**, and 3 tablespoons **olive oil** or salad oil. Add 1⅓ cups **unbleached all-purpose flour**; mix to blend, then beat until dough is elastic (3 to 5 minutes). Stir in about ½ cup more flour to make a soft dough. Turn dough out onto a floured board or pastry cloth and knead until smooth and springy (8 to 10 minutes). Place in a greased bowl; turn dough to grease top. Cover and let rise in a warm place until doubled (40 to 45 minutes).

FOUR SEASONS PIZZA
PIZZA QUATTRO STAGIONE
(Pictured on page 94)

Artichokes, mushrooms, strips of meat (coppa or salami), and cheese form four well-delineated triangles over the surface of this popular pizza. You can bake this pizza in two medium-size pans or one large pan.

	Pizza Dough (page 90)
¼	cup olive oil
½	pound mushrooms, thinly sliced
1	small onion, finely chopped
1	clove garlic, minced or pressed
1	large can (15 oz.) tomato sauce
1	teaspoon dry basil
¼	teaspoon oregano leaves
2	tablespoons grated Parmesan cheese
1	package (9 oz.) frozen artichoke hearts, cooked according to package directions
1	cup thin strips sliced coppa or salami
2	cups (8 oz.) shredded mozzarella or jack cheese

Prepare pizza dough; while it is rising, prepare sauce and toppings. Heat 2 tablespoons of the oil in a large frying pan over medium heat; add mushrooms, and brown lightly. Remove with a slotted spoon and set aside. To same pan add onion and a little more of the oil, if needed. Cook, stirring, until onion is soft but not brown. Add garlic, tomato sauce, basil, and oregano; cook, stirring occasionally, until thick (about 5 minutes). Remove from heat, stir in Parmesan cheese, and set aside.

With some of the remaining oil, brush 2 medium-size (11 to 12-inch-diameter) pizza pans (or 1 large one, 17 to 18 inches in diameter). When dough has risen, punch down, knead on a lightly floured surface, and shape into a smooth ball (divide in half if making 2 pizzas). Roll out dough to ¾-inch thickness and place on pans; stretch pizza dough to fit pans. Spread evenly with tomato sauce. Mark each pizza into 4 equal sections. Over one section of each pizza arrange mushrooms. Then arrange artichokes over second sections and brush them with remaining oil. Cover third sections with sausage, and fourth with cheese.

Bake on lowest rack of a 450° oven for 15 to 20 minutes (about 25 minutes, if large) or until crust is well browned. Serve hot. Makes 1 large or 2 medium-size pizzas, or 4 servings.

ITALIAN FLAT BREAD
FOCACCIA

Long before pizza became popular the world over, Italians in Genoa and elsewhere along the Ligurian coast baked a tantalizing flat bread called focaccia. Similar in texture to a thick pizza crust but lightly seasoned, it makes a good hot bread with meals. In Rome, the virtually unseasoned version is called pizza bianca (white pizza).

1	package active dry yeast
1	cup warm water (about 110°)
2	teaspoons sugar
¾	teaspoon salt
¼	cup olive oil or salad oil
2⅔	to 3 cups all-purpose flour
	Toppings or flavorings (directions follow)

In a large bowl, sprinkle yeast over warm water and let stand for 5 minutes to soften. Stir in sugar, salt, and oil. Add 2 cups of the flour; mix to blend. With a heavy-duty mixer or wooden spoon, beat until dough is elastic (about 5 minutes). Stir in about ⅔ cup more flour to make a soft dough.

Turn dough out onto a board or pastry cloth floured with some of the remaining ⅓ cup flour; knead until dough is smooth and springy (10 to 15 minutes). Place in a greased bowl; turn dough to grease top. Cover and let rise in a warm place until doubled (about 1 hour).

Punch dough down; knead briefly on a lightly floured board just to release air. Roll and stretch dough to fit bottom of a well-greased 10 by 15-inch shallow baking pan. With your fingers or the end of a spoon, press holes in dough at 1-inch intervals. Add toppings or flavorings as directed. Let dough rise, uncovered, until almost doubled (15 to 20 minutes).

Bake in a 450° oven for 12 to 15 minutes or until well browned. Cut bread into 12 equal pieces. Serve warm or at room temperature. Makes 12 pieces.

Raisin Bread. After dough has risen and been punched down, knead in ⅓ cup **raisins** until well distributed. After placing dough in pan, brush dough with 3 tablespoons **olive oil** or salad oil; sprinkle with 1 teaspoon **sugar.**

White Pizza (Pizza Bianca). Brush dough in pan with 3 tablespoons **olive oil** or salad oil.

Pizza Bread. Spread ½ cup canned **pizza sauce** evenly over dough in pan. Sprinkle ⅓ cup each **grated Parmesan cheese** and thinly sliced **green onions** over sauce; then drizzle with 3 tablespoons **olive oil** or salad oil.

Onion Bread. Brush dough in pan with 3 tablespoons **olive oil.** Sprinkle lightly with 1 teaspoon **coarse salt** and ½ cup thinly sliced **green onions.**

CRUSTY TURNOVERS
CALZONE

They taste like pizza, look like big turnovers, and are called calzone. These crusty turnovers can be filled with a spicy sausage or cheese-vegetable filling for lunch or supper.

Crusty Dough (recipe follows)
Sausage or Vegetable Filling (recipes follow)
Olive oil or salad oil
Cornmeal

Prepare Crusty Dough. While dough rises, prepare filling of your choice.

After dough has risen, punch it down and divide in half for 2 large turnovers, in quarters for individual-size turnovers. On a lightly floured board, shape each portion into a round ball; roll large balls into 11-inch circles, small ones into 8½-inch circles. Brush surface of each circle lightly with olive oil or salad oil.

Spread half (for large calzone) or a quarter (for small calzone) of the filling over half of each dough circle. Fold plain half over filling, then press edges together. Roll ½ inch of pressed edges up and over; then seal and crimp. With a wide spatula, transfer turnovers to greased and cornmeal-dusted baking sheets. Prick tops with a fork and brush lightly with olive oil or salad oil. Bake in a 475° oven until well browned (15 to 20 minutes for either size). Serve hot. Makes 4 servings.

Crusty Dough. Sprinkle 1 package active dry yeast over 1 cup warm water (about 110°) and let stand for 5 minutes to soften. Stir in ½ teaspoon salt and 2 teaspoons olive oil or salad oil. Gradually mix in 2½ to 3 cups all-purpose flour to make a soft dough. Turn out onto a well-floured board and knead until smooth and nonsticky, adding more flour as needed (¼ to ½ cup more). Place in a greased bowl; turn dough to grease top. Cover and let rise in a warm place until doubled (about 1 hour).

Sausage Filling. In a wide frying pan over medium heat, cook 3 (about 10 oz. total) mild Italian sausages (sliced) until browned. Add 1 small onion (sliced), 1 clove garlic (minced or pressed), ¼ pound mushrooms (sliced), 1 small green pepper (seeded and sliced), and 1 small carrot (thinly sliced). Cook, stirring, until vegetables are limp. Stir in 1 can (8 oz.) tomato sauce, 1 can (2¼ oz.) sliced olives (drained), 1 teaspoon dry basil, ½ teaspoon each oregano leaves and sugar, and ¼ teaspoon crushed red pepper.

Reduce heat and simmer, uncovered, for about 5 minutes. Let cool. When ready to assemble calzone, stir in 2 cups (8 oz.) shredded mozzarella cheese and ½ cup grated Parmesan cheese. Add salt and pepper to taste.

Vegetable Filling. Follow directions for Sausage Filling but omit sausage. Cook vegetables in 2 to 3 tablespoons olive oil or salad oil and increase mushrooms to ½ pound. Also increase oregano leaves to 1 teaspoon and add ½ teaspoon fennel seeds, if desired. Increase mozzarella to 2½ cups, Parmesan to ¾ cup.

VENETIAN SUGAR BUNS
FOCACCINE VENEZIANE
(Pictured on page 86)

Light, golden rolls, sugar-sprinkled and delicately flavored with lemon and vanilla, make a nice breakfast or brunch treat.

1	package active dry yeast
¼	cup warm water (about 110°)
½	cup warm milk (about 110°)
2	tablespoons butter or margarine, softened
¼	cup sugar
½	teaspoon salt
3	to 3¼ cups all-purpose flour
1	teaspoon each vanilla and grated lemon peel
2	eggs
2	tablespoons coarse sugar or crushed sugar cubes

In a large bowl, sprinkle yeast over warm water and let stand for 5 minutes to soften. Mix in milk, butter, sugar, and salt, stirring until butter melts. Add 1½ cups of the flour; mix to blend. With a heavy-duty mixer or wooden spoon, beat until dough is elastic (about 5 minutes). Beat in vanilla, lemon peel, and 1 of the eggs. Separate remaining egg, reserving white for glaze. Beat yolk into dough. Stir in 1 cup more flour to make a soft dough.

Turn out onto a board or pastry cloth floured with some of the remaining ½ to ¾ cup flour; knead until dough is smooth and springy and develops small bubbles just under surface (about 15 minutes). Place in a greased bowl; turn dough over to grease top. Cover and let rise in a warm place until doubled (1¼ to 1½ hours).

Punch dough down; knead briefly on a lightly floured board just to release air. Cover and let rest for 5

minutes. Divide dough into 10 equal portions. Roll each into a smooth ball. Place about 2 inches apart on greased baking sheets. Cover lightly and let rise until puffy and nearly doubled (20 to 30 minutes).

Beat reserved egg white lightly with 1 teaspoon cold water. Brush lightly over rolls. Sprinkle tops evenly with sugar. Using a floured razor blade or sharp knife, make ½-inch-deep crisscross slashes in top of each roll.

Bake in a 375° oven until rolls are richly browned and sound hollow when tapped (20 to 25 minutes). Serve warm, or cool on wire racks. Makes 10 rolls.

SICILIAN EASTER RING
CIAMBELLA SICILIANA PASQUALE
(Pictured on page 86)

The influence of Greek cooking is clear in this handsome braided Easter bread.

1	package active dry yeast
¼	cup warm water (about 110°)
⅔	cup warm milk (about 110°)
2	tablespoons butter or margarine, softened
⅓	cup sugar
¾	teaspoon salt
3¾	to 4 cups all-purpose flour
½	teaspoon each cinnamon and vanilla
2	eggs
5	hard-cooked eggs, colored red or deep rose (use an egg-dye kit or food coloring)
1	egg yolk beaten with 1 teaspoon water

In a large bowl sprinkle yeast over warm water and let stand for 5 minutes to soften. Stir in milk, butter, sugar, and salt until butter melts. Add 2 cups of the flour; mix to blend. With a heavy-duty mixer or wooden spoon, beat until dough is elastic (about 5 minutes). Beat in cinnamon, vanilla, and eggs. Stir in about 1½ cups more flour to make a soft dough.

Turn out onto a board or pastry

cloth floured with some of the remaining flour knead until dough is smooth and springy and develops small bubbles just under surface (15 to 20 minutes). Place in a greased bowl; turn dough to grease top. Cover and let rise in a warm place until doubled (about 1½ hours).

Punch dough down, turn out onto a floured surface and knead lightly just to release air. Divide into 3 equal portions. Roll each portion to form a strip 25 inches long. Place strips side by side on a large greased baking sheet and braid loosely. Curve braid to make a circle, pinching ends tightly to seal. At evenly spaced intervals, gently separate braid strands and press in the colored eggs (pointed ends down). Cover lightly and let rise until very puffy (40 to 45 minutes).

Brush bread lightly with egg yolk mixture. Bake in a 350° oven until braid is richly browned and sounds hollow when tapped (30 to 35 minutes). Let cool for at least 15 minutes on wire rack before slicing; serve warm or cool. Makes 1 round braid.

GOLDEN CHRISTMAS BREAD
PANDORO DI VERONA
(Pictured on page 86)

A specialty from Verona, this loaf has a characteristic "vertical" texture—if the bread is pulled apart, the pieces strip off in fragile fibers from top to bottom.

1	package active dry yeast
¼	cup warm water (about 110°)
3	tablespoons sugar
¼	teaspoon salt
1	tablespoon melted butter or margarine
3	whole eggs
3	egg yolks
2	teaspoons vanilla
1	teaspoon grated lemon peel
	About 2½ cups all-purpose flour
½	cup (¼ lb.) butter or margarine, softened
	Powdered sugar
	Butter (optional)

(Continued on next page)

Green artichokes for spring, red coppa for hot summer, earthy brown mushrooms for fall, and white cheese for winter snow. Four Seasons Pizza (page 92) is a whole year's worth of colors and flavors in one round pizza-calendar.

In a large bowl, sprinkle yeast over warm water and let stand for about 5 minutes to soften. Stir in sugar, salt, melted butter, eggs, egg yolks, vanilla, and lemon peel. Add 1 cup of the flour; mix to blend. With a heavy-duty mixer or wooden spoon, beat in another 1 cup flour until smoothly blended, then work in thoroughly another ½ cup flour. Scrape dough down into the bowl; cover, set in a warm place, and let rise until more than doubled in volume (1½ to 2 hours).

Vigorously beat dough with spoon to release all air bubbles. Pour soft dough onto a well floured board or pastry cloth, turning to coat sticky surfaces. Gingerly knead dough for 5 minutes or until quite velvety and springy; the dough is unusually soft but easy to handle if you take care not to puncture the surface with your fingers.

Wrap dough in flour-dusted plastic wrap and chill for about 20 minutes to make dough easier to roll. Cover rolling pin with a stockinet cover for easier handling, and roll out dough on the floured board or pastry cloth to make an 11 or 12-inch square. Gently and evenly spread the ½ cup softened butter to within 1 inch of the edges. Fold in overlapping thirds, then roll out again to a 12-inch square.

Fold in overlapping thirds again, this time folding the dough at right angles to the preceding fold. (Protect dough with ample flour as you work; dust off excess before enclosing folds.) Roll to a 12-inch square; repeat this fold-and-roll procedure two more times, crossing each fold at right angles to the preceding one. Cover with plastic wrap and chill for about 20 minutes to firm dough slightly, then fold and roll four more times.

Fold the 12-inch square in half, then roll up snugly from a narrow end and fit dough, folded edge up, into a heavily buttered and floured 3 to 4-quart tall mold (plain or fancy).

Cover and let rise until dough fills mold about two-thirds full; this usually takes at least 1 hour in a warm place.

Place on a low rack in a 350° oven and bake for 40 to 45 minutes or until bread is richly browned and a wooden skewer inserted in center comes out clean. Invert mold over a wire rack, tapping to release bread; leave bread upright, bracing, if needed. When the bread is cool enough to serve, trim a bit off the base, if necessary, to make it sit steady. Serve warm or let cool.

You may wrap bread airtight and store at room temperature for up to two days, or freeze for longer storage. To reheat, wrap bread (thawed, if frozen) in foil and place in a 350° oven for about 20 minutes.

To serve, place bread on a platter and dust with powdered sugar. Slice thinly from the top, cutting at a 45° angle and taking every other slice from the opposite side of the loaf. Serve plain or spread with butter. Makes 12 to 16 servings.

GENOESE FRUIT & NUT BREAD
PANDOLCE GENOVESE

A plump, round loaf, studded with Marsala-soaked raisins, nuts, and candied orange peel is a Genoese version of the Milanese yeast panettone. From the same dough, augmented by more nuts and candied fruits, you can create Mataloc — a festive bread from Bellagio on Lake Como.

2	**packages active dry yeast**
⅓	**cup warm water (about 110°)**
3	**tablespoons sweet or dry Marsala**
1	**cup raisins**
⅓	**cup butter or margarine, melted and cooled**
3	**eggs**
⅓	**cup sugar**
¼	**teaspoon** each **salt and fennel or anise seeds**
1	**tablespoon orange flower water or 1½ teaspoons vanilla**
3¼	**to 3½ cups all-purpose flour**
⅓	**cup pine nuts or slivered almonds**
¼	**cup candied orange peel**
	Glaze (directions follow)

In a large bowl, sprinkle yeast over warm water. Let stand for about 5 minutes to soften. In a small bowl, pour Marsala over raisins; set aside. To yeast mixture add butter, 2 eggs, and 1 egg yolk (reserve egg white for glaze), sugar, salt, fennel seeds, orange flower water, and 2 cups of the flour; mix to blend.

With a heavy-duty mixer or wooden spoon, beat until dough is smooth and elastic (about 5 minutes). Stir in raisins and their liquid and about ¾ cup more flour to make a soft dough.

Turn dough out onto a board or pastry cloth floured with ½ to ¾ cup of the remaining flour; knead until smooth and springy (10 to 15 minutes). Place in a greased bowl; turn dough to grease top. Cover and let rise in a warm place until doubled (1 to 1½ hours).

Punch dough down, then knead in pine nuts and orange peel. Shape dough into a round ball. Place on a greased baking sheet; cover with an inverted bowl. Let rise until almost doubled (45 minutes to 1 hour). Brush with glaze.

Bake in a 350° oven until bread is well browned and a wooden skewer inserted in center comes out clean (30 to 45 minutes). Cool on wire rack. Makes 1 loaf.

Glaze. Beat reserved **egg white** with ½ teaspoon **each powdered sugar** and **water** just until well mixed.

Fruit & Nut Bread (Mataloc**).** Follow directions for Genoese Fruit & Nut Bread, but increase **raisins** to 1½ cups, omit fennel seeds, and use the 1½ teaspoons **vanilla** instead of orange flower water. Expect each rising to take 1 to 1¼ hours. Use ½ cup slivered **almonds** instead of pine nuts. Omit candied orange peel. With almonds, knead in ½ cup coarsely chopped **walnuts** and ¾ cup chopped **mixed candied fruits**. Divide dough in half and shape into 2 balls. Using a floured razor blade or sharp knife, cut an X in top of each just before baking. Bake until richly browned (35 to 40 minutes). Cool on wire racks. Sprinkle loaves with **powdered sugar** before slicing. Makes 2 small loaves.

MILANESE COFFEE CAKE
PANETTONE

(Pictured on page 91)

A moderately sweet, cakelike bread, panettone is one of the specialties of Milan. Leavened either with baking powder—as this version is—or yeast, it's traditionally baked in a high, round metal mold or in a pan with a paper collar, resulting in a lofty, domed shape.

Inventive Italian-American cooks found that a small paper bag was easier to use than the tied paper collar (for many years, the molds were not readily available outside Italy).

1	egg
2	egg yolks
¾	cup sugar
½	cup (¼ lb.) butter or margarine, melted and cooled to lukewarm
1	teaspoon grated lemon peel
1	teaspoon *each* anise seeds and anise extract
¼	cup *each* pine nuts (pignoli), raisins, and coarsely chopped, mixed candied fruit
3	cups all-purpose flour
2	teaspoons baking powder
½	teaspoon salt
1	cup milk

Fold down top of a paper bag (lunch-bag size, measuring 3½ by 6 inches on bottom) to form a cuff, so bag stands about 4 inches high; butter inside generously and place bag on a baking sheet (or use a greased, flour-dusted panettone mold 6 inches in diameter and 4 inches deep).

In a large bowl, beat egg, egg yolks, and sugar together until thick and pale yellow. Beat in melted butter, then add lemon peel, anise seeds, anise extract, pine nuts, raisins, and candied fruit. In another bowl, mix flour, baking powder, and salt. Blend half the flour mixture with batter. Stir in half the milk, add remaining flour mixture, and mix well. Add remaining milk and blend thoroughly. Pour batter into prepared paper bag.

Bake in a 325° oven for 1¾ to 2 hours or until bread is well browned and a wooden skewer inserted in center comes out clean.

To serve hot, tear off paper bag and cut bread into slim wedges. To serve cold, wrap bread (still in bag) in a clean cloth, then in foil, and let cool completely to mellow flavors. To re-heat, remove foil, then cloth; rewrap bread (still in bag) in foil and place in a 350° oven for 45 minutes. Makes 1 loaf.

TUSCAN ALMOND-CRUSTED FLAT BREAD
SCHIACCIATA

(Pictured on page 86)

A chunky topping of almond paste and sliced almonds crowns these round, flat loaves of rich bread. Underneath the crust is a moderately sweet bread flavored with candied orange peel, raisins, and anise. This is one of the most elaborate versions of flat breads, called schiacciata.

1	package active dry yeast
¼	cup lukewarm (110°) water
¾	cup very soft butter or margarine
¾	cup granulated sugar
⅓	cup milk
½	teaspoon salt
1	tablespoon *each* grated orange peel and anise seeds
4	eggs
1	egg yolk
	About 4¾ cups all-purpose flour
1	cup *each* raisins and diced candied orange peel
1	egg white beaten with 1 tablespoon water
	About 7 ounces almond paste
1	cup sliced almonds
	Powdered sugar

In a large bowl, sprinkle yeast over warm water and let stand for 5 minutes to soften. Stir in butter, sugar, milk, salt, grated orange peel, anise seeds, eggs, and egg yolk.

If you use a dough hook, add 4¾ cups flour and mix at medium speed until dough pulls from bowl sides (about 10 minutes). Cover and let rise in a warm place until almost doubled (1½ to 2 hours). Stir dough down and turn out onto a well-floured surface.

Flatten dough and place raisins and candied orange peel on top. Fold dough over and knead lightly just until fruit is well distributed.

If you use an electric mixer (without dough hook), add 2 cups of the flour and beat at medium speed for 10 minutes. With mixer at low speed, or with a spoon, mix in 1 cup more flour until thoroughly moistened. With a spoon, stir in remaining 1¾ cups flour until thoroughly moistened. (Do not knead.)

Cover and let rise in a warm place until almost doubled (1½ to 2 hours). Stir dough down and turn out onto a well-floured surface. Knead for about 10 minutes, adding as little flour as possible to board, until dough is very smooth and velvety. Flatten dough and place raisins and candied orange peel on top. Fold dough over and knead lightly just until fruit is well distributed.

Divide dough into two equal parts and shape each into a ball. Place each ball on a well-greased baking sheet and pat into a flat round about 9 inches wide. Cover shaped dough lightly with clear plastic film and let rise in a warm place until puffy looking (40 to 45 minutes). Uncover; brush with beaten egg white mixture. Crumble almond paste into ½-inch chunks and sprinkle half the chunks over each round; then sprinkle half the almonds over each round and press lightly into dough.

Place baking sheets on middle rack of a 350° oven. (Or stagger them on the 2 racks closest to middle of oven; racks should be at least 4 inches apart.) Bake for about 30 minutes or until richly browned. Transfer breads to wire racks to cool. Dust generously with powdered sugar and serve warm or cooled. Makes 2 loaves.

8

DESSERTS &

PASTRIES

When it comes to the finishing touch to a meal in Italy, the choices are amazingly diverse, ranging from utter simplicity to artistic grandeur.

For simplicity, try fruits of the season, fresh or cooked. A wedge of robustly flavored or rich cheese (page 61) served with or after fruit is another easy but elegant **finale alla Italia.**

For those with a yen for more elaborate desserts, we present the Italian classics: Zabaglione (page 101) Zuppa Inglese (page 101), and Spumone (page 106), to name just a few. You'll also find lavish tortes and cheesecakes, as well as festive holiday cookies and confections. Where possible, we've broken down complicated preparations into easy steps that can be completed in advance.

Whip together egg yolks, sugar, and wine for a dramatic one-act Zabaglione show at the table. The simple concoction turns into a rich, golden foam in about five minutes. Poured into delicate glasses, Zabaglione (page 101) adds the perfect touch of elegance to conclude a special dinner.

WINE-POACHED PEARS
PERE AL VINO ROSSO

In autumn and winter, platters of poached pears standing in their own sweet cooking liquid are a common sight on the sideboards of Roman restaurants.

Bartlett pears, already tender, only need to be heated through. If you use winter pears, though, they'll need slightly longer cooking.

1¾	cups dry red wine
1	cup sugar
¼	teaspoon anise seeds
2	whole cinnamon sticks
2 or 3	thin lemon slices
6	firm-ripe medium to large Bartlett pears or medium-size Anjou or Bosc pears

In a pan large enough to hold all the pears side by side, combine wine, sugar, anise, cinnamon sticks, and lemon slices. Bring wine mixture to a boil over high heat.

Meanwhile, remove core from bottom end of each pear; leave stems in place. Peel pears, if desired. Set pears into boiling mixture and reduce heat to medium; cover and simmer until

Bartlett pears are heated through and still hold their shapes (8 to 10 minutes), or until Anjou or Bosc pears can be pierced easily with a fork (12 to 15 minutes). Turn fruit occasionally so all portions are at times in syrup. With a slotted spoon, lift pears from syrup and transfer to a serving dish.

Boil syrup over high heat, uncovered, until reduced to ¾ to 1 cup. Pour hot syrup over and around pears. Serve warm or at room temperature. Makes 6 servings.

CHESTNUTS MUDDLED IN PORT
CASTAGNE AL PORTO
(Pictured on page 102)

These chestnuts are more an after-dinner snack than a dessert. Accompany with port for sipping, and moistened napkins for cleanup.

1	pound fresh chestnuts
½	cup port
¼	cup sugar

With a sharp pointed knife, cut a slit about ½ inch long through shell into meat of each chestnut (this keeps

(Continued on page 100)

them from exploding in the oven); discard any chestnut with mold. Arrange nuts in a single layer on a baking sheet; bake in a 400° oven for 40 minutes.

(To cook in a microwave oven, place chestnuts in a shallow dish. Microwave uncovered on high (100%) for 2 minutes; turn over after 1 minute. Stir well and microwave on high (100%) for 1 more minute or until soft when squeezed.)

Mix port and sugar in a deep bowl. Remove chestnuts from oven. Using a thick potholder to protect your hand, squeeze each nut to pop the shell open so it can absorb the port; drop nuts into port-sugar mixture, stirring with each addition. Let stand, stirring occasionally, until cool enough to touch comfortably. Transfer nuts to a serving bowl.

Peel nuts with your hands. Makes 6 to 8 servings.

CHRISTMAS FRUITCAKE CANDY
PANFORTE DI SIENA
(Pictured on page 102)

A cross between fruitcake and candy, panforte (strong bread) from Siena is solid with whole nuts. Serve it in small wedges with espresso, tea, brandy, or dessert wines.

About 2½ tablespoons butter or margarine
2 cups (¾ lb.) whole unblanched almonds, or 1 cup each whole unblanched almonds and filberts
1 cup candied orange peel, coarsely chopped
1 cup candied lemon peel, minced
1 teaspoon each grated lemon peel and ground cinnamon
½ teaspoon ground coriander
¼ teaspoon each ground cloves and ground nutmeg
½ cup all-purpose flour
¾ cup each granulated sugar and honey
Powdered sugar

Heavily butter bottom and sides of an 8 or 9-inch cake pan with re-movable bottom. Line bottom with brown paper, then butter paper and dust with flour; set aside. In a bowl, mix almonds with candied orange peel, candied lemon peel, grated lemon peel, cinnamon, coriander, cloves, nutmeg, and flour until flour coats each particle.

In a deep pan over high heat, combine sugar, honey, and 2 table-spoons butter. Stirring frequently, cook quickly to 265° (hard-ball stage) on a candy thermometer. Pour hot syrup into almond mixture and mix thoroughly. Pour into prepared cake pan and spread evenly.

Bake in a 300° oven for 45 min-utes, then cool thoroughly. Panforte should be firm to touch. Loosen sides of cake from pan with a knife, then invert cake onto a large sheet of wax paper heavily dusted with powdered sugar.

Remove pan bottom and brown paper, cutting away paper, if neces-sary. Heavily dust top of panforte with more powdered sugar to coat completely. Serve immediately or wrap airtight to store indefinitely. Serve in small wedges. Makes about 2½ pounds confection.

MERINGUE COFFEE-CREAM TORTE
MARENGO CAVOUR

Essentially this impressive dessert is Florentine, but the coffee flavor in the chocolate-studded whipped-cream filling is an embellishment from the New World. The torte should be made ahead; standing overnight in the refrigerator makes the meringue layers easy to cut and serve.

4 egg whites
½ teaspoon cream of tartar
1 cup sugar
1 teaspoon vanilla
Cream Filling (recipe follows)
Sweet ground chocolate or cocoa (optional)

In an electric mixer bowl that holds at least 6 cups below top curve of beater, combine egg whites and cream of tartar. Beat at highest speed just until frothy (there should be no bottom layer of free-flowing viscous white). Continue beating and add sugar, 1 tablespoon every minute, sprinkling it gradually over the mixing whites. When all the sugar is incorporated, add vanilla and beat for 1 or 2 more minutes. When beater is lifted out, whites should hold very stiff, sharp, un-bending peaks.

Grease two baking sheets and dust with flour; trace an 8-inch circle on each. Using a pastry bag with plain tip (or a spoon and spatula), pipe or spread half the meringue onto one baking sheet, making a plain disk. Shape remaining meringue in an 8-inch solid disk with a decorative surface of puffs and swirls (use star tip on a pastry bag, if you wish).

Bake meringues in a 250° oven for 1½ hours (color should be pure white to faint amber). If you have two ovens, position each meringue just below the center in each oven. If you have one oven, position meringues just above and below the center, then switch their positions halfway through baking.

Turn off heat and leave meringues in closed oven for 3 to 4 hours to continue drying; then remove from oven. While pans are still warm, flex them to pop meringues free, but leave meringues in place to cool. Store them airtight at room tempera-ture for as long as 5 days.

Prepare Cream Filling. Place plain meringue on a flat serving dish; spread all the cream filling evenly just on the top. Place decorative me-ringue on top of filling. Cover and refrigerate for 8 hours or until next day to mellow for easy cutting. If desired, dust top lightly with sweet ground chocolate. Cut into wedges to serve. Makes 8 to 10 servings.

Cream Filling. In a cup, blend 1 teaspoon **instant coffee powder** and 4 tablespoons **coffee-flavored liqueur** (or 2 additional teaspoons instant coffee powder, 2 tablespoons water, and 1 teaspoon vanilla). In a bowl, whip 1 pint (2 cups) **whipping cream** until stiff, then fold in liquid coffee mixture and 1 large bar (about 5 oz.) **milk chocolate**, coarsely chopped.

FROTHY EGG PUDDING
ZABAGLIONE
(Pictured on page 99)

One of the best one-act food shows we know of is the dramatic, at-the-table preparation of zabaglione. To perform this, you cook just three ingredients over a denatured-alcohol flame in a round-bottom zabaglione pan. The egg yolks, wine, and sugar can be whipped to a gold, velvety foam in about 5 minutes. Then pour it into fragile stemmed glasses from which the zabaglione is eaten with a spoon, accompanied by crisp Almond Macaroons or delicate rolled Cialde (page 107).

If you prefer to skip the dramatics, you can cook the zabaglione just as well in the kitchen in a double boiler. Also, any number of fine variations of zabaglione are possible. This basic recipe gets you started; the three variations that follow will set you soaring.

8	egg yolks
3 to 4	tablespoons sugar
½	cup **Marsala**, sweet or dry

In a round-bottom zabaglione pan or the top of a double boiler, beat together egg yolks, 3 tablespoons of the sugar, and wine. Place round-bottom pan over direct heat or set double boiler over gently simmering water. Whip mixture constantly with a wire whisk or electric mixer until it is thick enough to retain briefly a slight peak when whisk or beaters are withdrawn (about 5 minutes).

Taste the mixture for sweetness; then beat in the remaining 1 tablespoon sugar, if desired. Pour Zabaglione into stemmed glasses and serve at once. Makes 6 to 8 servings.

Zabaglione with Grenadine. In place of Marsala, use a **dry white wine**, such as Soave; add ½ teaspoon **vanilla**. Pour ½ inch chilled **grenadine** into bottom of each serving glass, fill with **Zabaglione**, and dust each serving with **ground nutmeg**.

Anisette Zabaglione. In place of Marsala, use a **dry white wine**, such as Soave; add 2 teaspoons **anisette** or other anise-flavored liqueur, and ¼ teaspoon grated **lemon peel**.

Zabaglione with Cream. Spoon a little sweetened, ice-cold **whipped cream** into bottom of each serving glass; top with hot **Zabaglione**.

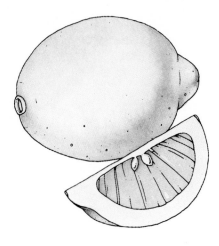

RUM CUSTARD CAKE
ZUPPA INGLESE

More cakelike than some versions of this popular dessert, this zuppa inglese tastes and serves best if made a day in advance.

ORANGE CAKE

4	eggs, separated
1	cup each **sugar and sifted cake flour**
¼	teaspoon baking powder
½	teaspoon salt
2	tablespoons each **hot water and lemon juice**
2	teaspoons grated orange peel
½	teaspoon cream of tartar

ORANGE-RUM SYRUP

6	tablespoons each **sugar and water**
1	teaspoon grated orange peel
½	teaspoon grated lemon peel
⅓	cup light rum

CUSTARD

4	eggs
⅓	cup sugar
1	pint (2 cups) half-and-half (light cream)
1½	teaspoons vanilla
2	tablespoons light rum
1	cup whipping cream

FROSTING

½	cup whipping cream
	Sugar
	Slivered toasted almonds (optional)

Grease and lightly flour a 9 to 10-inch spring-form pan (at least 2¾ inches deep). In a large bowl, beat egg yolks until thick and light-colored; gradually beat in sugar, beating until thick and pale. Sift flour with baking powder and salt. In a small bowl, combine hot water, lemon juice, and orange peel. Add flour mixture to beaten egg yolks alternately with hot water mixture, stirring to blend after each addition.

Using clean beaters, beat egg whites with cream of tartar until soft peaks form. Stir a fourth of the beaten egg whites into flour mixture, then fold in remaining egg whites carefully but thoroughly. Pour batter into prepared pan.

Bake in a 350° oven for 40 to 45 minutes or until cake is golden brown, begins to pull away from sides of pan, and springs back when touched lightly in center. Let cool completely in pan on a wire rack.

To make syrup, combine sugar, water, orange peel, and lemon peel in a small pan over high heat. Bring to a boil, then cook rapidly for 3 minutes. Remove from heat and let cool; blend in the ⅓ cup rum.

To make custard, place eggs and sugar in top of a double boiler and mix thoroughly. Scald half-and-half; gradually stir into egg mixture. Place double boiler over gently simmering water. Cook, stirring constantly, until custard coats a metal spoon in a velvety smooth layer (10 to 15 minutes). Remove from heat and mix in vanilla. Place top of double boiler

(Continued on page 103)

...Rum Custard Cake (cont'd.)

into ice water to stop cooking; stir custard frequently until cool. Stir in rum. Whip 1 cup cream until soft peaks form when beaters are lifted. Fold into cooled custard.

To assemble dessert, remove pan side from cake, leaving cake on base. Carefully cut cake horizontally into 3 equal layers and lift off the top 2 layers. Replace pan sides around pan bottom holding the remaining cake layer.

Drizzle cake bottom layer with a third of the syrup, then cover with a third of the custard. Carefully place the middle layer of cake on the custard, sprinkle this layer with another third of the syrup, then another third of the custard. Set top cake layer in place, sprinkle with remaining syrup, pour on remaining custard, and spread evenly. Cover cake lightly to protect top. Refrigerate for at least 6 hours or until next day.

Remove pan sides. Whip the ½ cup cream until stiff, sweeten slightly with sugar, and spread on cake sides. Garnish top of cake with nuts, if desired. Cut in wedges. Makes 10 to 12 servings.

RICOTTA CRUMB CAKE
TORTA DI BRICIOLE E RICOTTA

A specialty of Lo Scaldavivande Cooking School in Rome (though its origin is Sicily), this rather elaborate but spectacular cake resembles

Buon Natale! Merry Christmas Italian-style might include a buffet of sweets such as these. Panforte di Siena (page 100) at top center is a fruitcake so rich it's virtually a candy. Glistening Chestnuts Muddled in Port (page 98) fill a silver bowl in the center of the buffet. To the right you see Amor Polenta, (page 104), a Florentine pound cake made with cornmeal; to the left a platter of Twice-Baked Cookies (page 108) and fruit. Offer espresso and a sweet dessert wine to go with such Christmas delights.

cheesecake. Buttery almond crumbs bake like a crust around a creamy ricotta filling studded with pine-nut brittle and chocolate chunks.

⅓	cup granulated sugar
⅔	cup pine nuts (pignoli) or slivered almonds
3½	cups (1¾ lbs.) ricotta cheese
2	tablespoons light rum or ½ teaspoon rum flavoring
¾	cup granulated sugar
4	ounces semisweet chocolate, coarsely chopped, or ½ cup semisweet chocolate chips
	Almond Crumb Crust Mixture (recipe follows)
	Powdered sugar

Place the ⅓ cup sugar in a wide frying pan over medium heat. Cook, shaking pan frequently, until sugar liquefies and turns golden. Stir in pine nuts; then immediately turn out onto a buttered shallow pan. With a buttered spoon, press mixture to flatten slightly. Let cool, then break into ½-inch pieces.

In a bowl mix together ricotta, rum, and the ¾ cup sugar until blended. Stir in chocolate and pine nut brittle; set aside.

Prepare Almond Crumb Crust Mixture and spoon half into a buttered 10-inch spring-form pan, piling mixture slightly higher around edges; do not press firmly. Spoon ricotta mixture into center, and spoon remaining crust mixture over ricotta all the way to sides; gently pat down to form an almost flat top.

Bake in a 350° oven for 45 minutes or until lightly browned. Let cool thoroughly. If made ahead, cover and refrigerate until next day.

Before serving, remove pan sides and sprinkle top of cake with powdered sugar. Serve at room temperature or chilled. Makes 10 to 12 servings.

Almond Crumb Crust Mixture. Spread ⅔ cup blanched almonds in a single layer in a pan and toast in a 350° oven, shaking pan occasionally, for about 10 minutes or until lightly browned. Then whirl in a blender or food processor until finely ground.

In a large bowl, stir together 3¼ cups all-purpose flour, 1 tablespoon

baking powder, ⅔ cup firmly packed **brown sugar**, and the ground almonds. With a pastry blender or 2 knives, cut in ⅞ cup (½ lb. less 2 tablespoons) cold **butter** or margarine until fine crumbs form. Beat together 1 **egg** and 1 teaspoon **vanilla**; pour over dry ingredients and toss with a fork just until evenly moistened. Mixture should remain crumbly; do not overmix.

SUMMER CHEESE TORTE
TORTA DI MASCARPONE

Elegant mascarpone (Italian cream cheese) or homemade Fresh Cheese flavors the rich, luscious cream in this layered dessert. Mascarpone is available in food specialty shops and some Italian delicatessens.

3	eggs, separated
6	tablespoons sugar
1	cup Fresh Cheese (page 57), made with whipping cream; or ½ pound (about 1 cup) mascarpone
4	to 6 tablespoons Marsala or rum
11	to 12-ounce frozen pound cake, thawed, or packaged pound cake
1	to 2 cups strawberries

Beat egg whites at high speed with an electric mixer until foamy, then gradually add 3 tablespoons of the sugar; continue beating until whites hold stiff peaks. Beat egg yolks with remaining 3 tablespoons sugar until very thick. Place cheese in a large bowl and gradually beat yolk mixture into cheese until smoothly blended. Fold egg whites into cheese mixture along with 2 tablespoons of the Marsala.

Cut cake into ¼-inch-thick slices. Line a pretty, wide dessert bowl (at least 12-cup size) with half the cake and sprinkle with 1 to 2 tablespoons more Marsala. Spoon cheese mixture into bowl, spreading evenly. Top attractively with remaining cake slices and sprinkle with another 1 to 2 tablespoons Marsala.

Cover and chill for at least 6 hours or until next day. Garnish with strawberries. Makes 8 to 10 servings.

SUMMER CHEESECAKE
TORTA DELL' ESTATE

This creamy cheesecake is most festive with sweetened fresh berries or sliced peaches.

1½	cups finely crushed arrowroot biscuit crumbs
6	tablespoons butter or margarine, melted
2	cups Fresh Cheese (page 57), made with milk; or 1 pound cream cheese, softened
1	cup sugar
2	teaspoons vanilla
2	tablespoons lemon juice
4	eggs
2	cups sour cream (optional)

In a bowl, blend crumbs and butter. Press mixture evenly over bottom and about 1 inch up sides of a 9-inch spring-form pan.

Place cheese in a bowl. Beat in ¾ cup of the sugar, 1 teaspoon of the vanilla, and lemon juice. Add eggs, one at a time, blending well with each addition. Pour cheese mixture into crumb-lined pan. Bake in a 325° oven for 40 minutes.

Meanwhile, combine sour cream, remaining ¼ cup sugar, and remaining 1 teaspoon vanilla; mix well. When cake has baked for 40 minutes, remove from oven and spread sour cream mixture evenly over top. Return to oven for 10 minutes more. (Or you can omit the sour cream mixture and bake the cake for 50 minutes or until it appears set when pan is gently jiggled.)

Let cool, then chill before serving. Makes 10 to 12 servings.

LOMBARDY STRAWBERRY TART
CROSTATA DI FRAGOLE

A cooked strawberry base covered with fresh strawberry halves provides a delightful flavor and texture contrast in this tart from Milan.

If you make your own anise sugar, begin it ahead of time; it needs to stand for several hours before it's used. Or buy imported anise sugar in specialty food shops.

	Anise Sugar (recipe follows)
	Butter Pastry Shell (recipe follows)
4	cups strawberries, washed, hulled, and drained well
½ to ⅔	cup sugar
2	tablespoons each cornstarch and lemon juice
	About ¼ cup peach jam

Prepare Anise Sugar and Butter Pastry Shell.

Set aside 2 cups of the prettiest whole berries. Coarsely mash remaining 2 cups berries; place in a medium-size pan. Blend ½ cup of the sugar with cornstarch and add to mashed berries along with lemon juice; taste and add more sugar if desired. Place over high heat and, stirring, bring to a boil; continue to cook until thickened and clear. Set aside to cool slightly, then pour into baked Butter Pastry Shell and chill for about 1 hour.

Cut remaining berries in halves and arrange, cut sides up, over cooled berry filling. Force peach jam through a wire strainer and heat, stirring, until bubbling. Brush jam over berry halves to glaze them. Chill tart until ready to serve (as long as 4 hours). Just before serving, remove pan rim and sift about 2 tablespoons of the Anise Sugar over tart. Makes 6 to 8 servings.

Anise Sugar. To make your own, whirl ½ teaspoon **anise seeds** in a blender, or crush in a mortar until powdery. Blend with ¼ cup **powdered sugar**, cover tightly, and let stand for 2 to 3 hours or until next day. Sift through a fine wire strainer before using. (Or use purchased anise sugar and crush it to a fine powder before using.)

Butter Pastry Shell. In a bowl, mix 1 cup **all-purpose flour** with 2 tablespoons of the **Anise Sugar**. Add 6 tablespoons firm **butter** (cut into pieces). With your fingers or a pastry blender, work in butter until mixture is of even texture. With a fork, stir in 1 **egg yolk**. With your hands, compress mixture into a ball.

Place dough in a 9-inch pan (cake, tart, or cheesecake) with removable bottom. Press dough evenly over bottom and ½ inch up the sides.

Bake in a 300° oven for 30 minutes or until pastry is golden brown. Cool in pan on a wire rack.

FLORENTINE CORNMEAL CAKE
AMOR POLENTA

(Pictured on page 102)

This unusual cake is basically a pound cake with the pleasing crunch and nutlike flavor of cornmeal added. Traditionally it bakes in a special pan (with a rounded, ridged bottom) called either a deerback, saddlemold, or nut bread loaf pan. It can also be baked in a small loaf or tube pan.

Many recipes do not direct you to sift all-purpose flour. For reliable results here, though, sift and measure cake flour carefully.

⅔	cup butter, softened
2⅔	cups sifted powdered sugar
1	teaspoon vanilla
2	whole eggs
1	egg yolk
1¼	cups sifted cake flour
⅓	cup yellow cornmeal
	About 2 tablespoons powdered sugar

In a large bowl, place butter and the 2⅔ cups sugar; with an electric mixer, beat until creamy. Beat in vanilla; then add eggs, one at a time, and the yolk, beating well after each addition. Mix flour to blend with cornmeal. Add flour mixture, a portion at a time, to batter, mixing well after each addition.

Generously grease and flour-dust either a 10-inch deerback pan, an 8½ by 4½-inch loaf pan, or a 3½- to 4-cup tube pan. Spoon batter into pan and spread evenly.

Bake in a 325° oven for about 1 hour and 15 minutes or until a wooden pick inserted in center comes out clean and cake springs back when lightly touched in center.

Cool cake in pan for 3 minutes,

then turn out onto a wire rack. Sift the 2 tablespoons sugar over warm cake. Let cool completely, then cut into thin slices. Makes about 15 servings.

RICE CAKE
TORTA DI RISO
'DEGLI ADDOBBI'

As part of the Easter festival in Bologna, homes are cleaned, decorated, and then blessed. Often this simple country cake is prepared as a gift to the priest. Its homespun flavor is reminiscent of rice pudding. You can serve it any time.

3	cups milk
¼	cup long-grain rice
½	cup sugar
¼	teaspoon salt
2	tablespoons butter or margarine
½	cup blanched almonds, chopped
	Press-in Pastry (recipe follows)
3	eggs, lightly beaten
¼	teaspoon almond extract

In the top of a double boiler, combine milk, rice, sugar, salt, and butter; place over simmering water. Cover and cook, stirring occasionally, for 2¼ to 2½ hours or until rice is soft.

Meanwhile, spread chopped almonds in a shallow pan and toast in a 325° oven, stirring occasionally, for about 15 minutes or until golden. Prepare Press-in Pastry.

Pour part of the cooked rice mixture into eggs, then stir all back into remaining rice mixture. Stir in toasted almonds and almond extract. Pour into baked crust and bake in a 400° oven for about 20 minutes or until center is firm when shaken. Remove pan sides. Serve warm or cooled. Makes 6 servings.

Press-in Pastry. In a bowl, mix 1 cup all-purpose flour with 2 tablespoons sugar. Add 6 tablespoons firm butter or margarine (cut into pieces). With your fingers or a pastry blender, work in butter until mixture is of even texture. With a fork, stir in 1 egg yolk. With your hands, compress mixture into a ball.

Place dough in a 9-inch round cake pan with removable bottom. Press dough in a firm, even layer over bottom and up sides of pan. Bake in a 325° oven for 30 minutes or until golden; cool.

LEMON ICE
GRANITA DI LIMONE
(Pictured on page 2)

Italian ices and other frozen desserts occupy a special place in the memory of just about anyone who has ever visited Italy. This lemon ice makes use of a food processor to achieve the smoothly slushy consistency typical of Italian water ices.

1	small lemon
1	cup sugar
4	cups water
	Dash salt
	About ½ cup lemon juice

Cut zest (colored part of peel) from lemon with a vegetable peeler. Squeeze lemon, then strain and reserve juice. Cut zest in ½-inch pieces. Using metal blade of food processor, process zest and sugar until zest is finely chopped. Place in a 3-quart pan with water and salt. Heat just until sugar dissolves; let cool. To reserved lemon juice add enough additional juice to make ⅔ cup. Stir juice into cooled sugar mixture. Freeze mixture in divided ice cube trays. When frozen, you can

transfer cubes to plastic bags; return to freezer.

To serve, use metal blade of food processor to process 4 to 6 cubes of lemon purée at a time. Use on-off bursts at first to break up cubes, then run processor continuously until you have a velvety slush. Scoop into serving dishes or process ice and store, covered, in freezer until ready to serve. Makes about 4½ cups.

TRICOLOR ICE CREAM BOMBE
CASSATA GELATA

Vanilla ice cream forms the outer layer, followed by chocolate ice cream and a heart of whipped cream studded with candied fruit: a dessert to make children's eyes light up. And grown-ups', too!

1½	quarts vanilla ice cream, softened slightly
1	quart chocolate ice cream, softened slightly
1	cup whipping cream
1	tablespoon maraschino liqueur or 1 teaspoon vanilla
1	egg white
2	tablespoons *each* powdered sugar, chopped candied red cherries, chopped candied citron, and chopped candied orange peel
	Whole candied red cherries and pieces of candied citron

Line bottom and sides of a 2-quart mold evenly with vanilla ice cream. Freeze at about 0° until very firm. Cover firmed vanilla ice cream evenly with chocolate ice cream; freeze until very firm. In a bowl, whip ½ cup of the cream until stiff; blend in maraschino. In another bowl, beat egg white until soft peaks form, then beat in powdered sugar until stiff. Fold beaten egg white into cream along with chopped cherries, citron, and orange peel. Spoon this mixture into center of molded ice cream; spread to make a smooth bottom layer. Cover and freeze until firm (as long as 2 weeks).

To unmold, dip mold to the rim in hot water for about 6 seconds, then invert onto a cold serving plate. If ice cream does not come free immediately, dip in water again for 2 or 3 seconds. Return to freezer for at least 30 minutes to refirm surface before serving (or you can wrap unmolded cassata and store in freezer).

Whip remaining ½ cup cream until stiff and use to decorate cassata, garnishing with whole cherries and pieces of citron. Allow to stand at room temperature for about 10 minutes, then cut into wedges. Makes 12 to 16 servings.

FROZEN ANISE MOUSSE
SPUMONE ALL' ANICE

A Roman specialty, this rich-tasting frozen mousse is flavored with anise liqueur.

½	cup chopped blanched almonds
1	cup sugar
¾	cup water
6	egg yolks
1	pint (2 cups) whipping cream
2	teaspoons vanilla
3	tablespoons anisette or other anise-flavored liqueur
	Whole strawberries (optional)

Spread almonds in a single layer in a shallow pan and toast in a 350° oven for about 8 minutes or until golden; stir frequently. Let cool.

In a pan over medium heat, combine sugar and water and bring to a boil, stirring, until sugar is dis-

solved. Continue to boil, uncovered, until syrup is 220° on a candy thermometer.

Meanwhile, in top of a double boiler beat egg yolks with an electric mixer until they are thick. Continuing to beat yolks, slowly pour hot syrup into them, carefully avoiding beaters. Place over slightly simmering water and continue to beat with mixer until stiff peaks form (about 7 minutes). Remove from heat and set top of double boiler in cold water; continue beating until mixture is cold.

Whip cream until stiff; flavor with vanilla and anisette. Fold cream and nuts into egg yolk mixture; pour into a 1¾ to 2-quart mold and smooth the surface. Cover and freeze at about 0° until firm; store in freezer for as long as 2 weeks. Unmold and refirm surface as directed for Tricolor Ice Cream Bombe (page 105).

Decorate with strawberries, if you wish. Cut in thick vertical slices to serve. Makes 8 to 10 servings.

FROZEN CHESTNUT TORTE
SEMIFREDDO DI CASTAGNE

The sweet, mellow flavor of chestnuts is quite popular in Italian desserts. This frozen torte, using whole chestnuts canned in water, is served with a raspberry sauce.

	Orange Crust (recipe follows)
1	can (10 oz.) canned whole chestnuts, drained
5	eggs, separated
⅓	cup water
⅔	cup sugar
½	cup (¼ lb.) butter or margarine, softened
1	teaspoon vanilla
2	tablespoons orange-flavored liqueur
¾	cup sugar
½	pint (1 cup) whipping cream
	Raspberry Sauce (recipe follows)
	Mint leaves

Prepare Orange Crust; set aside.

Purée chestnuts using food proces-

sor, or force through a food mill or wire strainer; set aside.

In a bowl, beat egg yolks until very thick and light in color. In a small pan combine water with the ⅔ cup sugar. Bring to a boil over high heat, stirring, until sugar is dissolved. Continue to boil, uncovered, until syrup is 234° (thread stage) on a candy thermometer. Pour hot syrup slowly into yolks and beat constantly, carefully avoiding beaters. Beat in chestnut purée, butter, vanilla, and liqueur.

With clean beaters, beat egg whites until stiff; gradually add the ¾ cup sugar, beating constantly until whites hold high, distinct, glossy peaks. In another bowl, whip ½ cup of the cream until stiff. Fold whites and cream into chestnut mixture until thoroughly combined. Pour mixture over Orange Crust. Cover and freeze at about 0° until firm (at least 8 hours).

To release pan side, dip a towel in hot water and wring dry; wrap around pan and hold in place for 30 seconds. Then remove towel and run a knife blade around edge of torte. Remove pan side. Set torte on serving dish. Whip remaining ½ cup cream until stiff and force through a pastry bag with fancy tip onto torte to decorate. Return torte to freezer; when cream is frozen, wrap airtight and store until ready to serve.

Prepare Raspberry Sauce.

Before serving, remove torte from freezer and place in refrigerator for 15 to 20 minutes before cutting. Garnish with a few raspberries from sauce and a few mint leaves. Cut into wedges and spoon some of the Raspberry Sauce over each portion. Makes 12 to 16 servings.

Orange Crust. Mix 1 cup finely crushed **arrowroot biscuit crumbs,** 1 teaspoon **grated orange peel,** and 2 tablespoons **butter** or margarine (melted). Pat crumbs evenly over bottom of an 8 or 9-inch spring-form pan (at least 2 inches deep).

Raspberry Sauce. Sweeten 2 cups washed and hulled fresh **raspberries** or 1 package (12 oz.) thawed frozen raspberries with **sugar** to taste. Gently mix in 3 to 5 tablespoons orange-flavored liqueur. Serve; or cover and refrigerate up to 1 hour.

ANISE WAFERS
CIALDE

Cialde are traditional holiday cookies. Like Pizelle (page 109) they are baked in special irons. You can use decorative cialde or pizelle irons or the Scandinavian wafer iron used for krumkake.

1	cup sugar
1	egg
2	teaspoons vanilla
2	tablespoons each whiskey and salad oil
⅔	cup milk
1	tablespoon anise seeds
1½	cups all-purpose flour
	Salad oil

In a bowl, beat together sugar, egg, vanilla, whiskey, the 2 tablespoons salad oil, and milk until well combined. Add anise seeds and flour; mix to blend, then beat until smooth. Place 5-inch-diameter cialde cooky iron directly over moderate heat until iron is hot enough (turn over occasionally to heat evenly) to make a drop of water sizzle and dance when it hits the open iron. Brush inside of iron lightly with salad oil.

Put a small spoonful of batter in center of one side of iron and close. After about 10 seconds, clamp shut or squeeze handles tightly to completely flatten cooky. (If some batter oozes out, scrape from edge of iron; you'll soon learn to judge exact amount.)

Cook, turning frequently, until cooky is a pale gold (about 30 seconds). Open iron slightly to check progress during baking and shift iron about on heat if one edge seems to cook more quickly than another. Carefully open iron and lift out cialde. Roll immediately into a cylinder; cooky becomes too crisp to roll if allowed to cool. Repeat to make each cooky.

Let cool completely, then store airtight. Makes 30 cookies, each about 5 inches in diameter.

ALMOND MACAROONS
AMARETTI

These popular crisp macaroons start with whole almonds, rather than the more usual canned almond paste.

1½	cups each blanched almonds and sugar
¼	teaspoon salt
¾	teaspoon almond extract
6	tablespoons egg whites (about 3 egg whites; beat lightly with a fork before measuring)
	All-purpose flour, if needed
	Whole blanched almonds or whole pine nuts (pignoli)

In a blender or food processor, whirl the 1½ cups nuts (about ½ cup at a time, if using blender) until nuts have consistency of coarse meal.

In a bowl, combine nuts with sugar, salt, and almond extract; mix well.

Beat egg whites into nut mixture until mixture holds together in a firm, slightly shiny mass. The mixture should not flow.

Test bake one cooky to see if dough is of a consistency to hold its shape. Measure out 1 tablespoon of the dough, shape into a ball, and flatten slightly onto a greased and flour-dusted baking sheet; bake in a 350° oven.

Within 10 minutes you can tell if the cooky will hold its shape. The ball will spread and flatten slightly, but should keep its round shape. If it spreads out thinly, add 2 tablespoons flour to the dough, mixing very well.

Test bake another cooky, if necessary. Continue adding flour, 2 tablespoons at a time, and test baking until dough has desired consistency (one or two tests will usually be adequate).

Shape remaining dough on greased and flour-dusted baking sheets: Make scant tablespoon-size mounds by forcing dough through a pastry bag without a tip (you may have to disengage the dough with your fingertips), or form dough into scant tablespoon-size balls and

flatten slightly onto baking sheets. Top each cooky with an almond or sprinkle with pine nuts, if you like.

Bake in a 350° oven for 18 to 25 minutes or until lightly browned. With a spatula, immediately transfer macaroons to wire racks to cool. Handle them carefully; they will be soft and will crush easily.

When cool and crisp, store in airtight containers or freeze for longer storage. Makes about 30 cookies, each about 2 inches in diameter.

FLORENTINES
BISCOTTI ALLA FIORENTINA

One of Italy's favored fancy pastries, these confectionlike cookies date back to the Renaissance. Sliced and finely ground almonds and chopped candied orange peel augmented by just a little flour form the buttery pastry. Each cooky is painted with a thin layer of chocolate.

1	cup sliced almonds
¼	cup whipping cream
⅓	cup sugar
4	tablespoons butter or margarine
½	cup candied orange peel, finely chopped
2	tablespoons all-purpose flour
¼	pound semisweet chocolate

In a blender or food processor whirl ½ cup of the sliced almonds until powdery; set aside. In a small sauce pan, combine cream, sugar, and butter. Place on low heat and cook, stirring occasionally, until butter is melted. Turn heat to medium high and bring mixture to a boil. Remove from heat and stir in ground almonds, remaining ½ cup sliced almonds, orange peel, and flour.

Drop by level tablespoonfuls on lightly greased, floured baking sheets (allow 6 cookies to each 12 by 15-inch sheet). Flatten with back of a spoon to about 2 inches in diameter.

Bake in a 350° oven for 10 to 12 minutes or until edges are slightly browned (centers will still be bubbling when you remove from oven). Let cool for 1 or 2 minutes. Carefully transfer each cooky from baking sheet to a wire rack. Cool, then turn cookies upside down on a piece of wax paper.

Melt chocolate over hot (not boiling) water. Using a brush, paint a thin layer of chocolate on back of each cooky. Let cool for several hours until chocolate has hardened. Store cookies airtight in a cool place for as long as 2 weeks, or freeze for longer storage. Makes about 15 large cookies.

SICILIAN CREAM ROLLS
CANNOLI

Crisp, cream-filled cannoli are a most tempting Sicilian pastry. They are based on dough that is rolled thin and wrapped around metal tubes, then fried to make crisp shells. From the same pastry, you can also make the special fried cookies called sfrappole that are traditional in Bologna during carnevale, the midwinter festivities preceding Lent.

You can use cannoli tubes purchased in a gourmet shop, or buy 1-inch-diameter lightweight aluminum tubing at a hardware store and have it cut into 4½-inch lengths. Both the shells and the ricotta filling can be made several days ahead, but they should be put together just before serving so the shells will stay crisp.

1¾	cups all-purpose flour
½	teaspoon salt
2	tablespoons sugar
1	egg
2	tablespoons firm butter or margarine, cut into small pieces
	About ¼ cup dry white wine
1	egg white, lightly beaten
	Salad oil
	Ricotta Filling or Fluffy Ricotta Filling (recipes follow)
	Powdered sugar
	Chopped milk chocolate and halved candied cherries

In a bowl, mix flour with salt and sugar. Make a well in center; break

egg into well and add butter. Stir with a fork, working out from center, to moisten flour mixture. Add wine, 1 tablespoon at a time, until dough begins to cling together. Use your hands to form dough into a ball. Cover and let stand for 15 minutes.

Roll dough out on a floured board or pastry cloth to about 1/16-inch thickness. Cut into 3½-inch circles. With rolling pin, roll circles into ovals. Wrap each oval around an aluminum cannoli tube; seal edges with egg white. Turn back ends of dough to flare slightly.

In a deep pan, pour oil to a depth of 2 inches and heat to 350° on a deep-frying thermometer. Add 2 or 3 dough-wrapped tubes at a time and fry for about 1 minute or until lightly golden. With tongs, remove cannoli and drain. Let cool for about 5 seconds, then, handling shell carefully, slip out tube. Cool shells completely. (At this point you may wrap airtight and store for as long as 3 days, if made ahead.)

To serve, use a plain large pastry tube to force Ricotta Filling into cannoli shells (fill only the number you plan to serve at once). Sift powdered sugar over shells, and garnish ends with chopped chocolate and candied cherries. Makes about 24 pastries (allow 2 for each serving).

Ricotta Filling. In a blender or food processor, whirl 2 pounds (4 cups) **ricotta cheese** until very smooth. (The next step can be done with processor. If blender was used, transfer cheese to a bowl before proceeding.) Beat in 1½ cups **powdered sugar** and 4 teaspoons **vanilla**. Mix in ½ cup **each** finely chopped **candied citron** and **candied orange peel,** and ¼ cup chopped **milk chocolate.** Cover and chill for several hours or for as long as 3 days.

Fluffy Ricotta Filling. Follow directions for **Ricotta Filling,** but prepare only half the recipe; whip 1 cup **whipping cream** until stiff, then fold into ricotta mixture.

Bolognese Carnival Cookies (Sfrappole). Prepare only the **cannoli dough** (no filling is needed), and roll out as directed. With a fluted pastry wheel cut dough into 1½ by 3-inch

strips. In a deep pan, pour **oil** to a depth of 2 inches and heat to 350° on a deep-frying thermometer. Fry 5 or 6 strips at a time until lightly browned (about 2 minutes per batch). Drain on paper towels; sprinkle cookies generously on both sides with **powdered sugar.** Makes 3 dozen cookies.

TWICE-BAKED COOKIES
BISCOTTI
(Pictured on page 102)

Some people call these hard, crunchy cookies wine-dunkers, for they're frequently served with wine and dipped into the beverage just before they are eaten.

2	cups sugar
1	cup (½ lb.) butter or margarine, melted
¼	cup each anise seeds and anisette (or other anise-flavored liqueur)
3	tablespoons whiskey, or 2 teaspoons vanilla and 2 tablespoons water
6	eggs
5½	cups all-purpose flour
1	tablespoon baking powder
2	cups coarsely chopped almonds or walnuts

In a bowl, mix sugar with butter, anise seeds, anisette, and whiskey. Beat in eggs. Mix flour with baking powder and stir thoroughly into sugar mixture. Mix in nuts. Cover and refrigerate for 2 to 3 hours.

Directly on greased baking sheets, shape dough with your hands to form flat loaves about ½ inch thick, 2 inches wide, and as long as baking sheet. Place loaves, two to a pan, parallel and well apart. Bake in a 375° oven for 20 minutes or until lightly browned.

Remove from oven and let loaves cool on baking sheets until you can touch them, then cut into diagonal slices ½ to ¾ inch thick. Place slices close together, cut sides down, on baking sheets, and bake in 375° oven for 15 more minutes or until lightly toasted. Cool on wire racks and store in airtight containers. Makes about 9 dozen.

Italian Fruit Cookies. Follow directions for Twice-baked Cookies, but in place of the 2 cups nuts, use 1½ cups diced mixed **candied fruit** and ½ cup whole **pine nuts** (pignoli) or slivered almonds. Second baking will take only 12 to 15 minutes to toast lightly.

STAR COOKIES
PIZELLE

Thin wafers imprinted with a star pattern from the special pizelle iron are delicious to nibble with ice cream or fruit.

2	eggs
6	tablespoons sugar
¼	cup salad oil
2	teaspoons vanilla
1	teaspoon grated lemon peel
1	cup all-purpose flour

In a bowl, beat together eggs, sugar, oil, vanilla, lemon peel, and flour until smoothly blended. Place fluted 5-inch-diameter pizelle cooky iron over moderate heat and heat as directed for cialde iron (page 107) but do not brush iron with oil. Put 1 rounded tablespoon batter in center of iron; close and cook, turning frequently, until cooky is golden.

Carefully lift pizelle from iron at once and place flat on a wire rack to cool. Repeat to make each cooky. Store airtight. Makes about 14 large cookies.

COOKY BEANS
FAVE DEI MORTI

Similar to Cooky Bones these "beans of the dead" cookies are intended for dunking. Ground nuts make them richer than the Cooky Bones.

1¼	cups whole unblanched almonds
⅔	cup pine nuts (pignoli)
1¼	cups sugar
½	teaspoon baking powder
¼	cup all-purpose flour
2	egg whites

In a blender or food processor, whirl almonds and pine nuts (a few at a time, if using blender) until they have a flourlike consistency. In a bowl, mix nuts with sugar, baking powder, and flour. Stir in egg whites with a heavy spoon, mixing until dough sticks together.

Shape in teaspoon-size balls and flatten slightly on a greased baking sheet; do not allow cookies to touch. With a teaspoon handle, gently push in side of each cooky so that baked cooky will resemble a lima bean in shape.

Bake in a 375° oven for 10 to 12 minutes or until pale brown. Cool on wire racks; store airtight. Makes about 5½ dozen cookies.

CRUMB COOKY
TORTA FREGOLOTTI

It looks like a cake, but think of it as a giant break-apart cooky. A specialty of Veneto, torta fregolotti starts as a pile of buttery crumbs; but after baking, it has a shortbreadlike consistency. Serve it in chunks with ice cream. The recipe calls for grappa, an Italian brandy.

1	cup blanched or unblanched almonds
2⅔	cups all-purpose flour
1	cup sugar
	Pinch of salt
1	teaspoon grated lemon peel
1	cup (½ lb.) plus 2 tablespoons butter or margarine, softened
2	tablespoons lemon juice
1	tablespoon grappa, aquavit, brandy, or water

In a blender or food processor, whirl almonds until finely ground. In a bowl, mix ground nuts, flour, sugar, salt, and lemon peel. With your fingers or a pastry blender, work in butter until mixture forms uniform crumbs. Sprinkle lemon juice and grappa over mixture and toss together lightly until blended. Mixture should be crumbly.

Spread mixture in a buttered and floured 12-inch pizza pan (do not press into pan). Bake in a 350° oven

until browned (50 to 60 minutes). Let cool on a rack.

When completely cooled, wrap well and let age for at least 1 day. Break into chunks to eat. Makes 2 to 3 dozen pieces.

COOKY BONES
OSSA DA MORDERE

Dunk these hard, pale cooky "bones" in tea, wine, or strong coffee for a favorite Italian afternoon snack.

3	egg whites
1¾	cups sugar
½	teaspoon grated lemon peel
½	teaspoon baking powder
1½	cups very coarsely chopped blanched almonds
1¾	cups all-purpose flour

With an electric mixer, beat egg whites and sugar with lemon peel and baking powder until smoothly blended. With a heavy spoon, work nuts in thoroughly, then flour.

Lightly flour your hands, then pinch off tablespoon-size lumps of dough and shape like short sturdy bones. Place cookies slightly apart on greased baking sheets and bake in a 375° oven for 10 to 12 minutes or until pale brown. Cool on wire racks; store airtight. Makes about 3½ dozen cookies.

INDEX

METRIC CONVERSION TABLE

To change	To	Multiply by
ounces (oz.)	grams (g)	28
pounds (lbs.)	kilograms (kg)	0.45
teaspoons	milliliters (ml)	5
tablespoons	milliliters (ml)	15
fluid ounces (fl. oz.)	milliliters (ml)	30
cups	liters (l)	0.24
pints (pt.)	liters (l)	0.47
quarts (qt.)	liters (l)	0.95
gallons (gal.)	liters (l)	3.8
Fahrenheit temperature (°F)	Celsius temperature (°C)	5/9 after subtracting 32